Nothing But the
Truth
So Help Me God

Nothing But the
Truth
So Help Me God

73 Women on Life's Transitions

Author
ABOW

Editors
Mickey Nelson and Eve Batey

NOTHING BUT THE TRUTH, LLC

SAN FRANCISCO

Nothing But The Truth, LLC
980 Magnolia Avenue, Suite C-6
Larkspur, CA 94939
Nothing But The Truth So Help Me God: 73 Women on Life's
Transitions™ and Nothing But The Truth So Help Me God: 73 Women
on Life's Transitions Cover Design are trademarks of Nothing But The
Truth, LLC.

For information about book purchases please visit the Nothing But
The Truth website at NothingButtheTruth.com
Also available in ebook.

Library of Congress Control Number: 2014936237

Nothing But The Truth So Help Me God: 73 Women on Life's
Transitions
Compiled by A Band of Women
Eve Batey, Editor. Mickey Nelson, Editor.

ISBN 978-0-9883754-6-8 (paperback)
ISBN 978-0-9883754-7-5 (ePub ebook)
ISBN 978-0-9883754-8-2 (Kindle ebook)

Printed in the United States of America
Cover design by theBookDesigners, Fairfax, CA
First Edition

Contents

Artwork

Introduction

Shasta Nelson, author of *Friendships Don't Just Happen!: The Guide to Creating a Meaningful Circle of GirlFriends*

"Just when the caterpillar thought the world was over ... it became a butterfly."
—Anonymous

We open this book about transitions with the recognition that each of us is in the midst of our own evolution.

Maybe we've just suffered the greatest loss of our lives or are just starting to hear the hushed whisper of a new desire. No matter what form our transition takes, we are changing. We are, undoubtedly, within one of three stages of transition in some part of our lives, be it an ending, the unknown-in-between, or the new beginning. If not at this moment, we've been there so many times and have a quiet knowing that we'll be back. So we take a deep breath as we hold this book filled with the voices and stories of women, and we acknowledge the prayer in our hearts that says, "Speak to me with honesty. Resonate with me so I know I'm not alone. Inspire me so I can feel hope." And it's a prayer that will be answered.

The Difference Between Change and Transition

Few of us are taught the distinction between transitions and changes. To confuse the two makes our job of aligning ourselves more difficult. And it's alignment that is the ongoing job description of our lives.

William Bridges is clear in his book, aptly titled *Transitions*, that "Change is situational. Transition, on the other hand, is psychological." In other words, what happens outside of us is the change; the internal reorienting process is transition.

In some cases, the change comes first: We're fired, we find out we're unexpectedly pregnant, a parent dies, a new opportunity presents itself with a phone call. Our invitation in those moments is to align our internal world to these new external changes. We have to metaphorically try on a new identity, imagining ourselves in the new way of life, brainstorming options, and recognizing the losses and gains that will come with this change. We have to come to terms with what it means for us to be recently unemployed, a new mom, or a daughter without a living parent. To find our ultimate peace we have to align our hearts and minds with our new reality.

In some cases, the transition comes before the change. We search for love, choose to switch jobs, strive for a goal, and dream of retirement long before we create the possibility for it in our lives. At these times in life, we do all the internal work first, until we have the courage, the clarity, or the resources to bring about the change that will align our external world to the world we have already prepared for ourselves internally.

Sometimes we're the one who initiates the divorce, triggering the change that reflects the internal choices we've already made. And sometimes we're the one receiving that news from the other and have to do the internal processing since the change is set into motion. Either way, both parties are called to constantly practice the dance of transition and change, internal movement and external situations. Back and forth, little by little, we think one provocative thought at a time, make one courageous move, and then circle back to shift the thought a little more. We make the dance up as we go, seeking to find a rhythm between what we feel on the inside and what we see on the outside. Two dance partners that are seemingly at odds will soon flow as one.

Whether the transition or the change occurs first, we are always seeking to align what we know is true on the inside with what is on the outside. We find peace in bringing the two together as much as we can.

Understanding the Stages of Transition

Beyond seeing the distinction between change and transition, understanding that within every change and transition are three stages can bring clarity. There is always an ending, the unknown-in-between, and the new beginning. The three truths this offers are: First, there is no such thing as an ending without a new beginning. Second, there is never a new beginning apart from some ending. And third, just because we can't yet see the next stage doesn't mean it's not there. To remember that beginnings and endings come hand-in-hand allows us see the forest, and not just the trees.

Of course, if the change is something we want—marriage, a new baby, a big promotion, or early retirement—it's easier to focus on the new beginning than what has to end to make way for the new. But just because we don't validate the loss doesn't mean it's not there. As a culture, we are so uncomfortable with loss that we think it's something to be avoided. But if we neglect to recognize that with the desired baby also comes some loss of freedom, or we abandon the reality that a certain passing away of our self-identity or some amount of grief accompanies responsibility, then we are deluding ourselves.

To pretend that new beginnings are without endings puts us at risk of depression, a result of not being in alignment. We may have produced the change we wanted, but we haven't fully transitioned ourselves if we insist only on celebrating and not also on grieving. To move into a new dance step means leaving the space we occupied before. Creating any new chapter in our life necessitates the turning of a page and the ending of the previous chapter. The good news is that the reverse is just as true: you cannot have an ending without a new beginning.

It would certainly make sense for the caterpillar that is being completely demolished inside a dark cocoon to wonder if life is over, but the emerging butterfly shows otherwise. When our relationships end, our loved ones die, and our dreams are dashed, we are left looking at the explosion of loss around us. Chapters do end, lights do go dark, and fear can settle on us like a suffocating blanket. But when our ending was born, so was our new beginning, even if we don't yet have eyes to see it.

There are many meanings given to the well-known story of Jesus' death thousands of years ago, but one of my favorites is that death isn't the end of the story. There is a resurrection, a new life, a new hope, and a new chapter. I won't pretend to know what is on the other side of a literal death, but I can attest that new life always follows the figurative deaths in our lives. The human experience is one of many new beginnings; I believe this is a reminder that hope beats out fear and that in the end, love wins.

What sometimes makes this hard to believe is that, like Jesus being in the tomb for three days, there is a middle stage of transition, between that ending and the beginning, where we don't yet see a way to let go and aren't ready to see the light of newness that is coming. Every transition model has a phase that is described with words like "the unknown zone," "depression," "the neutral zone," or "the place of acceptance." That's the time Jesus was still in the tomb or the caterpillar was stuck in the cocoon. We know this stage from our own lives—the months after the loss when we haven't yet realized its purpose or what awaits us.

We will do well to remember that loss isn't to be avoided or denied in new beginnings any more than hope should be shunned in our respective endings. Both hope and loss are tools making us something new, something we will look back on with gratitude for who we became in the process.

Some of us, while we read this book, may not yet be able to visualize our new beginnings. All we can see is the loss. This is where we lean into the stories of others to remind us that life is transformative. Our belief in what is possible will be strengthened as we hear the stories of others who attest to the recreating that always happens.

The Power of Stories and Rituals in Transition

Many of us know the power of rituals for connecting our feelings with circumstances. Rituals can be big public events that scream our milestones or as common and unpretentious as the action we engage in that calms us, centers us, or expands us. Perhaps it's the receiving of our driver's license at sweet sixteen that makes us feel more grown up. Or maybe it's when a ring is placed on our finger that the loving words feel more real. Perhaps the ritual is a hike behind our house that gives us room to think. Or maybe it's the passing down of a family heirloom that reminds us we're part of something much bigger. Perhaps it's the annual camping trip that alerts us that summer is finally here, or the restaurant that is embedded with years of fancy dinners that have celebrated our lasting love. It could be as flashy as the dream wedding, or as private as buying your first box of condoms. Rituals are anything we do outside of us to help guide our alignment to our hearts.

In some cases, rituals lead us to accept what is, whether it's the lowering of the coffin that prevents our denial or the fortieth birthday party that forces us to ponder life. In other cases, we create rituals to reflect what is ready and true for us, whether it's showing up at our first AA meeting to put a stake in the ground to help us keep a recent promise or the throwing away of our birth control pills to try for something we now want.

Rituals—whether ceremonies, unchanging patterns, repetitive behavior, a system of rites, or a one-time formal act—are used to bring us alignment between our situation and our feelings.

Stories serve the same purpose, but instead of being something that happens outside of us, they move invisibly within. Hearing the stories of others can expand what we thought possible, give a roadmap to those who feel lost, and provide a menu of options for us to consider as we make our own choices. A story can instantly move us to action or settle into some recess of our mind waiting for a moment, perhaps years from now, when its wisdom is needed. Stories invite us to self-reflect, ponder, dream about, sit with, and consider.

When we hear a story, we have an opportunity to self-examine our own lives. That reflection demands that we challenge our own biases and deeply held beliefs. With fresh thoughts comes the courage to act in a changed, bigger, more honest way. As we take steps, we can think about our lives in even more inventive ways. In this way, we are ever bringing alignment between the actions we make and the thoughts we think: one moving ahead, enticing the other to catch up, only to later switch places like members of the same team in a relay race. But it is this very game that leads us to the alignment we crave, the meaning of life we seek, to know ourselves intimately and create the lives that matter to us.

Preparing for Our Own Transition

As we seek alignment between what is outside of us and what is inside, stories are one of the most powerful tools we have to guide us. This book that you hold in your hands is filled with stories that can help us self-reflect as we move through the stages of our own transitions. Some of us will hear a voice between the lines of ink that will compel us to lunge forward with a voracity never before seen in our lives, while others among us will be pressed to the floor and told to sit and rest. Some of us will forever know the very page that clarified a decision or willed us to look back to a moment in history for our healing, while others of us will reach "The End" with more questions than answers. But all of us will self-reflect, identifying with the actions of those who dared make public their very poignant memories and feelings.

Their stories will reverberate with us in some way, because transition is a universal notion. So many of us know what it feels like to be weighted with insecurity, doubtful whether we're loved, fearful of failure, nervous about success, filled with angst, wounded by crippling events, and too weary to stand back up. The ability of these stories to put the human heart into words will shift something in us. That's what stories do. Stories move our heart by letting us try on new ideas, helpful language, and possible outcomes.

Much attention is given to the changes in our lives, but rarely do we talk about the transitions. For that, I applaud Christine Bronstein, the editor of this book and a woman I greatly admire, for inviting us all to come sit and share our stories. This book is like a tangible campfire, a gathering place where we can pass around our own stories and glean wisdom from the tales of others.

You'll see some stories in which the women chose their transitions and the work was in bringing about the change to match what they had already decided. And you'll be moved by the testimonies as many of them had change thrust upon them, forcing them to eventually choose the internal work of growing into something new. Watch carefully and you'll see where rituals showed up and where stories guided. Some authors may focus more on the change outside of them, but all of them will pull back the curtains on the transitions within. Some of the endings and beginnings will be obvious, some more subtle. And whether or not they each articulate that mysterious, scary place of the unknown-in-between, you'll know it's there.

Next to each scar, wrinkle, or pain that the stories on these pages have caused their authors, you will see a light shining brightly. For that's what we do: We fall, we heal, we nurture, we grow, we hope, we expand, we shine, we dance!

Above all, we become the next thing we're meant to be. We trust that while we may no longer recognize the caterpillar that we were, we will serve the world in bigger ways with whatever we're about to be.

Blessings on you, not only as you receive these stories of transitions but as you continue the journey of your own.

Section One

Moving On, Letting Go

Love You Hard

Abby Maslin

I observe my husband closely as he struggles to balance his coffee cup while slamming the car door shut. I stretch my arm outward, prepared to catch the falling cup, but he surprises me by tucking it in the corner of his arm and methodically maintaining his balance. When he dresses in the morning, I stand nearby watching closely as he buttons his shirt and pulls on his sweater. As always, his button-down shirt hangs awkwardly on the right side, the seam of his sleeve not quite matching the position of his armpit.

I deliberate silently about when to intervene and when to keep my mouth shut. Do I gently wipe the food from the right side of his face? Do I pull his shirt a smidgeon to the left, helping him to appear fractionally more composed? Do I turn the other way and pretend not to notice the trillion subtle differences that mark this changed man from the independent, consummate professional he was before?

Every day my head rings with questions as I continue to walk the delicate tightrope that accompanies the dual roles of caregiver and wife. I've all but forgotten the feeling of not being needed. It strikes me as nearly inconceivable that a year ago my husband was capable of flying around the world giving presentations to bigwigs on the future of renewable energy. Life Part II is all about relearning the basics.

"What is your name?" I ask.

"Dan . . . Daniel," he responds. The weakness in his right muscles has transformed his formerly strong voice. Every utterance in his new voice is marked by a slight slur, lisp, or change in tone.

"When is your birthday?" I prompt.

"September. September third." He gets this one correct.

I move on to the tough questions. "Where are you from?"

"September," he answers quickly. He can tell from my expression that he is wrong. "Oh wait, that's not right."

He tries again. "September."

I fail to conceal my wince.

"Uggh," he groans in frustration. "Why do I keep saying that?"

And so begins the conversation that marks each and every day of our new life.

"Because you're brain injured," I respond. "And sometimes your brain needs extra time to process what it has just heard."

"It makes me feel stupid," he complains. "Like I'm mentally wrong."

Mentally wrong. I like that expression. My husband's broken language has introduced some of the most apropos phrases I've ever heard. I often think his healing brain is wiser than the minds trying to fix it. In many ways, his unusual thinking seems far more analytic and intuitive than it was in his days as a young analyst in the energy world.

My husband is only thirty, yet he has worked harder in his life than most eighty-five-year-olds. From modest upbringings, he pushed his way through college and grad school with a resourcefulness and drive so intense I often wonder how he ended up with a middle of the road, chronic procrastinator such as myself for a wife. Seven months ago, when a group of young men struck him over the head and robbed him of his phone on his walk home, I wondered what kind of universe would ever require such a decent and hardworking man to pave his tough road to success twice.

My husband doesn't think in these terms. He rarely resents the difficult path in front of him. He doesn't dwell on the life we had before or his lost independence. He views the obstacles ahead as necessary challenges in becoming the best version of himself. In terms of anger, sadness, and resentment, he has let go.

For me, the task of letting go is tremendously painful. I don't want to let go. In the late hours of the night, I pour over my laptop screen as I indulge in hundreds of old photos and home movies featuring my husband of before. I am a voyeur of my past life, relishing in minute details and savoring the sound of his old voice. In these moments, I must try to silence my own inner voice as it incessantly begs for one more chance to hear him speak, watch him walk, or laugh as he roughhouses on the floor with our son.

Letting go of our pre-assault, pre-injury life is like quitting any addictive habit. Once you've quit, you're free. But you never stop mourning the addiction itself. I can't truly grieve my husband because he is still alive. But I'll never stop missing the man I married, the one who isn't coming back. It is an ambiguous, torturous grief that I struggle to articulate. How can I reconcile my mixed feelings of gratitude and grief as I rebuild my life in the presence of a living ghost?

Each day my husband grows stronger, and I learn to trust in the power of his recovery. I have witnessed the miracle of his rebirth: from a nearly dead, comatose state, past the progression of small milestones, to an emerging partial independence. I have hovered over him like a protective mother, fought in his defense like a warrior, and soothed his soul like a knowing healer.

As his eyes begin to shine brighter and the pace of his step quickens, I must learn to carry the weight of our family's trauma and gradually step back into the role of wife. I must let him go. Back into the outside world, where young men equate a man's life with the value of his cell phone, and where people often look unforgivingly upon the disabled, I must let my husband return. In his own time and with his own unique challenges, he will overcome this horrific chapter.

Until then, he kisses me intently and looks knowingly into my weary eyes.

"I love you so hard," he proclaims.

I silence my correction and offer my most genuine smile.

"I love you too."

Abby Maslin

Abby Maslin is a teacher for DC Public Schools with dual master's degrees in education and creative arts therapy. In August 2012, her husband was the victim of a brutal assault in their Washington, DC, neighborhood. As she and her family cope with the aftermath of severe traumatic brain injury, Abby has been documenting their struggle on her blog, abbymaslin.com, and as a regular contributor for the website Brainline.org. She is also in the process of writing a memoir about the experience, based on her prize-winning essay *Love You Hard*. When she's not busy writing or wrangling two-year-old son Jack, Abby can be found in the yoga studio, replicating her favorite Barefoot Contessa recipes, or participating in family dance-offs.

The Shopping Trip

Leslie Lagerstrom

Tucked in the front pocket of my jeans is the list, handwritten in purple ink, the color chosen specifically because it always makes me feel better. A completely mundane list by anyone's standards—the kind you could probably find in the purse, pocket, or palm of most shoppers entering Target that day. But mine is different for a reason no one would ever guess, and only a few people—only those who have walked in my shoes—might truly understand.

Toothpaste. Shampoo. Cat litter. Storage containers. Paper towels. Laundry detergent. These seem like the most basic of items, but in reality, five of them are decoys. Diversions in the form of innocuous sundries to convince me this excursion is not out of the ordinary and that what I am purchasing is routine. But it isn't what I'm buying that makes this shopping trip seem so surreal. It's the *why*. The *reason* I am here is what pulls at my heartstrings as I grab the red cart with one rattling wheel and head deliberately into the store.

Proceeding down the main aisle, the flashbacks begin almost immediately. Like a made-for-television movie, each department of the store corresponds with a different memory in my head—the only thing missing is a melodramatic soundtrack to accompany the scenes playing at a dizzying pace in my mind. Passing child-size mannequins holding bedazzled miniature purses and wearing girls' clothing in varying shades of pink, I swallow hard to dislodge the lump that has formed in my throat. It was here, just a few years earlier, that I received some of the first clues from our gender-variant child that there was a disconnect between her mind and body. Simple conversations always led to arguments followed by tears as Sam rejected wearing anything feminine the store had to offer. "Boys don't wear dresses," she would explain matter-of-factly, while I tried in vain to convince my five-year-old daughter otherwise.

Accelerating my pace to escape the discomfort elicited by the innocent attire, I come upon racks of boys' apparel. The rough-and-tumble wear was always a magnet for my little girl who knew she was really a boy. "But I want Spider-Man underpants," her young voice echoes in my mind, the words evoking feelings of sadness even after all this time. "Can I wear swim trunks like Dad this summer?" Sam would ask, holding the boys' swimsuit bottoms up to her waist for me to approve. My approval did not come easily. Instead, I avoided the gaze of her eager, puppy-dog eyes, which accompanied her naive requests to wear masculine clothing featuring footballs and hockey pucks—the only type of clothes that made this child feel whole. I rationalized that it was my job to stand firm and remind her she was really a girl.

Now I find myself six years later—after extensive research, doctor's visits, and counseling sessions—on a shopping trip that represents the start of a journey down a different path for my child, and the beginning of a new chapter for our family. "Here in Aisle 22, of all places," I laugh nervously to myself at how strangely funny that seems. I am here to buy a container that will be used to store the last remnants of proof that our first child was born biologically female. A hoarder by nature, all the mementos I have accumulated over the years are nothing but painful reminders to Sam that his mind and body did not match. It was time for them to go, or at least be hidden from view, as he began to truly live his life as a boy.

"Throw them all away," Sam instructed, but I could not bear the thought of discarding my child's history. The Girl Scout Brownie vest adorned with Cookie Super Seller patches. A framed birth announcement proudly proclaiming Samantha Carole's arrival. Sports trophies with girl figurines bouncing basketballs and holding bats. Art projects emblazoned with her feminine given name, carefully created by tiny fingers wrapped around a favorite green crayon. An "I'm the Big Sis" T-shirt worn to the hospital on the day our second child was born. And the photos . . . oh yes, the photos. Gathering them from the fireplace mantel, taking them down from our refrigerator door, and removing them from all the nooks, crannies, and bookshelves where they had resided throughout our home for the last ten years . . . that probably hurt the most. But I knew these artifacts needed to be packed away so that Sam's correct identity could not only survive but also thrive.

"It's hard to decide when you have this many options," a young mother standing next to me amongst the sea of plastic containers offers, breaking my train of thought. A little girl no more than four years of age sits in her cart, tenderly holding a faded brown bear that has obviously been loved. I smile and nod, remembering once more those early days of Sam's childhood, and I am suddenly overcome with a sense of relief. Relief because I finally recognize this trip does not represent a loss, but rather another step in the direction we must travel together to help him become whole. In that instant, I understand the magnitude of his sense of self, and my heart wells with pride, knowing he has already achieved something many people will spend a lifetime trying to accomplish. At about the same tender age as the child before me in that cart, Sam already knew who he was and has never wavered from being true to himself. Indeed, this was not a good-bye, but rather a long-awaited acknowledgement of the person my beautiful child has always been. His whole life ahead of him, he will now continue on with his head held high and his family proudly by his side. As a parent, I could not wish for more.

Leslie Lagerstrom

Leslie Lagerstrom is the proud mom of two children, who, after retiring from a twenty-one-year corporate marketing career, is focusing her passion on being a writer and advocate. In 2011 she created the blog Transparenthood™, which chronicles her experience raising a transgender child. Leslie is a regular contributor to *The Huffington Post*, and *MORE Magazine Online* has also featured her essays. Committed to spreading awareness on the subject of gender-variant children, Leslie, along with her family, appeared on *The Jeff Probst Show* in November 2012. A speaker for Welcoming Schools—an initiative by the Human Rights Campaign to foster safe classroom environments—Leslie frequently shares her family's story with K-12 teachers throughout Minneapolis and St. Paul.

The Last Drop

Sierra Godfrey

Childbearing women pass a lot of milestones, from the first time we hear our baby's heartbeat to the big twenty-four-week gender-revealing ultrasound. There's that magical thirty-seventh week, when the baby can be born without being called premature. Then there's the birth itself, and the two-week-old mark at which our previously angelic sleepers turn into fussy, nonsleeping demons. There's the point at which we can have sex again, and the day we resume menstruation. But there's one significant milestone that we don't talk about. It's an intense, emotional moment that can be both bad and good all at once. It's the day the last drop of milk we'll ever make falls from our breast.

That's it. You're done. You've had your children and you're not having any more. Whether your baby is four months, a year, or two years, you've transitioned from supporting that baby with your body. These thoughts have been on my mind as I move toward complete weaning of my last baby. I don't mean weaning from breast to a cup. My baby is no longer much of a baby at nearly two years old. He's talking and laughing and somehow saying "butthole" in front of guests. He's also still nursing once a day. I have only a trickle, but still we hold on because bidding adieu to those sweet days forever isn't as easy as I thought it would be. He's my second and last child. I'm moving into a period that is officially classified as perimenopausal. It hardly seems fair when I could still pop out a few more kids if I wanted.

I liken the feeling about the last drop to how I have a hard time giving away the last baby outfit or baby book, even though my kids clearly aren't going to wear or read them. That little zippered sleeper with the Winnie the Pooh adventure map printed all over in size 0–3 months? Yeah, that's tucked away in a box. It's not going anywhere.

When I'm eighty, I'll pull it out and hold it and remember my children's babyhood. We become sentimental hoarders as our children become kids with their own personalities and wills. And although you might keep a frozen bag of breast milk that you pumped out in the early days of nursing, when your boobs were spraying milk like Tommy guns, hidden in the bottom of the freezer under a package of short ribs, you know you really can't keep the last drop.

Emotion over the end of nursing your baby picks up speed when you see other people continue to drip. My neighbor and I were pregnant at the same time with our second children. Both of us experienced aching, stiff pregnancies that left us cranky and less than eager to go through it again. I knew my second would be my last. My neighbor wasn't so sure. Less than two years later, she's pregnant again with her third. At first this horrified me. *Three* kids? The expense! The chaos! The toddler tantrums compounded by three! But of course, that's three children to love and kiss. Three people sharing the cost of your nursing home is surely better than two, right? I could have another one! I'm healthy, still in my thirties. But I'm not going to. Instead, I'm moving on to a place of physical freedom, and my toddler is moving on toward school days and interests of his own—none of which will include my breasts.

The last drop my baby drinks will be my very last connection to the world of childbirth and babyhood. In her book *The Nursing Mother's Guide to Weaning*, author Kathleen Huggins says that the last drop of milk is our last connection with our childbearing bodies, and it's an unmarked but incredibly poignant moment. The World Health Organization recommends breastfeeding your baby for two years. The American Academy of Pediatrics recommends breastfeeding for the first year. However long we do it—even if for a few days—the last time your last baby sucks is the last time we have a part in that special babyhood time.

There's an emphasis in Western culture on moving quickly from nursing to fast, big-kid stuff, and we don't talk about this. We don't say, wait a minute! The last time we nurse matters! It's the remaining connection to those nearly ten months the baby spent inside you. It's the last link to our ability to nourish and grow another human being, and maybe even the last time the bond with our baby will be as thick. Some women aren't as affected, of course—some don't consider it a milestone. Some are glad to be done with the mess and the tied-down feeling. I can certainly understand that. But when my friend Kate could no longer squeeze a drop of milk from her breast, she cried. For women who are forced to stop nursing before they want to, it's probably devastating.

There are good things that come with the end to nursing. We'll have more freedom—fewer ties to the baby, more time for ourselves. The physical toll on our bodies will decrease. Pregnancy and nursing gingivitis, we hope, goes away. The suck, if you'll pardon the pun, on our calcium supply lessens. When we take medications, we no longer have to pause because we're not in the "if you're pregnant or nursing, ask your doctor first" category. We can have guilt-free glasses of wine. And yet, that last drop is so final. Maybe it's because after we stop having children, we're old. We might as well be grandmothers. It's like saying we're no longer able to have children, which is a terrible feeling if you want to have them. Maybe it taps into a primal desire to reproduce, to mother, to nourish.

Whatever it is, my last drop of milk will truly be my last connection to that sweet quiet that descends when your baby leans into your breast to suck and the only sound is the gentle drinking sound and your heart and your baby's heart. I'll no longer be in the childbearing game. As my mother-in-law advised, "Enjoy that baby now. You won't get to again until you have grandchildren."

So while I look forward to that older stage of childhood, the interaction and conversations, the running and jumping and all-day adventures, and their ability to wipe their own butts, I'm going to have a moment of silence for that last drop.

Sierra Godfrey

Sierra Godfrey is a writer and graphic designer. She has enjoyed the art of storytelling for as long as she can remember and is passionate about making sense of the world through words. She has a BA in conceptual design and an MS in technical communication, and her writing has been featured in online publications. People say she's sassy, but she's pretty sure she's sweet—especially when the lighting is right. She lives in the San Francisco Bay Area with her husband, two little boys, and one very bad cat. She can be found on Twitter (@sierragodfrey) or at sierragodfrey.com.

Finally Fall

Ashley Collins

I worried our weather would jump from summer to winter without the beautiful autumn for which the East Coast is famous. I felt caged. I wanted to tear at my skin and shred my clothes, become a wild animal, one that belongs in this forest. That's how completely the incessant rain and gray curtain of thick air that settled around everything affected me. It seemed like a derivative of fog. Real fog is beautiful in its texture and chiaroscuro. But this was cloying wet air with no dimension—it was opaque and suffocating. Combined with the tangled green jungle surrounding my new home, I was so claustrophobic. I didn't even enjoy walking the dogs. Everybody said it was unusual. Perhaps it was post-hurricane weather, or maybe it was my fault for bringing the rain from Seattle. But this wasn't Seattle weather. This felt like a swamp.

I'm homesick for northwest air. I miss the soaring pines and firs, the high sky, mountains and water that decorate the land like jewelry. I miss mist that has transparency, and dew that sparkles like diamonds, highlighting spider webs spun in such beautiful artistry there must be a divine source. I miss the crows that descend this time of year in such great numbers it feels like dark magic at work, even though I know they are feeding on the trees of the arboretum. I miss the eagles and herons that sit like sentries on platforms in Lake Washington, good omens as I drove over the bridge. I miss my house. I miss my friends and my family. But most of all, I miss my boy.

Fall is the dying season, when leaves dry up and fall off trees, flowers stop blooming, grass stops growing. The earth prepares itself for winter, for dormancy. It feels like that is happening to my heart. I knew it would be painful. I saw my friends wander around with unseeing eyes that first fall after a child left the nest, grief etched on their faces.

Now I'm one of them. I wear that lonely place in my soul like a secret scar because his childhood is over and my job is finished. When he returns, he will be a man, never needing me quite the same way again. It's a necessary cycle of life, like leaves falling from a tree—beautiful and poignant. The wind has taken this leaf of mine on a journey far away. He has changed colors by now. But he said, in the lines of a poem he wrote before he left, that I would still recognize him.

I thought I would escape the pain of separation. I was fleeing from it at the same time he was falling away from me, in the frenetic process of moving from West Coast to East. As long as I kept moving, literally as well as figuratively, maybe I wouldn't feel the loss so acutely. And it worked for a while. I still had two girls entering a new school, a new house to unpack, the animals to settle, and a new life to create. But after the rush at the end of summer, when the lion's share of work was done, there were moments of quiet when my mind sneakily let in thoughts of my boy. I missed his energy as I missed the cacophony of crows at dusk in Seattle. I missed his playing the piano when he knew I needed cheering up. I missed his chatter every night at dinner while his father read the wine bottle and his sisters ate in stony, adolescent silence. He wasn't in college in America, where I could have delivered him new sheets and towels, a bucket of Red Vines, and met his roommate. There was no transition. He went to Africa.

I watched him plan his gap year out of the corner of my eye while I was planning good-bye parties and putting our house on the market. I saw him carry REI bags to the basement while I was meeting with the moving people. I heard him on the phone with African and Indian consulates while I typed new school applications for his sisters, bracing myself for his graduation. I didn't want to help him.

The barometer did finally fall. The air cooled and dried out. The leaves turned from green to yellow and started falling. I can see through the forest. The sun has scattered my demons, revealed them to be internal rather than external. The dogs look at me knowingly. Winding roads lined in old stone walls have regained their bucolic charm. Mailboxes are decorated with cornstalks and hay bales, scarecrows and pumpkins, pots of red and yellow mums. We saw a young deer on the lawn of the school the other night, small antlers gleaming in the moonlight. There is magic here too.

Ashley Collins

Ashley Collins is married with three children and lives with her family in Greenwich, Connecticut. She graduated with a BA in anthropology from Stanford University in 1987. Her first job was at *Vogue* magazine, having failed to realize *National Geographic* had moved their editorial offices to Washington, DC, before arriving in New York. She has traveled extensively, following her husband's career, as well as her own wanderlust. She has lived in New York City, London, and Seattle prior to moving to Greenwich. She currently writes a blog about her family and their animals, and competes as an equestrian show jumper.

Home(less) and Gardens

Heather Kristin

The day I searched for my father, whom I had never met or seen a photo of, I wandered into Adam Purple's garden. I was ten years old and newly homeless with my family. While my peers attended school, I spent the day walking all over Manhattan, staring at businessmen's facial features and hot dog vendors' thumbs. If they had my pointy nose combined with my flat thumbs shaped like big toes, I had nothing to lose by marching right up to them and asking, "Are you my father?"

Nobody matched my description.

I continued my hunt, skipping past vacant buildings and crossing to the other side of the street when I saw drug dealers, prostitutes, and mounds of trash. Having been born and raised in New York City in the 1980s, I knew which blocks were safe and which would get me killed.

After an hour, I was thankful to have reached the five abandoned, city-owned lots on the Lower East Side. Cornstalks grew tall next to tenements. The World Trade Center shined like Oz in the distance. Someone at the shelter had told us that Adam Purple often handed out (for free!) fruits and vegetables. I hoped to be so lucky.

His community (yet illegal) garden was a lush place. Overgrown plants, flowers, trees, squash, blackberries, asparagus, carrots, beans, and radishes were all arranged in the shape of a giant yin-yang symbol. Sunlight reflected off a cracked window and onto a man with a ragged trucker's cap who wore all purple. He had my long nose, but I couldn't see his hands. They were covered in gardening gloves. More hipster than Daddy Warbucks, I pretended for a few minutes that he was my father.

I stayed for a few hours, crunching on carrots and apples. By the time the city lights began twinkling in the dark, I wasn't sure he was my father and felt too insecure to ask him. I had to find my mother somewhere on the streets and return to the shelter.

For the next year, my family slept in shelters, strangers' beds, and subways. My needs changed. I spent what was left of my childhood more worried about finding my next meal and a place to sleep than finding my father.

I hadn't seen Adam Purple for about twenty-five years, but recently, on one of my daily walks, I thought I saw the eighty-something-year-old zoom by on his bike. I wanted to flag him down, tell him we had all survived, but I wasn't sure it was him, and if it was, if he would even remember me or respond to the question I still had: Are you my father?

Daisy, my two-year-old daughter, strapped in her stroller, glided downhill on the Williamsburg Bridge. I held tight, careful not to let go. In the distance, an elderly man with a long white beard pulled his bike up the hill toward me. Every few steps, he crashed his bent-in-half body and bike into the rail. I picked up my pace, fearful that the steep incline would cause him to collapse. Within a minute, I stood in front of him and noticed he had dried bloody gashes combined with fresh ones on his arms and legs.

"You OK?" I asked as Daisy squirmed in her stroller, seeming afraid of the strange man.

"Fine," he answered.

A Hasidic mother slowed down and a runner stopped. He asked if the man needed water or an ambulance. He waved them away and told me to keep walking. But I couldn't. Underneath his baseball cap and dark sunglasses, I knew who it was.

"Are you Adam Purple?"

"That was my name. Before the city bulldozed and destroyed my Garden of Eden," he said, panting. He groaned, shuffled ahead, and then crashed his bike into the rail again.

Hoping to cheer him up, I introduced him to Daisy, the light of my life and most proven source to make any stranger smile on the subway. He barely glanced at her and kept trudging up the hill. An enormous drip of clear mucus poured out of his nose. He didn't wipe it away. Then I told him how I admired his tenacity years ago to pick up manure from the Central Park horse carriages, carry it on his bike, and bring it back to his garden to create soil. He didn't say a word. I told him how shortly after the destruction of the garden, I traced the footsteps he painted all over town like DNA, stretching from the Upper East Side to the Brooklyn Bridge and winding their way to the garden.

He kept moving, ignoring me, and crashing his bike every few steps into the gate. Then he snarled. Daisy gripped her dolly tighter. I kept a healthy few feet from him but kept pace with him as he tested my compassion. I convinced myself that it was easier than walking away out of fear. I decided that even if he wasn't in his right mind, I'd walk back over the bridge with him. I owed it to him. He had once fed me. I would watch over him.

"Do you have kids?" I asked.

"Yes."

I held my breath, wondering if now was the time to ask him if he was my father. I might never see him again, or worse, he might die. He didn't look so good. Daisy looked up at me as though we should stay away. Without warning, his skeletal frame climbed onto his bike and he miraculously weaved all the way down the bridge and out of sight.

I was sad I'd never be able to follow his purple footprints on the pavement again, down a yellow brick road to some hippie home. I couldn't run after him, pushing Daisy in the stroller, screaming, "Are you my Dad?" I'd scare her too much. The wind tried to push me forward on the bridge, but I remained paralyzed. I didn't want her to see me act crazy. I finally had a normal life and was healthy. My husband was my rock, and my daughter loved me more than anything. Plus, I didn't want to take care of another family member who could be schizophrenic, bipolar, or have borderline personality disorder.

I stared at the new World Trade Center, just rising over the city, and knew I couldn't stand there forever. Life was too fragile to be lived with anger and regret. I could no longer hold on to my parents and the Internet, for that matter, for answers, and be defined by disappointment and sorrow. I could forgive, reclaim, and build upon what I had lost. My search for my father left me feeling empty, but it was no longer about me, it was about my daughter. I would protect her in ways I had never been protected.

With Adam Purple gone, Daisy looked relieved.

"Go home to daddy?" she asked.

"Yes," I said, knowing I'd created a loving family from the ruins and thankful to plant my own garden in a place I now called home.

Heather Kristin

Heather Kristin's essays have appeared in *Glamour, Slate, The Huffington Post,* the *St. Petersburg Times, Narrative, Smith,* and the anthology *Live and Let Love,* which was featured on *Good Morning America* and *Chelsea Lately.* Oprah's Lifeclass "The Truth Shall Set You Free" featured Heather live after a segment with the memoirist of *The Glass Castle.* Recently, Heather was honored by the State of New Jersey General Assembly for her dedication to women's issues. She is thrilled to be reading with Gloria Steinem this spring with Girls Write Now, a nonprofit where she has been mentoring an at-risk teen for the past six years.

I Think I'll Make It

Kat Hurley

It was hardly a secret growing up that psychologists had predicted I would never lead a truly happy and normal life. It is doubtful those words were intended for my ears, yet that's just how I learned most things in those days. There was no telling what surprising morsels of un-sugar-coated facts would either fly straight out of the horse's mouth or trickle their way down through the boys until they hit me, the baby.

I was five when I went to therapy. Twice. On the second visit, the dumb lady asked me to draw what I was feeling on a piece of plain construction paper. I was staring at the few crayons next to the page when I told her politely that I'd rather not. I'm sure it had been *suggested* that I go see her, because, truth be known, my Grandma Kate thought psychologists were a "bunch of quacks." When I said I didn't want to go back, nobody so much as batted an eye. And that was the end of that.

When I draw up some of my earliest and most vivid memories, what I see reminds me of an old slide projector screening crooked, fuzzy images at random. In the earliest scenes, I am lopsidedly pigtailed, grass stained, and in clothes painfully clashing. In one frame I am ready for my first day of preschool in my bright red, pill-bottomed bathing suit. I am standing at the bottom of the stairs where my mom has met me, and through her contained laughter she explains that a carpool isn't anything near as fun as it sounds. In another, I am crouched down in the closet playing hide-and-seek, recycling my own hot Cheerio breath, patiently waiting to be found, picking my toes. Soon, Mom would come home and together we'd realize that the boys weren't *seeking* (babysitting) me at all, they'd simply gone down the street to play with friends.

I replay footage of the boys (Ben and Jack) pushing me in the driveway, albeit *unintentionally*, toward the busy road on my first day biking without training wheels, and (don't worry, I tattled) *intentionally* using me as the crash-test dummy when they sent me flying down the stairs in a laundry basket.

I have the image of me cross-legged on my parents' bed, and my mom's horrified face when she found me—scissors in hand—thrilled with what she referred to as my new "hacked" hairdo. That same bed, in another scene, gets hauled into my room when it was no longer my parents', and my mom, I presume, couldn't stand to look at it any longer. I can still see the worry on her face in those days, the disgust on his. I see the aftermath of the few fights they couldn't help but have us witness.

Had I known I should have been squirreling away memories as precious keepsakes, I would have scavenged for more smiles, clung to each note of contagious laughter and lingered steadfast in every embrace.

Truth is that I was just a regular kid before I was ever *really* asked to "remember." Up until then, I'd been safe in my own little world: every boo-boo kissed, every bogeyman chased away.

I was my daddy's darling and my mommy's little angel—

Then—without warning—I wasn't.

"Tell us everything you know, Katie. It is very important that you try to remember everything you saw."

August 11, 1983

I am five. I'll be in kindergarten this year, Ben is going into third grade, and Jack will be in seventh. It's just Mom and me today. We're on our way to Dad's office. Not sure why, again, except that "they have to talk." Ever since Dad left and got his new townhouse with his new girlfriend, it seems all they do is *talk*.

Mom pulls into a space in front of the office. "You can stay here, sweetie pie, I won't be long." I have some of my favorite coloring books and a giant box of crayons; I'll be fine.

Time passes in terms of works of art. Goofy, Mickey, and Donald are all colored to perfection before I even think to look up.

Then, out of nowhere, I hear a scream. Like one I'd never heard before, except on TV. *Was that her?* I sit still for a second, wait for another clue. *That wasn't her.* But something tells me to check anyway—just in case.

I scramble out from the way back, over the seat, and try to open the door, but I'm locked in. *Locked?* I tug at the lock, let myself out, scurry to the front window of my dad's shop, and on my tiptoes, ten fingers to the ledge, I can see inside. Everything looks normal, like the last time I was there. *Where are they?*

Then, through the window, I see my mom. At the end of the hall I can see her through the doorway—but just her feet and part of her legs. She is still. I don't get it. *Why is she on the floor?* I try to open the door, but it's locked.

I'm sure I knocked; I must have banged. Then again—

It wasn't her. It sounded like it came from down the street, I tell myself; someone was probably just playing. Shaking the sound from my head, I get back in the car.

Only two pages are colored in this time. Not Mickey and friends, Snow White now. Fairy tales. My dad knocks on the window, startling me, smiling. "Hey, Princess! Mom is on the phone, so you'll just see her Monday. You're coming with me, kiddo; we have to go get your brother."

Everything I've seen is forgotten. My dad's convincing smile, tender voice, and earnest eyes make all my fright disappear. He told me she was on the phone and I believed him. How was I supposed to know that dads could lie?

Two days later, we were at the beach on a job with Dad when Grandma and Grandpa surprised us with the news, "Your mother is missing." And it was only then, when I sensed the fear they tried so intently to wash from their faces, that the realization struck me as stark panic, that I was brought back to the scene for the first time and heard the scream I understood *was* really her.

My testimony would later become the turning point in the case—reason enough to convict my father, who in his cowardice had covered all his traces. Even after his conviction, it would be three more years until he fully confessed to the crime. I was eight when I stood, uncomfortable, in a stiff dress at her grave for the second time—more flowers, same priest, same prayers.

Thankfully, the darkness was always graced with laughter and lullabies and being a kid and building forts and, later, learning about my period from my crazy grandma. If I got any special attention, I didn't know it. Life went on. Time was supposed to heal all wounds. My few memories of her, despite my every attempt, faded with each passing holiday.

I was in Mrs. Dunne's third grade class when my dad finally confessed. We faced a whole new wave of reporters, news crews, and commotion. They replayed the footage on every channel: me, five years old again, clad in overalls, with my Care Bear, walking into the courtroom. And just like before, my grandpa taped all the newsreels, so we'd never forget, he said.

For our final TV interview, my grandparents, the boys, and I sat in our church clothes in the front room to answer the reporter's questions. I shifted around on Grandma Kate's lap in my neatly pressed striped Easter dress. Everybody had a turn to talk. I was last. "Katie, now that the case is closed, do you think you will be able to move on?"

I'm not sure how I knew it then, especially when so many years of uncertainty were still to come, but I was confident: "Yeah," I grinned. "I think I'll make it."

Kat Hurley

Kat Hurley is an author, freelance writer, blogger, and slam poet. She studied journalism in college, yet spent seven long years teaching high school mathematics "gathering material." Kat is excited to be back in the US after a year perpetually lost in Southeast Asia, where she was amazed to find enough quiet to write her first book. She recently ran a successful Kickstarter campaign for her upcoming memoir, *I Think I'll Make It*, which will be published later this year. Kat lives in Brooklyn with her fiancé. She can be spied online at kathurley.com, ithinkillmakeit.com, and (her newest project) gratitudeisthenewsexy.com.

One Thought to Keep

Sierra Trees

Someone I once cared for deeply told me that the most interesting people he had met were those who had known failure, hardship, defeat, and loss. They possessed an undeniable gratitude, a sensitivity and appreciation that filled their souls with an unstoppable fire sealed with kindness, compassion, and pure strength. He told me these people came from the depths of living a real life. They did not simply happen, they were tested, and what made them so interesting was who they became afterward.

I woke up that morning with the feeling that the day held the contents of any other Monday. A slight sun peeped through the fog that hazed across the Golden Gate Bridge, a common sight as the San Francisco Bay entered the first days of June. The morning embraced a simple perfection—the clarity of the sky, the rare light to my eyes as the 6:00 AM alarm resounded against my bedroom walls. I remember my breakfast of scrambled eggs and half-burnt toast to have been indisputably better than most. I now see this day, this beautifully simple day, as the day I was tested.

At the inexperienced and sheltered age of fourteen, my knowledge of death was limited. It took cover distant from my adolescent brain and out of reach from my childish hands. I had lived a sheltered life with my single father for many years. He shaped our lives in order to keep the uneasiness of a real existence at bay. Even my parents' early divorce and my older sister's sickness were sugar coated for me. My father mastered the art of painting a happy picture for me, and with his death the picturesque depiction of my life came crumbling down around me.

I found myself, at fourteen, doing my best to find that stability for myself that I'm not sure existed to begin with. Somewhere deep inside, I knew this life always waited, always lurked in the corners of our big white house and family Christmas cards. For fourteen years, I had chosen ignorance. The day the courts gave my dad full custody of me, I chose to believe it had nothing to do with my mother's behavior. The winter my beautiful sister came back from boarding school as thin as a rake, I elected to trust it must have been a high school phase. I could choose to see my life in this way, because my dad let me hide and seek comfort in his caring blue eyes and supportive hands. My naiveté was no longer possible after that Monday in June when I lost the one piece of glue that kept the Trees family together, my father.

I moved to Santa Barbara, unpacked my San Francisco life into a small boarding school dorm room in Carpinteria, and began to grow. There is an isolation that comes along with being fourteen years old, no matter the circumstances. High School years are inevitably some of the toughest for all of us. As I entered mine, I searched for familial support that no longer existed. I was alone. While my friends worried about what to wear and who to kiss, I was concerned with my new life. With a sister falling apart before my eyes and a mother fighting to fill the shoes of the impossible, I found myself lost. With time I realized there is no explanation for a loss like that, and I found my heart settling the less I searched for it. My father left a void with his passing, and I handled my grief by trying to fill that place the best I could. I pulled my young mind together, hired a lawyer, cared for my lost sister, worked hard at a relationship with my mother, and found myself stepping into my dad's shoes.

To say it happened in those four easy steps would be an insult to the process. There was a new sense of independence that I found with this new life I was entering, and with independence came great responsibility. I found myself looking to memories of my father to guide me through this new responsibility that my young hands were not equipped to handle. It's incredible how you find support in the most unexpected places. I built a new family for myself; my friends and my writing became my support system. There were times when all I wanted was someone to hide behind once more; his strong hands and caring blue eyes called to me as I reached young adulthood at an impossibly fast rate. For the first time in my life, at fourteen, I was worried about financially supporting my mother, taking care of a sister I didn't understand, and figuring my own life out all at once. These were all aspects of life that my father had taken care of for me. As much as I wanted to hide away and break down, that was not an option for me.

With time, I came upon happiness much like that I had with my father. Only this time, it was truthful, it was real. I found a new person within myself: a young woman who could handle a real existence. There have been ups and downs since the passing of my father, and I've built a great support system to help me through those times. If my father hadn't died when he did, I wouldn't be the woman I am today. I am strong, I am independent, I am my father's daughter. I look back at that Monday, my perfect Monday in June, as the day I became a real person.

Sierra Trees

Sierra Theresa Trees was born on her father's apple farm in Springdale, UT. At a young age, her family moved to San Francisco, where she grew up. She attended Katherine Delmar Burkes School, an all-girls middle school, until she moved to Southern California to live with her mom in Santa Barbara and attend a boarding school, Cate. Sierra spent many of her years focused on the arts—reading books, writing, and studying history, ceramics, and drawing. Sierra attended her first year of college at University of Oregon, where she declared her English major. Sierra is now transferring to Fordham University in Manhattan to continue her college years and hopes to become a writer.

Bloom Where You Are Planted

Christine A. Krahling

Friendships can develop in many ways. Some are expected: when kindergartners find themselves sharing a snack, say, or when two moms meet at the gym and find they love both spending time with their children and finding precious time away from them. Some friendships take you by surprise, which is how it happened with Ginny and me. We met through a mutual friend almost ten years ago. Ginny had a home-based craft business, and I called on her often to make one-of-a-kind gifts for friends and their children, as well as to create keepsakes for my daughters' various milestones. There were chocolate birthday party favors, a high school graduation quilt made of T-shirts, and many a dance recital costume that needed altering. Ginny was always happy to oblige, even when I couldn't give her much notice.

When it came time to tell friends and neighbors that my family and I were moving out of state, I called Ginny personally, as the thought of her passing my house on the way to the park and seeing a "for sale" sign with no warning seemed insensitive. While we'd never so much as gone out for coffee in all the time we'd known each other, we shared many a chat in my foyer when she stopped by—her newborn sleeping in the car at times—to pick up what needed mending or drop off one of her latest creations. We talked about all kinds of things—mostly parenting and the challenges that come with having children more than a few years apart. We were grateful not to be taking part in that "crazy busy" community of moms who overscheduled their children and then complained of exhaustion incessantly. We thought that we were good parents and good planners, focused on quality time with our children.

It was Ginny who was one of my biggest cheerleaders when I landed a position as a local magazine editor. I joked that she was part of a small but exclusive fan club who'd tell me each issue that they'd actually read my editor's letter and liked the magazine's content. Ginny never failed to lift me up, always complimenting my achievements whether personal or professional, always telling me what a great person she thought I was. It was Ginny who talked me off the ledge when my older daughter's prom gown returned from the drycleaners with a stain on it (this was before the prom) and listened to my "dance mom drama." After seeing my failed attempt at securing elastic with a stapler to my daughter's recital top hat, she laughed and asked, "Has she had her tetanus shot?"

It was Ginny who listened to my concerns once our "for sale" sign went up—that my husband and I were now tackling a commuter marriage until we could move at the end of the school year, how concerned I was for my younger daughter and how she'd adjust to fitting in at the tender age of eleven, how my widowed mom would fare after we left, and on and on. Ginny listened with support, and we continued meeting in my foyer, wrapping up final projects: good-bye gifts for teachers and the women at the salon; one last set of dance-recital-themed candy bouquets.

So it was no easy day when Ginny made her last delivery to me one morning: this time a quilt of woven T-shirts for my younger daughter, one that included bits and pieces of the life she had made from preschooler to middle-schooler. I gave Ginny a handwritten note that expressed all that she and our chats had meant to me over the years and how much I would miss not only her many talents but her friendship too. A special bond had been made in my foyer, but now it was time to move on. Like they say, to everything a season. My future—and that of my family—was now daunting and uncertain.

After Ginny gave me my daughter's quilt, she handed me a bag. As I reached in, I realized that while I had gifted many of Ginny's custom-made creations over the years, I would now have something that I could call my own. I pulled out a beautifully embroidered pillow, on it stitched the words, "Bloom Where You Are Planted."

Ginny—fighting the tears we promised we wouldn't shed—told me that many years ago, when she herself had moved to a strange place—no family or friends to be found—she had come upon this saying and had made herself a pillow with the same words stitched upon it, similar to the one that I was now holding. She said that until she found her way, she looked at that pillow each and every day, until eventually, she "bloomed." She said she had faith that I would do the same. Suddenly, my future didn't seem so intimidating. I packed that pillow into one of our "open immediately" boxes so that I would feel as if I had some sense of familiarity in our new home, and perhaps an angel looking over my shoulder.

Ginny and I still keep in touch. In fact, one day she told me that she had been at the supermarket (the only other place we had run into each other over the years) and thought she saw me. We said we missed each other, and our chats.

The pillow now rests on a chair in the sitting room of my new home, surrounded by other things that give me great comfort—my yoga blanket, my books, and the gift of a true friend.

Christine A. Krahling

Christine A. Krahling is a Writer's Digest Award–winning writer, blogger (celiacsavvy.wordpress.com), and former editor of *Lehigh Valley Marketplace*. She has developed a presentation titled "When a Child Has Celiac Disease: A Guide for Educators and Health Care Professionals," and is available for speaking engagements. Christine's essay *The Most Meaningful Legacies Can't Be Measured* appears in the Hallmark book *50 Truths Worth Knowing*. She is a contributor to the book *Tell Me What to Eat If I Have Celiac Disease*. Christine has been a book club facilitator for more than ten years. She lives with her family in Syracuse, New York.

Elderly

Eileen McIntyre

On the threshold of turning sixty-five, the age most countries term "elderly," what does a woman do?

This woman sings in the shower—no apologies. I dance at home with my husband, although the "fast" dances have gotten fewer and the slow ones have gotten slower. I have traded in my high heels for "sensible shoes," although I confess to asking for and getting a pair of red 3½" heels for Christmas from my husband—whoa! OK, they are burgundy, and I wear them with the skinny jeans I bought on a whim. I hear the gasps!

I walk. I will admit I sometimes run when no one is looking. Ziplining is a dream. I go to lunch accompanied by a book. I jump on the bed occasionally on a devilish whim to wake up my husband with a laugh and a kiss.

One of my favorite things to do is walk on the beach, raise my hands skyward when no one is watching, twirl around, look up, and breathe in the salty air, offering a prayer of thankfulness. At times I squirm into a bathing suit; more often I slide on shorts and a T-shirt. I find I am into comfort these days. I rush to feel the chill or warmth of the water on my skin, burrow my toes in the wet sand as waves roll over my feet. Watching the sun as it prepares to go to sleep, I marvel at the changing colors brush-stroked across the sky. I savor lying down on a hammock and drinking in the stars. I go to the movie theater, internalize a chick flick, and let the tears run down my cheeks as I laugh or cry.

I study crafts that I dream of mastering and travel to places unmarked by my footprints. I vary my way home. I talk to people I have never met and compliment them, or at least leave them a smile along the way. I speak love letters and thank-you notes to family and friends, and on occasion put pen to parchment.

There are cons on this journey to "elderly." I glance and other times stare in the mirror at the face that doesn't look familiar with its gorges and cracks, facial hair that peeks out like blades of grass begging to be mown, and dry and brown patches that claim territory during sleep. The invasion is spreading to the outer banks as I am working on acceptance. My body is beginning to make itself known with unpleasant sensations, but I am on the upper crust of the earth and not under the dirt. I try not to stress when the glasses I am looking for are on the top of my head or the car keys are not in the place they call home or I can't recall someone's name when I am standing in front of them. I don't have to like these things.

I awake each morning thankful to God, who has granted me one more day. I have the urge to fit in as much as I can in that twenty-four hours, including moments of quiet—moments where if I listen, I can hear my breath.

I am more afraid of not living than I am of dying.

So, my action plan for dealing with the transition to "elderly" is to keep on going for as long as I can and to refuse to be reined in by a term that others mark on me. I am blessed. After I am dead, fallen like a tree, others can count my rings. The rings can't whisper my story.

Elderly? I'm not feeling it in my soul—how about you?

Eileen McIntyre

Eileen McIntyre is a new writer living her dream. She is currently writing her first contemporary women's fiction novel. Flash fiction is her favorite genre, and her writing has been published online at 100wordstory.org and fiftywordstories.com. Eileen is retired and lives in Magalia, California, with her most ardent fan—her husband Michael. She loves life and enjoys attending writer's conferences and networking with other writers.

Building an Empire to Investing in What I Love

Janet Hanson

In 1995, my husband and I launched Milestone Capital, an institutional money management firm. We worked really hard and had one big lucky break—we formed a strategic partnership with Bear Stearns, and as they say, the rest was history. By 2000, we were managing over $2 billion in assets and we loved the thrill of running our own business.

By 2002, we were flying high and had moved to Bedford, New York —a bucolic horse town about ninety minutes north of New York City. We bought a seventeen-acre property with a 7,000-square-foot house and a stunning pool out back. We built a squash court for our son, Chris, to play on, which was a very novel thing to do. Our daughter, Meredith, stabled her horses at a great barn not far from our home. We were "Team Hanson" and had a dazzling, amazing life.

In September 2002, I was diagnosed with breast cancer. Next up, I was told that I should have my ovaries removed because my doctor thought there was an extremely high probability that I would develop ovarian cancer. So I did that, and in the ensuing months had to contend with several bouts of skin cancer (face, chest, and leg). I was extraordinarily depressed and for the first time in my life was put on several different antidepressants. That was when the wheels started to come off the cart.

But being a type A, I figured that if I continued to move at the speed of light, I could outrun all my demons. By 2004, I had agreed to step down as the CEO of Milestone Capital to work for Joe Gregory, the president and COO of Lehman Brothers. I signed a three-year contract that allowed my husband to exit Milestone and launch what would become his own very lucrative consulting business.

One of the few things that made me really happy was investing in other women. I invested in women running for political office and women starting their own businesses, and I hired a ton of women to help me run 85 Broads, a global network I had launched in 1997.

Then it all crashed and burned. In September 2008, Lehman Brothers went under, and life as I knew it pretty much imploded.

My husband exited our marriage, which caught my kids and me by complete surprise. In 2009, I sold our house in Bedford for peanuts, bought a tiny cottage on Nantucket, and tried to figure out how I was going to stay afloat financially. Downsizing from 7,000 square feet to 1,500 square feet is a very humbling experience. I gave away almost the entire contents of our home and discovered that less was not more, it was just less.

I was, in a word, distraught. I wanted to go back in time and try to figure out how this horrible trauma could have happened, but I had to compartmentalize my grief and think about my two kids. I was now responsible for every single aspect of their lives, which was frightening and overwhelming. At the time, my daughter was a sophomore in college and my son was a senior in high school.

I have no doubt that my inner strength came from the women in 85 Broads, who were fearlessly blazing amazing trails of their own. I found myself cheering loudly for every single one of their professional successes, which was exactly the antidote I needed to offset my profound sense of personal sadness. In many ways, 85 Broads was my "village," as the women who had needed my help and guidance now returned the favor many times over. Bottom line, when you are in a position to give, you should give unconditionally. When you are no longer in a position to be the giver, those you helped won't have to be called upon; they will show up on your doorstep.

For the last five years, I have invested in what I love, my two fabulous children. Mer now has her own art boutique/gallery on Nantucket and is just crushing it! She is dazzlingly talented. Chris recently graduated from Dartmouth and is pursuing a career as a professional squash player. He was named one of the top ten best college players in the US for three of his four years at Dartmouth. He also won the Kenneth Archibald Prize—the highest athletic award given to a graduating senior who has shown athletic and academic excellence as well as high moral character during all four years of college. Given that both of my kids have only one parent in their lives, I have been blown away by their courage, resilience, and faith in themselves and in me.

My latest transition has been to exit the stage as CEO of 85 Broads and turn over the reins to Sallie Krawcheck, a former Wall Street rock star. Now I can laser-focus on investing in what I love—Mer and Chris!

Janet Hanson

As the founder and former CEO of 85 Broads, Janet Hanson has built a global network community of 30,000 trailblazing women whose mission is to generate exceptional professional and social value for its members. She has a BA from Wheaton College and an MBA from Columbia Business School. She has worked in Fixed Income Sales & Trading at Goldman Sachs and been the CEO of Milestone Capital and the MD/Senior Advisor to the President and COO of Lehman Brothers. She serves on the board of the Christopher and Dana Reeve Foundation and is a former Wheaton College trustee and an Associate Fellow of Pierson College at Yale University. She was the Middlebury College honorary degree recipient in 2007. Janet's No. 1 passion is her children—her daughter Meredith and her son Chris.

Starting from the Edge

Belva Davis

Someone once told me that to get red wine out of a white carpet, you are to start at the outermost edges of the spill and blot gently as you work your way to the center of the stain.

Too bad I didn't know that when I attempted to clean up the biggest stain of my life. Instead of starting with the easy parts at the edges of the problem and working my way into the core of the issue, I jumped right into the eye of the storm with a big splash to force a change, without a plan or any sense of direction.

The truth is, I didn't know much when I decided to embark on the biggest transition of my life. I just knew that I needed a change. On an instinctual level, I knew I needed to rid myself of dangerous self-devaluing habits and beliefs. Even now, all these years and experiences later, I still count that as one of the most difficult—but necessary—things a woman can do.

I started by leaving my husband, giving him the house, taking my small children, and disappearing into the night. I was running away. It would be years before I could acknowledge that the move had addressed only the nucleus of my stain—though it was surrounded by a million other spots that were bleeding outward, asking to be changed too—trying to teach me the lesson that I needn't keep yielding to others and to fear.

This is how I described that first jump in my book *Never in My Wildest Dreams*, and these are the words that got me out the door that night:

"Get over it—divorce is not acceptable in this family. I'd rather see you dead than go through a divorce."

* * *

I had to get out of there.

For three months, I schemed with the precision of plotting in a detective novel. First I informed the Navy that I would not be returning from maternity leave and requested my full retirement disbursement: $3,000. I paid cash for a used car—a huge blue-and-white Plymouth sedan—that I bought only on the condition that I could store it on the sales lot until I needed it. I spent hours hovering over the counter at the AAA office, perusing cheap motel listings and maps as I plotted our route along desolate country roads that meandered south toward Los Angeles. And I hired a moving van, which was to appear at our house at 9:30 a.m., about an hour and a half after Frank left for work, to load up the furniture, toys, and clothing the children and I would later need and deposit them in a rented storage space. To avoid confrontation, the timing had to be perfect.

An opaque fog enveloped us as we sped through the night, our own headlights reflecting back to cast a luminous halo around our lumbering Plymouth. Tule fog is notorious in California's Central Valley—it causes more weather-related deaths than any other force of nature in the state. For the most part, I avoided venturing onto any easily traceable highways. Our greatest danger was that if we needed help, no other living soul was around for miles.

For the sake of my children, I feigned calmness. But I was inexperienced behind the wheel—an awful driver who kept hitting the brakes at the slightest cause. The bassinet on the backseat, with baby Darolyn tucked inside, would tumble forward; six-year-old Steven would grab it and slide it back into place. He asked where we were going. I told him only that we couldn't live with his father anymore and needed to find someplace else to be for a while. Mostly he was quiet.

We changed motels every night, and at each we propped a chair against the door. None of us slept soundly.

In Los Angeles, I checked us into a flashy Hollywood motel with a shimmering blue swimming pool on the Sunset Strip. We stayed three nights, giving Steven a chance to swim, relax, and pretend to be on vacation. A phone conversation with my mother shattered our fantasy refuge: Frank's mother had put a private eye on our trail. Mrs. Davis was a strong-willed woman who was devoted to her grandchildren, and I knew she would never give up. For a few frantic hours, I considered driving us into Mexico. Then the rational part of my brain kicked in, and I realized I couldn't speak a phrase of Spanish and we would have no one to help us. Besides, I was running out of money.

I could only hope that Frank's temper was similar to my father's, and that with the passage of time, he would simmer down. For all my masterminding of this elaborate escape, I really had no plan for what would come next.

* * *

Transitions—be they big or small—cannot happen unless there is an openness to change, and to be truly open to change, one has to be willing to take risks. Risk has been a keyword on my journey to newness, a journey that started when I fled from that toxic marriage and continues for me still today.

I risked the threat of bodily harm to my children and to myself. I risked failure as I ventured out on my own, and again as I sought a new career as a writer. I risked public ridicule as I put myself forward into vulnerability as an untrained television journalist. But what was my alternative to taking these risks? Never being fully confident or realizing the authentic "me" inside of me? That prospect was—and still is— much scarier than the unknown.

As unbelievable as it may seem, because of my latent issues with self-value, I found it easier to see myself as a pioneer in the world of media than as a competitor trying to measure up head-to-head with another person's skills.

Six years after the blue-and-white Plymouth's drive across California's Central Valley, I landed my dream job as Belva Davis, Television Reporter. I found comfort in the fact that my audience and I would learn together what it was like to be the first black woman television reporter in the western United States.

Almost fifteen years after that drive, I was in Cuba reporting on Fidel Castro.

Thirty years later, I count Maya Angelou, Nancy Pelosi, and Dianne Feinstein among my colleagues and have published my own memoir.

Over the course of many years lived and many risks taken, there have been glorious rewards, to be sure, but there have been many roadblocks. I have learned from those roadblocks that diving into the center of an obstacle blindly, as I once did, can mistakenly make matters worse. Similarly, if you apply pressure to the center of a red wine stain, it actually sends the red wine outward, broadening the stain.

It was a hard-earned lesson that real, lasting, inward transition takes time, support, and tender loving care. With this lesson in hand, I have spent a lot of time in my wiser years blotting around the edges of issues that might have been much larger if I had handled them impatiently. Starting from the edge of anything, you can absorb more guidance, preparation, and perspective on what it is you are dealing with.

Fortified by awards and honors, I've kept moving closer to the center of where the real work of self-realization must take place. I've begun to accept the fact that removing every trace of a spill is not necessarily a good thing, for the same reason that not taking risks is not a good thing.

Even now, in my eighth decade on this earth, I face risks. For example, on any given night on live television, I am aware that I could blow fifty years of my work. One of those blank moments that sometimes occur at my age could be caught on camera, and it could become the most memorable thing I have ever done. Still, I will continue to go on camera. I will continue to take risks. Denying my ability to rise above fear and insecurity would be denying the self-worth I have spent decades cultivating.

Belva Davis

Award-winning journalist Belva Davis has been working as a journalist in the San Francisco Bay Area for nearly fifty years. She has anchored news programs at KPIX-TV, KQED Public Television 9, and KRON-TV. She has been the host of *This Week in Northern California* for more than nineteen years.

Vati's Hühner, by Barbara Libby-Steinmann

Artist Statement:

I am waking up this morning in my childhood bedroom on my parents' farm listening to familiar sounds of my childhood. The rooster is crowing his morning song, and a little further in the distance I hear the soothing ding of cowbells. It is 6 a.m., and the milking machine just turned on. I hear my brother's footsteps coming down the stairs. In the room next to me, I hear my mom getting up. Both of them are getting ready to work the morning milking shift. I am thinking that I will hear my dad soon, getting himself ready for his routine on his farm. It is all so familiar, the way it has always has been.

But no, it seems so surreal! Vati, you are not fastening your boots to get ready this morning for yet another day's work on the farm. We all miss you so very much. The animals on the farm are wondering, where you are? The beautiful heirloom chickens you have raised so proudly are awaiting you to bring them their grain. You would have never missed a day's work; the routine on the farm was your daily breath. You were always devoted, passionate.

We said good-bye to you last night. As I was stroking your hair, still light brown in color with hardly any gray, I kept thinking, "You are going to wake up." I imagine you holding my hand gently and then squeezing mine in yours, strong and calloused, as you did so many times when I was a little girl. You would tell me, "Be strong; you are not alone. Together we will get through this."

Yes, together we will get through this. Vati, you will always be with me. Your presence on the farm will always be there.

Love you always,
Your daughter Barbara

My upbringing on a dairy farm in Switzerland built the foundation of my deep connection with nature and the land. My passion is to be outdoors, breathing in the fresh cool air of a new day, feeling the sea breeze on my skin, climbing a mountain and enjoying stunning views. As I spend time outdoors, either on bike rides or hikes, nature's beauty is awe inspiring to me. I might notice vast shapes, textures, lines, contrasts, colors, and the delicate details of a bird's feather. My eye might catch the simple beauty of the spiral on a small shell. As I exercise, fragments of ideas or entire concepts pop into my head with the rhythmic movement of my body and breath. I use a camera to document what I see. My photo archive is an invaluable tool for my creative process.

In capturing nature's beauty on my canvas, I like to trust my instincts and stay fresh. I experiment with simplifying shapes and lines, moving towards the abstract, but never completely losing touch with the essential details. My color palette is vibrant, and with the use of complementary colors I am able to give my paintings subtle movement.

Barbara Libby-Steinmann

Barbara Libby-Steinmann is an elementary school art teacher and painter. She creates a challenging curriculum that facilitates all students in discovering and developing their artistic and creative skills. Barbara sees herself continuing to travel down the road of painter and art educator. She will use her enthusiasm to nurture innovation and passion in every subject, perfecting her knack for creating beautiful paintings. Born and raised in Switzerland, she now resides with her husband and two cats in West Marin, California. She earned a Bachelor of Department Store Merchant Designer from Gestalterische Berufschule in Zürich, Switzerland, a BFA in illustration from California College of the Arts, and a Single Subject Art Teaching Credential from Dominican University.

Section Two

Growing Pains

Monkey Bars

Kerri Devine

My daughter runs her dimpled hand over the shoulder of my soiled green T-shirt, down the length of the sleeve, stroking my arm the way you would a stray cat. "Niiiice mommy," she says. Hardly, I cringe, thinking about all the times today I wished I could lose her. It's noon. Already we've wrestled with getting dressed ("Doooon't *want* a sweater!"), played restaurant (I made a grilled cheese while she cut plastic root vegetables with an imaginary knife), and colored. "Draw a cat," she demands, tossing her Dora coloring book on the floor and handing me a crayon. "Purple!" Her fine blonde hair skims the top of her cheeks where her creamy skin is newly dotted with freckles. When I leave the kitchen to put the damp dishtowels in the laundry room, I hear her calling from her high chair, making sure I'm still near, "Waaaant to see Mommy?"

Each day they come. Somewhere between lunch and arts and crafts, items from my to-do list appear in my mind—a running catalog of resentments: Take up yoga. Make gazpacho. Clean out the hall closet. I'm angry I have no time alone anymore and wondering how long this phase will last.

"Whiskers!" Lulu says, reminding me to add a few brown lines fanning out from the cat's face. Her hand is warm, and she smiles at me as we hold the bent crayon together and trace the cat's tail. Her sweetness washes over me like the high from a grade-school crush.

That's the way it is now. These feelings come in pairs, difficult to reconcile. I'm never quite sure whether I want to hold her or cry, exhausted as I am by her neediness.

I hired a sitter, a girl down the street, to come for an afternoon or two so I could catch up on things. Stripping the sheets from the bed,

I watch them from the upstairs guest room. My daughter is running around in circles on the grass, dizzying herself until she takes a tumble. I can hear her through the open window: "all . . . fall . . . *down!*" She is both taller and leaner than I remember, but her legs still hold those last folds. I know when summer ends, they'll be gone. I see her running across the lawn with Kelly, running away from me. Soon she'll be in school. I want to run after her, tumble to the ground together, hear her ask, "Tickles?" and do a belly laugh when I blow loud raspberries on her bare feet. I worry there won't be enough moments like this before she goes to school, prefers her friends' company to mine, and each one I give away to someone else brings a temporary twinge, the subtle pain of something missing, a memory we won't share.

As I fold her clothes, I notice the framed photo of us on my dresser. Lulu is wearing one of those heathery skullcaps with ears so they make your children look like newborn bear cubs. Her face is pressed against mine, and I have the distant look of a new mother who is at once besotted and overwhelmed. The photo is in black-and-white; the finish holds the blur of those early moments together. They say infants don't know where they end and you begin until around six months. My daughter just turned two, and I'm still trying to figure it out.

I remember those days. I was a jumble of nerves and neuroses—afraid to go outside, paralyzed by her crying, worried I might dislocate her tiny arm every time I changed a onesie. Yet as insecure as I was then, I miss my daughter's babyhood. I miss the roundness of her, the scent of pink lotion even when she wasn't wearing any, the way her entire body moved when she breathed against my chest after an inconsolable cry.

The sitter is gone now. After Lulu's nap, we head off to the swing set. Before I can get to her, she's on the top rung of the monkey bars, the one I didn't even know she could climb. "Stop on the top step," I say, nervously. "That's for the big kids."

I scoop her up and into the swing, tickling the inside of her thigh as I slide the plastic panel down the ropes to her knees. "Nice Lulu," I say, as I begin to push my big girl up to the sky.

Kerri Devine

Kerri Devine is a marketing and communications consultant to major corporations and nonprofit organizations, and a ghostwriter for important business leaders and public figures. She lives in New York. This essay represents the author's first piece published under her own name.

Into the Driver's Seat

Nancy Davis Kho

In three short months, my oldest daughter will officially be fifteen and a half and entitled to a learning permit for her California driver's license. When she was an infant, I thought I'd dread the moment I'd have to release her to the open roads. Turns out, not so much.

Part of my willingness to see her transition into the driver's seat is a product of the desperation that comes from four years of driving her and her younger sister back and forth to classes at their ballet school. The girls don't always attend the same classes, because that would be too convenient, so even with sporadic carpooling we're talking about a dozen round-trips between the house and the studio each week. The station wagon and I follow the seven-minute route faithfully, to the point where I suspect my car could teach Google a thing or two about self-driving automobiles. I'm thankful to anyone who will help break the monotony of chauffeuring, even if it's a kid who is still in braces and might sing One Direction songs into the gearshift.

Another factor in my lack of consternation is that my daughter continues to mature into an older version of the sensible, risk-averse girl she has always been. At five, while learning to ride her bike, she'd first make sure the white plastic basket attached to the handlebars was fully stocked with Band-Aids. Then, and only then, would she strap on her helmet and head grimly down the street, little legs pumping beneath her. She never forgets her house key, always has her bus pass, and will not even try a new dessert unless someone taste-tests it first. My guess is that she'll check her blind spot six times before making a lane change.

Maybe it's that I'm a little too trusting of blind luck, and here I speak of the strangers into whose cars I regularly climb, thanks to the only-in-the-Bay-Area "Casual Carpool" phenomenon. Casual Carpool operates like a free taxi service, enabling drivers to load up two passengers so they can cross the Bay Bridge in the less-congested carpool lane and pay a reduced toll, while providing a free ride to commuters who queue up in an orderly line and advance, two by two.

It's genius, when the driver obeys the rules of the road. But everyone who participates in it has a Casual Carpool horror story to whip out during a dinner party: of the lady in the powder-blue Corolla who putters along at thirty-five miles per hour as six lanes of traffic whip by her going seventy; the cigar-smoking driver in the Cadillac; or the jackass who steers with his knees while cradling his phone in one hand and using the other to fiddle with the radio station. Still, I haven't been mangled in a car accident. Yet.

But I think the real reason I've lost my reservations about my daughter getting her driver's license is that in the two years since she became a teen, I've realized that driving is the sole activity for a fledgling adult that comes with a concrete set of expectations and reinforcement from the legal community, not to mention seatbelts and airbags.

Navigating high school is at least as hazardous as driving a car, but its utter lack of security features makes an '85 Yugo look like an armored tank. Of course I talk to my daughter about safe sex, responsible drinking, and online predators until I am blue in the face. She could probably give those lectures herself, verbatim.

But wouldn't it be nice if there were something more than an arbitrary age minimum for alcohol and drug use, so you'd know your kid passed a multiple-choice test on substance abuse administered by the state before taking that first sip or puff? That airbags would deploy and punch a lecherous man in the nuts before he initiated a fateful interaction with your naive teenage daughter? That if kids participated in risky behaviors online, a virtual policeman would swoop onto the scene, maybe from a hidden chat window, and suspend their right to type for sixty days?

And those are the easy issues with my daughter, where at least I can clearly articulate what her dad and I consider acceptable standards of behavior. As a parent of a teen I'm continually confronted by issues where there isn't a black-and-white answer, where my words of wisdom —such as they are—are merely my best guess at saying the appropriate thing. Friendship dramas, academic choices, family dynamics: I never expected to find myself so tongue-tied so often as a parent, scrabbling not just for the right advice but for the right delivery, so that I don't give her the impression I lack faith in her ripening judgment.

I wish I had a map I could give her that shows landmarks like "True-Blue Friends" and "Respectful Boys" and "Dead-End Jobs" and "Knuckleheads—Road Closed—Detour." It would be so much easier to hand her a spiral-bound study guide of road signs to memorize that would help guide her safely into adulthood.

But we're talking about the fluid and shape-changing beast that is normal human development, the alternately dark and joyous places you have to pass through to become a grownup. Sometimes, when the house is full of the ecstatic gleeful energy that only a high school freshman girl can muster, I think being a teen is like Anaheim: nice place for a short visit, but I wouldn't want to live there.

I have no reason to doubt my kid. She's made great choices so far. Even so, I know she needs to hit a few bumps, run out of gas, and take some wrong turns in the process of moving from the passenger seat of childhood to the driver's seat of her adult life. It's important that my husband and I give her plenty of room to fail and learn, fail and learn, until she gets it right.

So as I get accustomed to my new role riding shotgun, I try not to pump invisible breaks or white-knuckle the dashboard as she confidently takes the wheel.

Nancy Davis Kho
Nancy Davis Kho is a writer in Oakland, California, whose work has appeared in the *San Francisco Chronicle, The Morning News*, TheRumpus. net, and *Skirt!* magazine. An avid music fan, she writes about the years between being hip and breaking one at MidlifeMixtape.com.

Waiting Between the Lines

Mihee Kim-Kort

Trying not to look at the timer on my watch, I'm running around upstairs doing anything to avoid the bathroom for three minutes. Folding towels. Refolding towels. Making up the bed we never make up after a sleepless night of tossing and turning. Adjusting the comforter too many times. Organizing piles of paper into new piles. Then moving them around. Wiping down the desk and bookshelves with the sleeve of my sweatshirt and collecting as much dust as possible, as if it's the shimmery remains of fairies' wings. The more fairy dust, the better the chances for those barely whispered wishes and sighs that have left my lips.

I let myself look down at my wrist. It's 3:09. I put the stick down at 3:06:47. With a few more grains of seconds left, I slowly walk back to the bathroom in measured steps, methodically counting them too. I look at the sink where the stick is lying face up. I reach for it, breathing quickly, my stomach filling with fireworks and shooting stars that I try to squelch because it's always too early to celebrate anything.

I see: One. Blue. Line. Immediately, I toss it into the trashcan.

I lie down on the floor on my stomach, head in my arms, and close my eyes. I breathe, inhaling the chemicals of floor and bathroom tile cleaner, not caring because I have nothing inside me to protect, nothing to shield from outside toxins, to worry over and be anxious about. Nothing. I begin to cry. Gasping for air, I turn over. It's only been a year. Some people try for ten years. *Get it together, girl.* It could be worse. Way worse. We've only tried for twelve months. We've only started the medication. We've only started tracking the weeks.

We've *only* . . .

They aren't helping—these words that have become a mantra

of sorts. Words that I've memorized—I say perfectly each time, like the proper and necessary closure. A magic spell. An incantation that makes me eventually rise from the floor like Lazarus from his tomb. *Only* isn't working now. Month after month for twelve months, it's been a turbulent flight amidst skies that hold these hopes—nauseating and thrilling, exciting and disappointing. Honestly, it's soul-crushing. *Only* doesn't make watching baptisms easier. *Only* doesn't dilute the headache of Mother's Day. *Only* doesn't keep my heart from shattering when I receive a surprise hug from a child or smell the top of a baby's head. *Only* doesn't prevent the stabs of agony inside me anytime I see a swollen belly or an infant seat.

But, I stand back up. *Only* finally works. Sort of. Even if it's *only* one blue line, I have to get up. So, I find the calendar hanging on the wall and mark another day in the month ahead. We hold our breath in the weeks in between as we count down the days. We make up stories about the strange cravings and miraculous expansion I will someday experience during those nine months. We dream, night and day, murmuring prayers for those two blue lines.

I sit for the first time in a room that would eventually become like a second home.

I am struck by the nameless, neutral color of the walls and the contrast between the innocuous and clichéd prints of babies and puppies and the various posters of the female anatomy. I look around, and my eyes linger on the intimidating diagnostic machines, the lone chair for the assumed support person, and the red hazardous-materials container—these seem like an odd combination for decor. Andy stands next to me, somehow managing to look both casual and jittery, which is accentuated by his six-foot-three frame. I can almost feel him vibrating next to me. As I lay back, I look up at the ceiling, where there is a poster of a bright-blue ocean reminiscent of the beaches in the Dominican Republic. It seems bizarre at first, but its sedating effect on me slowly makes sense.

I suddenly feel very serious. It's a moment we've been awaiting for almost two years now. *How much of this is wishful thinking? Have I made this all up? Are we really here?* My hands are tight with uncertainty and I can feel my toes curling down as I try to hold in any feelings of anxiety and stress. The doctor walks in and starts chatting immediately, before even sitting down. "How are you feeling this morning?"

"OK." I lick my lips, wishing I had my ChapStick. "A little anxious, I think," I mouth dryly.

"Well, go ahead and lay back, and we'll take a look in there," she says as she puts on some rubber gloves and brings one machine with a screen much closer. "Your beta levels were perfect, so let's see what we have here."

The assistant, who I had forgotten was there, turns off the lights. A foreign yet soothing humming noise comes on as the screen lights up. It's black, but there are white scribbles and a vague outline of a circle on the screen. And then—a sound—a steady throbbing. "OK, let's see." her eyes are focused on the images and she has a smile pulling at the corners of her mouth. "So, there's the embryo, and you can hear its heartbeat."

"Really???" I ask, straining to make sense of the unbearably tiny marble in the middle of the screen. "We can hear its heartbeat? Now?" Andy asks, again. "That's amazing!"

"It's smaller than a grain of rice, but yes, it has a heartbeat." She continues to look at the screen, doing something to make the images shift a little. "Aaaaaaaaaaaaaaaand . . . it's not the only one in there. See the other one? It's looking good too!"

I sit up a little on my elbows, straining to look at the screen. Andy and I look at each other with eyes bulging and unblinking. Andy starts to sway a little. "Holy . . . I mean, I'm sorry . . . what do you mean, "the other one"? The other one . . . stuck, too?" he struggles for words.

"Yup! Twins! Congratulations!" she says. "So, we'll be seeing you every week now . . ." She continues to talk very matter-of-factly, but the words swirl away from me as my mind attempts to speed forward toward the end of nine months.

I lie back down looking at the screen and then again at the ceiling. I search out the Caribbean Sea for some reassuring sign, even a glimpse of some fantastical creature or remnant of angels' wings in the skies. The sunlight glances off the impossibly blue water into my eyes. I look down at my hands. My legs. My feet. Two. *Two embryos.* Here we are looking at *them.* Both of *them. They* both made it. We'd tried so hard for so long, and all of a sudden, there was a *they. They* were there, with heartbeats glowing like flickering fireflies.

I put one hand down to my stomach. I cover my face with my arm. I start to laugh and weep.

Mihee Kim-Kort

Mihee Kim-Kort is a clergywoman married to a clergyman, and mom to three children in Hoosier country. She grew up in the mountains of Colorado, then spent time in graduate school on the East Coast before she and her family settled down in Indiana. Her passions include writing, parenting, college student ministry, and engaging in social justice. She blogs regularly at First Day Walking, miheekimkort.com.

Mothering Is Just One Thing After Another

Vicki Larson

Like so many 1950s-era girls, I grew up practicing to be Mommy. I mothered my dolls; I fussed after my twelve-pound Yorkie, Teddy, doomed to spend his life having his hair brushed to a satiny sheen and wearing pink plastic bow clips; I looked after my friends' younger siblings (although they might remember it as something more along the lines of "bossed around" rather than "looked after").

As far as I could tell, this mothering stuff seemed pretty easy, so I never gave it too much of my mental energy. There were no starry-eyed dreams about becoming a wife and a mom—you know, the fairy-tale wedding, the house with the white picket fence, the 2.5 kids. I accepted that there'd be .5 of a kid as easily as I accepted the idea that airplanes could fly and that radios played music without having to fully grasp *how* they did it. Being a mother was one of those understood things, too: I would have a great job and then I'd find a great guy and we'd have kids.

It would just . . . happen.

So there was no surprise when, despite a few "youthful indiscretions" that almost threw me off track, it did. At thirty, I met a great guy, and a few years later, I was married and pregnant.

The first indication that I might have underestimated the ease of motherhood was when I miscarried. I was devastated and blamed it on those youthful indiscretions. Was I being punished? But a few months later, a baby bump emerged, and despite some challenging moments—a near-emergency C-section—I gave birth to a beautiful, healthy son.

Like all newborns, he was perfect. Like many new moms, however, I was not.

Besides a stint as a mother's helper while I was in junior high, I didn't have much experience with kids, let alone babies. I'd never even diapered one until I brought my son home.

Despite my feel-good experience with my relatively patient and accepting Yorkie, it was pretty obvious that this baby wasn't going to be as gracious and forgiving for very long.

As my son went from baby to active toddler to a boy who had very definite ideas about things, like who could take him out of the car seat, and how his shoelaces should be tied, I would sometimes watch him and think, "Gee, that's kind of odd. Are all kids so fussy? Is this 'normal'?" But he was my firstborn; I figured his somewhat baffling behaviors were part of the package deal of having a son. I began to refer to them as his "things," little endearing quirks that made him who he was. The "things" didn't last long, a few weeks perhaps, and they were constantly changing. As one "thing" went away, a different one replaced it. They were so goofy that his dad and I would often laugh about them. "If they're not getting in the way of his life, don't worry," his pediatrician assured me. And they weren't. He was a sweet, funny, kind, generally happy boy.

Still, my idea that mothering was relatively easy was being as challenged as a Supreme Court nominee at a confirmation hearing. I wanted to believe my pediatrician, but I was struggling. I didn't want opinions, I wanted answers. That's when I became the kind of mother who began turning to The Experts. There was always a pile of parenting books at my bedside and I became a regular at the all-day Saturday parenting workshop conference circuit.

Each time I went, I hoped I would gather some insight into my son's "things." I was always hopeful some other mother in the audience would ask, "How do you handle a toddler who has to hide his shoelaces?" "What do you say to a fourth-grader who insists on wearing a too-small dorky sweatshirt tied around his waist every day, even in summer?" "How should you stop an eleven-year-old from sniffing his knee?" "Do you battle a ninth-grader who throws a fit about taking off the only pair of jeans and T-shirt he'll wear so they can be washed?"

I heard lots of parenting fears and frustrations, but no one ever asked anything even remotely similar, and so I was on my own. It felt lonely.

At some point, I started to suspect that what we were dealing with was truly unique to us, and then I felt embarrassed about his "things." I feared others would notice them, too, because they seemed so obvious. I searched the faces of family and friends—*do you see what I see?* But I couldn't bring myself to talk about it because I didn't think they'd understand what I couldn't even understand myself. No one said anything, but that didn't mean they didn't see. As much as I hated to do it, I sometimes compared him with other kids, kids who seemed "normal," including his younger brother. When I felt confused and alone and sorry for myself, the word "freak" crossed my mind. Then I felt ashamed, too.

Then came the Mother of All "Things." He was sixteen when he walked by me one day, holding what appeared to be a lobster in his hands. Common in Maine, perhaps, but not so much in the San Francisco Bay Area. "Hey, come back here," I said to him. "What's in your hands?"

"Nothing," he mumbled as he shuffled over—slowly and with attitude, as only teenagers can—and held them out for me.

He was right. There was nothing in his hands. The "lobster" *was* his hands: blazing red, swollen and chafed.

"Mom," he said, his voice cracking, "I have a problem."

And then I understood.

He had tried valiantly to hide his latest "thing," but this one wasn't easily dismissed. The numerous trips he'd make to the bathroom day and night, the inordinately long time he'd spend in there, the sopping mess he left in his wake—all of it drove me crazy, but I can only imagine the local water district loves my family.

I love my family, too, even though it looks somewhat different than what I expected. No one plans on having a kid with obsessive-compulsive disorder, and few of us accept it well at first. After all, it is such an irrational thing. Honestly, who can make a truly convincing case about how constantly washing one's hands actually solves anything?

I never thought I would have a child with a mental illness, and yet that is what I have.

After an intense and expensive year of therapy and medication, after our family vocabulary included words most people have no use for like "habituation," "SSRIs," "self-efficacy," and "benzodiazepines"— my son, now a young man at twenty-two, is in a much better place. We can talk about the days of his "things" and laugh about how random a disease it is. OCD is part of who he is and always will be.

Even though I still have moments in which I struggle to understand his OCD, I've let go of thinking in terms of "freak" and "normal," stopped feeling embarrassed and ashamed, no longer feel anxious if it seems like he's just a tad too long in the bathroom, and resist wondering what might trigger another episode.

Mothering didn't turn out to be quite as easy as I imagined, but it helped me learn how to be relatively patient and accepting, like Teddy, my Yorkie. I could not have asked for a sweeter, funnier, kinder son.

Or, as it turns out, one with cleaner hands.

Vicki Larson

After a long career as a journalist, Vicki Larson is amazed and delighted that she is still paid to do what she loves most—write for a newspaper. A mom of two wonderful young men, her writing can also be found at *The Huffington Post, Mommy Tracked: Managing the Chaos of Modern Motherhood, Knowing Pains: Women on Love, Sex and Work in Our 40s*, and on her blog, the OMG Chronicles. When not working on a book she's co-authoring, *The New I Do: Reshaping Marriage for Cynics, Commitaphobes and Connubial DIYers*, she can be found hiking, biking, and daydreaming around Marin County.

My Father Called for Me

Vanessa Hua

My mother begged me to stop.

I was sweeping stacks of junk mail, yellowing newspapers, and old brochures off her desk and into a paper grocery sack.

"Just give me an hour or two. Please, let me do it myself," she said, her voice shaky and eyes wet. Half a year ago, my father fell and struck his head in my childhood home in the East Bay. In the ambulance, he cried out my name, "Vanessa. Vanessa. Vanessa." He slipped unconscious before I arrived and passed away three days later.

Now, I grimly emptied the drawers, exhausted and near tears myself after leaving behind my house in Los Angeles, where my twin boys learned how to crawl, walk, and talk. The moving truck would arrive here tomorrow, on Sunday, to unload the belongings we had packed in a hurry on Friday. Although my mother had promised to clear her home office and make way for the nursery, she was far from finished. Without prodding, she would hoard the accumulation of three decades, boxes of science journals and racks of eighties power suits. Downstairs, our sixteen-month-old twins screamed as my husband fed them dinner, the boys cranky after an early wake-up and a daylong drive. Until we cleared space in the room, I couldn't set up their portable crib. "I'm not throwing anything away," I said, gently as I could. "I'm packing it up."

My father had called for me, and this was how I answered.

"He had a lot of faith in you," my brother told me. "That you'd know what to do." I'd inherited my father's quick wit and his temper. Using my skills as a journalist, I'd researched treatments for his Parkinson's. The middle child, I was the family peacemaker, the sibling who oversaw the logistics for vacations, Thanksgiving dinners—and for my father's funeral.

While helping sort out the estate, my brother remained at home for six months, telecommuting. He was prepared to move permanently until my husband and I volunteered. We'd planned to return to the Bay Area, and my brother, still single, had a life of his own in San Diego.

When we told family and friends we were moving home—not only to my hometown, but home, to the very bedroom where I'd grown up—most were astounded. The lack of privacy would hurt our marriage, they said. We would fight, they said. My mother should retire from the laboratory, they said, sell the five-bedroom house, and move closer to us.

To them, three generations under one roof represented defeat and retreat, the last resort of the financially strapped. They didn't understand that for many Chinese, for many immigrant families, such an arrangement is an ideal, if not an obligation.

When I was a child, my maternal grandmother, a widow, lived with us, helping raise my brother, sister, and me while my parents pursued their American dreams. She taught us Mandarin through stories and songs, and we learned English together from television, shouting "A new car!" along with Bob Barker on *The Price Is Right*. She grew rock candy on a string and fried up savory pink, white and green shrimp chips.

After our rough start, my mother began establishing new traditions with her grandchildren. Within days, she began putting on samba music and danced with the twins in the kitchen, raising her arms and stomping her feet on the tile floor. Giggling, they copied her, united by the beat that spanned cultures, continents, and generations.

My father called me, and this was how I answered.

The difference between then and now: My grandmother moved in with her daughter and deferred to my parents in every way. My husband and I moved into my mother's house, where we had to ask permission to impose our order on hers. The floral bedspread and Spuds

McKenzie poster were gone from my bedroom, but I found myself reverting, acting like a teenager again, curt and sighing with irritation.

We argued after she cooked rice and left it on the counter overnight and the next day. "You can feed it to the twins," she said.

"They're not garbage cans," I said. "Also, it's not safe. The rice has been left out too long."

"It's safe," she said. "I'm a scientist. I know."

Be patient, my husband said. She and I were both grieving for the man whose presence we felt keenly in the light-filled house he designed and wanted to pass onto his children. In the weeks after we moved, I found a pair of his paint-spattered loafers on the deck overlooking hills studded with oaks, as if he had just stepped away from his chores. I discovered contracts with the Chinatown associations he retrofitted, and the neurology clinic's check-up evaluation, which resembled a kindergarten report card: "Patient was agreeable and cooperative."

Sorting through my father's pill bottles, stored high in a kitchen cabinet, I began to understand the details of his suffering. Pills he had to take six times a day, three times a day, once before bed. Pills for insomnia, pills for his tremors, pills for infection. Supplements too—fish oil, essential fatty acids, q-gel, bitter melon, melatonin, chromium picolinate—all still sealed, hope in a bottle. Behind the medication, I found a stack of gold-rimmed, cream-colored fine china plates.

"I won't give them away until I die," my mother said. "Maybe we'll use them again." My father purchased two sets of eight, she said, because he envisioned a day when the family would expand with husbands and wives and grandchildren. I stroked the edge of a plate and continued the cleaning my mother couldn't bear to do.

My father had called for me, and this was how I answered.

Back when I was pregnant, my husband wanted to buy a minivan, but I had refused, fearing I'd become a frumpy suburban matron. We settled on an SUV with three rows, enough seating to accommodate my parents. Climbing into the rear was an acrobatic feat. Without the aisle of a minivan, I had to shuck off my shoes and vault over the center console, push aside sacks of toys, snacks, and diapers, and cram into the rear beside the folded double stroller. It was a cramped, awkward fit, but we could be all together.

Five weeks after moving home, we drove into San Francisco to see longtime friends, ones my mother had met many times. I invited her along, as I always did, because I didn't want her to feel left out. Often she joined, sometimes she didn't. Living under one roof, we were figuring out when to integrate and when to remain independent.

It was Chinese New Year, a day on which you must live as you would like to the rest of the year: free of debts, free of fights, and in a new outfit and a new haircut.

"I brought the whole family!" I said. My friends laughed and made room for us on the waterfront picnic benches. My mother chatted with my American-born Chinese friends, who understood our arrangement without question, and between bites we traded off chasing after the twins in the sunshine.

My father had called for me, and this was how I answered.

Vanessa Hua

Vanessa Hua is an award-winning writer and journalist. Her fiction and nonfiction has appeared in *The Atlantic, ZYZZYVA,* the *New York Times, Salon,* and elsewhere. She has worked as a staff writer at the *San Francisco Chronicle, Los Angeles Times,* and *Hartford Courant,* filing stories from Burma, China, Panama, and South Korea. She is a Steinbeck Fellow in creative writing. The daughter of Chinese immigrants, she is a graduate of Stanford University and UC Riverside's MFA program. She is working on a novel and a collection of short stories, and can be found online at vanessahua.com and threeunderone.blogspot.com

The Glue

A.C. Hyde

Not everyone gets the chance to play every role within a family— but I have. Technically, I have only been the youngest and middle child, but emotionally, my position has run the gamut: baby, middle, even the eldest. Seeing the world from these different perspectives made all the difference as I grew up—and the lessons I learned transitioning between them (rife with humor and challenges) still serve me today.

At ten years old, I was the younger of two daughters enjoying a normal, fun childhood in a sunny neighborhood in Berkeley with a strong, loving family. I lived in a safe, protected, happy bubble. My older sister Lynn and I participated in the occasional sibling rivalry, being only two years apart, but I had fine-tuned the art of getting my parents to take my side simply with a wide-eyed, innocent stare. I reveled in being the baby and the center of my family's universe. It's all I knew.

Lesson No. 1: Savor the fleeting moments of feeling like the world revolves around you. It doesn't.

One evening when I was twelve, my mom enthusiastically addressed the family as we ate: "Who'd like to add another child to our family? Let's take a vote." By that time, my parents had moved us to Marin County, and the youngest child in our family—me—was already in puberty. You can imagine the shock around that dinner table.

My mom's hand shot up like a rocket in support of her own suggestion. After a quizzical look at my sister, I copied her lead, and a pair of adolescent girls' hands slowly went up in unison. My dad's hands lay lifeless in his lap, and an unsettled look crept onto his face.

"No hope of an early retirement, I suppose," my dad finally signed in resignation, pushing himself back from the table.

I had no idea what this new addition might mean, but I was happy to be part of the majority vote. Little did I know that I had willingly given up my role as the center of the universe.

Lesson No. 2: Always do your research before you vote.

When my little sister Paige was born a year later, my life changed in an instant. At first, it was a complete party! People brought over pre-pared meals, Lynn and my cookie intake and TV watching was unlimited, and we stayed up way past our bedtime.

The soiree soon ended, however, and my parents' lack of censure gave way to even stricter rules, *"Quiet!"* being chief among them. Their attention was completely consumed by the baby's every breath. Until that time, my Dad and I had a nightly ritual when he got home from work: upon the opening of the garage, I'd run eagerly to the front door to greet him with a bear hug and kiss. Now, when he walked in, he quickly walked past me with a rushed, "Hey, kiddo. Where's the baby? Did you help your mom out today?"

It didn't take long playing second fiddle for self-doubt to creep in. *Was I not important anymore?* I started to feel vulnerable and rudderless and wasn't sure I liked this new intruder, however adorable she might have been. I missed being the baby of the family. I longed for the days when I sat on my mom's lap; now Paige eyed me coyly from that coveted spot. I missed watching TV from under the crook of my Dad's arm after dinner; the baby was now soundly asleep in his arms during the *Star Trek* hour. My wide-eyed stare had officially lost its power. I was hurt and unsure of my place in my family and—pardon the dramatization—the world.

Lesson No. 3: Life is not fair. If you can get used to that, you'll be a happier camper.

I felt I had no one to whom I could confide my distress. Who would want to listen to me, anyway? My parents were focused on the baby, and Lynn, going through the growing pains of starting a new high school, didn't want anything to do with me. She reinforced my suspicion that I was too young to know all the adult stuff that she knew, but too old to pout like a child. My days of being the baby in the family were long gone, and I was now the middle child, for better or for worse.

At any age, it's an unwelcome and jarring realization to feel important one day and replaceable the next, but at age thirteen, that realization may as well be the apocalypse. I found myself in an "in one day, out the next" situation with the Mean Girls at school as well, and before I knew it, I was "out." It was an arduous process to find some security amidst the feelings of fear and worthlessness—both at home and now also at school, where my insecurity was quickly bleeding over. I was in no-man's land.

Lesson No. 4: Self-criticism never does any good, but self-improvement does.

Eventually I grew tired of my own tears and realized that only way to improve my life was to change my own feelings. At school I learned to make new friends in the grades above and below me. At home I stopped complaining about changing diapers because I realized a clean baby is a happy baby. All I had to do was see things from a different perspective, and life didn't seem quite so bad.

No longer obsessed with feeling sorry for myself, I was able to watch my parents more closely with the baby. I observed with wonder the pure joy this perfect baby girl brought them, and I recognized that they had this same unconditional love for all three of their daughters. Once I gave into my new place in the family, my love for Paige grew exponentially and I embraced being an older sister for the first time. When she squeaked out a noise resembling my name, her tiny, sweet voice melted my heart. One afternoon when she was three, I took her out in a stroller and a passerby asked me how old my daughter was. I laughed and said, "My daughter?! This is Marin County, not the Deep South! She's my beautiful baby sister! Isn't she the cutest thing in the world?" Lo and behold, I was actually really proud of being an older sister.

Lesson No. 5: Life is full of surprises. Be open to them.

When Lynn left for college a few years later, I became the oldest child at home. I relished the fact that I was now the boss, my high school commands ruled, and Paige emulated my every move. I loved the fact that Paige idolized me, thought my eighties music was the coolest, and even tried to replicate my crimped hairstyle. I realized that this is how Lynn must have felt when it was just the two of us: absolute adulation and total authority. I felt in control and in charge, and I was in heaven.

When it came time for me to go off to college, my parents didn't fuss as much as I thought they might have—Lynn had already paved the way for that milestone, something I was appreciating more and more as I got older. The freedom I'd felt as the eldest child at home transitioned seamlessly into the freedom I felt in my new college life. I loved the ability to make my own choices, from what classes to take to what time to go to bed (if at all). I tasted autonomy for the first time, and I felt really appreciative of it.

Lesson No. 6: Be grateful.

Coasting along this happy segment of life took a precarious dovetail during my sophomore year, when a crazy freak accident during spring break left me clinging to life. And I do mean *freak* accident— when I tripped onto a small table with a porcelain frog at a friend's house, my throat bizarrely landed on the frog's chipped foot, and I lacerated my trachea and esophagus. I smashed one vocal cord and came very close to landing on my jugular vein. My trachea healed well, but my esophagus battled extensive scar tissue for which I faced a series of operations and long, fretful nights in the hospital.

I watched *The Sound of Music* and what must have been every episode of *Star Trek* from my hospital bed with my family faithfully by my side. Ironically, after my taste of autonomy, I felt like my parents' "baby" once again: they smoothed back my hair and held my hand as I was wheeled into one surgery after another. Witnessing their worry, I realized that there will always be times when we feel like the baby of our families and in fact, the baby in our own lives—when we are vulnerable, helpless, and not in control. And that is OK.

Lesson No. 7: Try to smile through pain, knowing "this too shall pass." Faith and courage are worth their weight in gold. (Also, watch out for porcelain frogs.)

Years later, I took on the role of being the oldest sister again, this time to both Paige *and* Lynn, for very different reasons. Sadly, my older sister Lynn faced a hellacious divorce at the same time that Paige was happily planning her wedding to the love of her life. As I waded into this unchartered territory, I could feel the fruits of the lessons I'd learned through my past roles in the family guide me forward.

The irony of one marriage ending while another one began was not lost on me. I had to be an emotional support system for each of my sisters in very different ways, commiserating with Lynn about the misfortune of love gone wrong while at the same time confidently sharing in Paige's hopefulness about a happily-ever-after marriage of her own. Through a lot of girl talk—and even more wine—both sisters made it through. That time in our lives illuminated the fact for me that everyone's journey—both content and timing—is different and special, and as it turns out, people *do* want to listen to me.

It was obviously difficult for Lynn and Paige to communicate with each other, given their extremely different situations, so I stepped in to facilitate. It was at that moment that I truly appreciated my place in the family: I was the glue. As the middle child, I listened well, cheered everyone on, empathized easily, and provided a buffer during conflict.

Lesson No. 8: Marriage can be overrated, love is not, and wine does help.

Giving is usually better than receiving, and as the middle child, I find I like to give a lot, whether caring for my younger sister or listening to my older sister. I like my role. And I like me, probably because I am the sum of many roles. Life will throw us many curveballs, but if you're open, love will always find you, so be flexible and roll with the transitions.

A.C. Hyde

A.C. Hyde has been an aspiring author for as long as she can remember. When not writing, she has explored many career paths: high school English teacher, director of marketing at an investment management firm, and currently a real estate agent at Coldwell Banker. She was recently published in the Local Einsteins Marin Real Estate 2013 resource book. A.C. grew up in Marin County and graduated from UC Santa Barbara with a BA in English. She is the proud aunt of three sweet nephews and one beautiful baby niece and is the loving owner of her small zoo of two dogs and two cats. A.C. lives in San Rafael, California, and loves to read, golf, hike, travel, and spend time with her cherished family and friends.

Hot Potato

Kelley Hayes

I met Derrick Mason in September 2000. He was one month into kindergarten and I was thirty-eight. His mother had been given the choice to get rid of her predator boyfriend or give up her kids. She chose the boyfriend. The children were brought to my house after their first foster placement bailed. Dumped twice in the same day, the three children stood in my living room, their clothes in a paper sack. The social worker said it was only for the weekend.

It was hard to get past Derrick to mother the children. He acted as the parent, and the other two ate, bathed, and went to bed on his clock. They barely spoke to anyone without a nod from him first. His brother, who was two years older and had learning disabilities, seemed physically attached to his siblings but unaware of their overall predicament. His younger sister clung to Derrick like a baby chimp. "Attachment" is a buzzword in the world of foster care and is as essential as oxygen. Derrick was bonding the best he could. He was five years old.

Derrick gradually let me relieve him of his parental duties. As his sister began to trust me, he began to relax. Days passed, and then weeks. When it became apparent that no one was coming back to get them, I put the boys in a public school near my house and their sister in daycare.

My parents, who lived beside us, had trouble adjusting to the children. The kids had predominantly survived on their own in a tiny apartment and on the street. Now they roamed fearlessly between our two houses, often arriving on the patio next door from over the fence or swinging into the courtyard on the wrought-iron gate. They were loud and wild, with no manners. They ran and screamed, upsetting my mother's white-tablecloth world. They ate with their fingers and talked with their mouths full. They jumped on her beds and waded through her fishpond.

At my house, the children marveled at clean sheets, gorged themselves on food, and mastered video games. Derrick did well in school and, for once, developed friendships aside from his brother and sister.

The Masons stayed for several months, and then one day a social worker came and took them home. The little girl was glad to see her mother. The brother was confused. Derrick saw reality. He would go back to work as parent, protector, and survivor. He clawed at the bed, the bedroom door, the front door, and me.

He was not ready to abandon his new world, and my heart was breaking. I remember sympathetic friends questioning the cruelty of foster care. I felt part of a brutal system. I thought I was doing a good thing, but watching Derrick fight to stay with me made me sick.

After they left, he called constantly. Could I pick him up from school today? Could I go with him on a field trip? Could he come over for the weekend? Each reunion was gleeful and each parting was devastating. I began to avoid his calls, hoping he would meld back into his family. He persisted. For years he spent school holidays and summer vacations at my house. He wanted to live with us permanently, but because his mother was abiding by the minimum rules of parenting, the Department of Human Relations would not allow it.

Finally, in 2010, his mother was diagnosed with bipolar disorder, and after much violence and turmoil, both Derrick and his sister were removed from her home permanently. His brother, then sixteen, ran away. Derrick was sent to live with his grandmother in a housing project forty miles from my town. He was in tenth grade and had attended eleven different schools in four different cities.

The grandmother was cruel to Derrick and demeaned his visits with me. She taunted him, calling him a "faggot." One night she stuck a knife against his neck after he argued with her daughter about how to cut a birthday cake. He ran to a neighbor's apartment and called me. The police brought him to our house, where he is now. He is asleep down the hall. Tossed from home to home, and finally the buzzer rang. No more moving. God's little hot potato laid permanently in my lap.

Derrick told me recently that one of his favorite childhood memories was a day I brought Rice Krispie treats to his third-grade classroom. He remembered another happy time, when after we ate supper on the back porch, my husband and I danced to the radio and Derrick danced with us. I remember him putting his arms around my legs, pressing his head against my back as we all three-stepped in-time, moving in a circle.

He will be eighteen soon and will graduate from high school. Yesterday he got his first letter of acceptance from a college. We squealed and held hands, bouncing in a circle in the kitchen.

My friends say I am a great person for helping Derrick and tell me "that kid is so lucky to have you." I say it was me who lucked out. He clung to me like a baby chimp. I tried to brush him off and hope for the best, but he refused to let me be less than noble. We will have a graduation party, to say good-bye, but this time he wants to go. He is ready to fly.

Kelley Hayes

Kelley Hayes is a writer, artist, student, world traveler, and former social worker in Decatur, Alabama. She is a wife and mother of three and daughter of one. She splits the remainder of her time between Alabama and Memphis, her birthplace. She earned her BA from Barat College, Lake Forest, Illinois.

Tears and Possibilities

Dawn Elyse Warden-Reeder

"I'm going to college," Amelia blurted out while placing an order for a Corona and handing over her ID. "I'm celebrating."

The waitress' expression read, "You go, girl," but I could see the wheels turning as she checked the ID. I restrained from explaining that "college" was a two-year life skills program for developmentally disabled adults, and that we'd just gotten the good news that Amelia had been accepted.

"Wow! That's exciting. Where are you going?" the waitress asked.

"Chapel Haven, in Connecticut," she said, taking care to not mix up the school's name with the town so I wouldn't correct her for the umpteenth time. "It's near where my cousin went to college."

"Yale," I interjected, anticipating the next question. "In New Haven."

"Cool town, I've been there. I bet your parents are really proud of you."

"Yep," Amelia nodded. "They are."

Eight weeks later, my not-yet fiancé, James, and I hit the road, with Amelia nestled in alongside several overstuffed duffels, a Justin Bieber poster and her collection of purses. I-95 was mercifully void of its typical traffic snarls, a detail that kept Amelia, and consequently me, from getting fretful about meeting up with Dad in time for shopping and lunch. The school's fence line came into view, and I took a deep breath. On the outside, we were all set to move our not-so-little girl into her new school, but on the inside, well, that remained to be seen.

Our feet had barely hit the ground before a group of students circled the car, eagerly introducing themselves and offering to carry something. I recognized a few faces from when we'd visited in the spring.

My strawberry-blonde, blue-eyed beauty had clearly made a positive impression, because these young men were all over her.

We followed the motley crew of admirers into the main building, where another warm welcome awaited us. Amelia giggled nervously through all the attention.

Annette, the admissions director, came over and put her hand on my shoulder. "How's mom doing?"

"Oh, I'll be tearing up in no time," I joked.

She grabbed a pack of tissues off the reception desk, clearly familiar with the soggy mom routine. "It's too early for that, but just in case."

While we were waiting for my ex to show up, we reviewed logistics: Amelia's apartment key and ID card, directions to Target, Bed Bath and Beyond, and CVS, and the next day's orientation lineup.

Right on schedule, Sam (a.k.a. Dad) walked in. He gestured behind him toward the courtyard where the students were congregating. "It seems these boys are no different than other college boys when a pretty new girl shows up."

Our eyes met, and I knew he was also thinking: *normal* with a twist.

It definitely didn't feel normal jumping into my car with James and Sam as passengers, but it didn't feel as awkward as I thought it might. James kept the conversation going, Amelia and I focused on the list, and Sam offered to pay for the big purchases. I had no clue what he was feeling, but Amelia seemed buoyed by our togetherness.

The day's controlled well of emotions spontaneously erupted during dinner. Sam had gone, but we'd taken Amelia out to a "hot" Yale sushi bar. Halfway into our pricey cuts of raw fish, Amelia started squirming uncomfortably. We jostled our way out of the tightly packed dining room and bee-lined for the restroom, but it was occupied. I glanced from the closed door to Amelia's off-color, panic-stricken face and knew she couldn't hold it. Vomit splattered everywhere, and there was nothing I could do but hold my daughter's hair and tell her it was OK. When the door finally opened, I didn't even try to explain. I pushed Amelia into the bathroom and feverishly yanked paper towels out of the dispenser. I wiped her face and mouth, propped her on the toilet with her head between her knees, and started scooping up puke.

"You're going to feel a lot better now that you got all your worrying out."

It killed me to leave her alone in her new room afterward; her roommate wasn't due until the next day, and the other girls were behind their own closed doors. I entertained the thought of sending James to the hotel without me, but he wouldn't have any of that.

"It's just going to make it harder tomorrow."

I wouldn't budge until he agreed to find one of the night staff and get a confirmation that one of them would check in on her a couple of times during the night. I programmed Amelia's phone with all of the school's emergency numbers, kissed her on the cheek, and shut the door behind me.

The following morning we arrived at orientation just in time to catch a glimpse of her going off with her fellow First Years.

"Let her be," James said, following my gaze.

Upstairs, all the new parents were taking seats in front of a projector screen. For the next twenty minutes, we watched an in-depth slideshow highlighting what our grown kids would be doing for the next few weeks and over the next two years. Then the director treated us to newly added slide: a photo of recent grads who had gotten married and moved into the community program. Just as Amelia had purged all of her anxiety the night before, eighteen years of maternal angst over what the doctors proclaimed our daughter would and wouldn't do came pouring out of me.

For the next three hours, separation anxiety floated between Amelia and I. Our jaws and shoulders tightened as we watched the other families dismantle. At 4:00 p.m., James gave me the signal. I inched over to Amelia, who was watching the school's director endure several tin plates of whipped cream being smashed into his face—a time-tested tradition to break the ice with the "kids." I wrapped my arms around her and pulled her close.

"Time to go, baby doll," I said gently while squeezing her even tighter.

James came over and wrapped his arms around her, too, but before he could get a proper hug, Amelia started bawling. Thankfully, Annette's assistant, Monica, who'd been a huge support to me during Amelia's visit in March, jumped in.

"Let's go watch Mr. Emerson get some more whipped cream in his face."

"I don't want to," Amelia whimpered, her eyes begging me not to leave.

I willed myself to keep it together. "Hey, little miss. Remember what we talked about? This is something you want. We have to tough it out. Remember how proud you were to get to come here?"

Twenty-one years later, and she still had that same heartbreaking pout. I hated leaving her this way. I reached out and pulled her chin toward me. I planted a kiss on both cheeks and looked her square in the eye. "I love you, Angel. You got this." Her teary eyes stayed on me as Monica started to lead her away, mouthing, *"She's going to be fine."*

James snuck up behind me and slipped my hand into his, pulling me in the opposite direction. "And so will you."

Dawn Elyse Warden-Reeder

Dawn Elyse Warden-Reeder (a.k.a. @eatDEWwrite) is a Philadelphia-based journalist and food writer turned publicist, copywriter, social media marketer, and blogger. Her appreciation for the entrepreneurial spirit and for those who've overcome obstacles to achieve their goals makes her a natural Pied Piper for the innovators, do-gooders, and risk-takers served by her PR firm, the warden ettinger group. In everything she does—including raising five children, one with special needs—Dawn brings a notable level of passion (her creative writing discipline notwithstanding). When she's not writing, tweeting, posting, or pitching, you'll find her in the kitchen feeding her culinary passion, something she enjoys almost as much as playing with words.

Lucky Drive

Karen Lynch

Whenever I used to hear someone claim their cancer was a blessing in disguise, I cringed, assuming the victim was practicing some sort of denial, the opposite of sour grapes. Then cancer happened to me. And why wouldn't it? I was an easy mark, living in the cancer capital of the world: Marin County. Plus, I'd made a deal with the universe that I was OK with getting cancer. But I'm getting ahead of myself. Let me tell you how I came to welcome the big C into my life.

It was the first rainstorm of the year, October 2009. My husband, Greg, and I were the nervous parents of a newly licensed son. Keenan, our seventeen-year-old, was commuting to high school in San Francisco from Novato. As I drove to work that morning, a viscous pool of water glistened in the fast lane of Highway 101, near Lucky Drive, and I ignored a wave of premonition that briefly crashed into me.

I was at my desk when my phone buzzed with a text from Greg: *Keenan in accident on my way there.*

I did what all terrified parents do. I prayed. Yes, I say *all*, knowing there are atheists among us. But I suspect even atheists pray in such moments, if only: *to whom it may concern.* My prayer session lasted the excruciating twenty-six minutes and thirty-four seconds it took Greg to arrive at Highway 101, near Lucky Drive. It was an intricate negotiation in which I begged God, Spirit, Jesus, Buddha, Allah, and/or Moses to please leave my son and his passenger unharmed. I promised God, in all his multicultural manifestations, I would accept anything at all in their place. *Please, Krishna-Jesus-Mary, take me instead!*

Keenan had hydroplaned over four lanes and careened into the guardrail. Inexplicably, he hit no vehicles, though the road was full of traffic. He and his passenger climbed out of my totaled car unscathed.

We dealt with the post-accident issues—towing the car and obtaining a loaner—without complaint, simply grateful to have been spared worse. I forgot about my deal, and had I have given it any thought at all, I would have assumed it would take some time, possibly years, before I would be required to make good on my bargain.

Not a week later, in my office again, my right hand sprang to my left breast in response to a caustic twinge. And there it was. A lump. I knew immediately it was cancer. I wasn't being dramatic; I'd had cystic breasts my entire life, and this sinister, pea-sized intruder was nothing like any of the other lumps I'd detected over the years. And it hurt. Contrary to what we've heard, cancer sometimes hurts, I later learned. Especially if it's the dastardly, fast-growing, triple-negative kind. But in the very same moment that I found my lump and recognized it for the nemesis it was, I nodded my head in surrender. *Oh yes, I had agreed to this.* Well, maybe not *this*, exactly. But I'd made a deal with the universe, and I accepted my fate with a bizarre sense of transcendence.

I know this isn't logical. I don't believe there is some malevolent spirit in the sky, doling out misfortune like wartime rations. But what I do know is that in my own mind, I had made a perverse agreement, and I had no regrets. Cancer was something I could handle; having a dead son was not.

And so I went through the cancer trifecta: surgery, chemo, and radiation. Nothing unusual to report there, except that my friends found my Zen-like attitude odd. They considered my lack of complaint tantamount to an act of heroism. I explained that I was no hero, and told them about my odd arrangement with the God of all things bad— how the accident and the cancer were unmistakably intertwined. They looked at me with confusion, maybe skepticism.

The next six months passed in a flurry of doctor's appointments. I soon learned the jargon of chemotherapy. I would be treated with the dreaded *red devil—Adriamycin*. I would lose my long hair and who knew what else, but I was still OK with the deal. My son was alive.

Sometime after surgery, a counselor prepared me for life after cancer. When I told her I was a homicide investigator, she seemed faintly amused, saying, "I doubt you'll want to do that after this." I laughed. Quit my coveted job as one of the few female homicide detectives in the country? Let down Gloria Steinem? What sort of wimp did she think I was? I had yet to acknowledge that spending my days consoling inconsolable parents of homicide victims had, no doubt, contributed to the demise of my health.

Meanwhile, other issues were brewing with my seven-year old daughter. When we adopted Kyra from China as a toddler, we accepted that she was not an affectionate child. As time passed, Kyra's persistent aloofness began to concern me, though I strongly resisted the idea she might have an attachment disorder. I knew I was fooling myself. From the day she was found, at ten days old, she had lived in Gao—an orphanage. In the fifteen months before Kyra was placed in our arms, she had changed caregivers multiple times. Kyra seldom returned our affection and disliked being held. But I fought the idea of bringing her to a therapist and having her labeled as abnormal in some way. Would naming the disorder turn it into a self-fulfilling prophecy?

In the month prior to my diagnosis, I had begun to question my lack of action. I searched intently for therapists specializing in adoption, and had settled on one when the cancer distraction took center stage. Kyra's issue was relegated to a backstage dressing room.

For the six months of treatment, I was home every day. Some days I felt weak, lacking the energy to leave bed. But on many days, I drove Kyra to school, packed her lunch, picked her up, read her stories, and played games with her. Sometimes I was crabby and greenish, but I was being a mom in a way I had never managed to be while working. As the months passed, Kyra began to make eye contact with me. She laughed with me, and occasionally hugged me, but only when I asked her to. When we watched movies, she asked me to scratch her back. Then one night, five months after my diagnosis, Kyra gave me an unsolicited hug and said, "I love you, Mom."

So, maybe the counselor had the last laugh in the end. I never did go back to work, at least not the kind of work that ate my soul and caused me to build a fortress-like tumor over my heart.

Kyra may never become an extremely demonstrative person, but she's well within the range of *normal*. Now, I'm home writing most days, and Kyra is a rambunctious ten-year old. So when I made that deal, I came out way ahead. I've become one of those crazy blessing-in-disguise cancer people. Maybe God really does move in mysterious ways.

Karen Lynch

Karen Lynch is a native San Franciscan. After graduating from UC Berkeley, she joined the San Francisco Police Department in 1981. She lives in Novato, California, with her husband and their three children, including Kyra, who was the subject of an essay that won the 2012 Notes & Words national essay contest. Her memoir, *Good Cop, Bad Daughter,* is the story of how growing up with a bipolar mother trained Karen to be a cop.

Scales

Abby Ellin

Finally, I'd had enough of America and its discontents and decided to spend 1987, my junior year of college, far, far away from school and all of its pain. As the main character in Carrie Fisher's *Postcards from the Edge* put it while sitting in a bombed-out bus stop in Jerusalem: "I wanted to go somewhere where my insides finally matched my outsides." I, too, longed to be in a place where the chaos around me mirrored the chaos inside me. I chose to do a semester at the University of Tel Aviv, which seemed distant enough.

I met my best friend for the year, Jen, on the plane to Israel. We were both from the Boston area, both aspiring hippies, and had both been to the Bob Dylan/Grateful Dead show at Foxboro Stadium over the summer. After spending fourteen hours in a space the size of a soup can, we felt as if we knew each other and decided to room together.

As soon as we reached the dorm, we unpacked our stuff. Clothes, Grateful Dead tapes, and other American luxuries—Maxi Pads, Marlboro Lights—were strewn about the room. Jen was the neater of us, and it took her twice as long to fold her clothes and store them in the faux Formica shelves. I vaguely tossed mine in: T-shirts on the top shelf, shorts and long pants on the next, aerobic-wear on the bottom. Bras, socks, bathing suits, and underwear went in one drawer; beneath them I placed my shoes. I threw mismatched sheets on my bed, which was really a narrow foam mattress on a rickety wooden frame. I took a sort of pleasure in this; this was, after all, my year to "rough it." Giving up futons and queen-sized beds seemed the least I could do, a hardship I should be able to endure.

I unzipped my duffel bag and removed the cardboard box hidden in a tangle of sheets and blankets. I peered over at Jen, who was methodically stacking tapes on a shelf. Quickly, I tore open the box and took out an oval-shaped white scale that I'd bought especially for this trip.

I didn't know what to tell Jen, how to explain the addition to our room; I tried to slip it beneath my bed and hoped she wouldn't notice, but I wasn't quick enough.

"You brought a *scale*?" she said, a pair of Suzanne Vega tapes in each hand.

My face flushed, and I folded the box in fours. "Well, uh, you always hear about people gaining weight here, so I decided to, you know, make sure I don't. You can use it whenever you want," I added.

"You don't look like the type of person who would care about her weight," she said.

I glanced down at my ensemble. I was sheathed in a wraparound skirt decorated with psychedelic peacocks, a flowing embroidered shirt, and Birkenstocks. A crystal the size of a small egg dangled from my neck, and my hair gave new meaning to the term "windblown."

"Well," she said, turning back to her stacking, "at least airport security didn't think it was a bomb." We laughed, even though I didn't find it particularly funny.

Over the next few months, our room became increasingly popular once people learned about my scale. The women shyly asked if they could slip in and borrow it; the men jumped on it irreverently, as if it were a trampoline, which caused me terrible anxiety. What if they broke a spring? Eventually I cleared space for it in the closet so people wouldn't come in and abuse it when I wasn't around. I set it down beside my sandals and Chinese slippers, but I always felt its presence: taunting me, glaring, alive.

In October, Jen and I headed to Europe for our fall break. We made plans for a three-week trek: Arrive in Amsterdam, depart from Rome, take the middle part as it comes. We bought Eurail passes, validated our student IDs, and took out hundreds of dollars in traveler's checks. I briefly considered bringing the scale, but ultimately vetoed that idea. Yes, Jen was supportive and understanding, listening when I moaned about how fat I was, turning away when I weighed myself, but I didn't want to push it.

By the time we reached Italy, we had been traveling for nearly three weeks. I'd eaten space cakes in Amsterdam, potato pancakes in Bonn, and chocolate bars everywhere in between. In Florence, I gave up.

"I'm fat," I said, collapsing outside the Uffizi. We had just finished admiring *David*, who, in his marble splendor, moved me more than any man I'd ever known. For a moment, while gazing up at him, I could almost forget about the flab bulging over my belt buckle and the three cannolis I'd inhaled the previous evening. "I can tell I've gained weight. My clothes are tight."

"You didn't," Jen said calmly, although I knew her nerves were shot. "But maybe you should stop eating so much chocolate and eat more normal meals."

I examined a postcard of *David*, a view from his backside. His shoulder muscles rippled like a bodybuilder's, and his ass was rock-hard. "Don't watch what I eat," I mumbled, running my finger along his calves.

"How can I not? We're together all the time."

I looked at Jen, my best friend, the person stuck dealing with my food problem. In a sense, she was a guinea pig: the way things went with her would determine how open I was with other people. I never talked about the food thing with anyone; it was mine.

"Maybe we should split up," I said, though that's not what I meant. What I really wanted to say is, "Let's go back to Israel, where it's safe and I know what type of food I can eat and I can weigh myself whenever I want."

"Don't be stupid," Jen said, and she was right. Instead, we reached a kind of compromise: she would ask me if I really wanted that extra tiramisu, and I'd promise not to get mad. We spent the remainder of the trip talking like this. When we returned to Tel Aviv, I stepped on the scale. I was down two pounds.

At the end of the semester, Jen went back to the states, but I stayed in the Holy Land. I'd planned it this way from the start: the minute I saw the silver wings of El Al glittering in the sunlight, I knew I'd be gone at least a year. I was a writer, after all. I needed to Experience Life. My goal was to take the semester off to find myself (or, ideally, someone else). I'm sure part of me hoped I'd be less obsessive about food, as if distance and space might somehow transform me.

Then my mother came to visit, and we traveled throughout Israel and Egypt. Before she left, I plied her with things to take home, keeping only the items of utmost importance: my Walkman, my Dead tapes, my journal, and, of course, the scale, which I buried deep in the pit of my backpack. It was like carrying a sack of cement, but this didn't bother me. I felt comfortable with it—safe, as if an old friend were trekking alongside me.

I read this now, twenty-five years later, and all I can think is: *How whacked was I?* Truly, pathetically whacked. And as so many of us know intellectually but don't really digest emotionally, there are no geographical cures. The craziness that lives with us in Greenwich Village travels with us to Zambia or Cuba or Tenafly, New Jersey. Our job is to figure out how to surpass—or at least manage—it, wherever we are.

I have not stepped on a scale, in any country, in nearly a decade. I refuse, even at the doctor's office. I know if I've been on a sugar rampage and my clothes are too tight. Nothing good can come from my knowing a meaningless number that will determine my mood for the rest of the day.

This realization did not come swiftly, alas. Nor did epiphany bash me over the head in a single "aha!" moment. Instead, over time, I simply tired of devoting precious brain space to weight. Why bother seeing the world if the only thing I was going to think about was the size of my thighs? Talk about gross narcissism.

Of course, I'd be lying if I said weight never crosses my mind. It rears its malignant head every so often, usually when my life feels unmanageable and out of control. I am hardly unique: I have yet to meet a woman in this culture who doesn't have some food or body issue (though I have never, *ever*, met anyone who traveled with a scale). My hope is that one day we will all gather together and toss our scales into a giant incinerator. We will eat and drink wildly, a Burning Man for the formerly weight obsessed. Now *that* would be a trip worth taking.

Abby Ellin

Award-winning writer Abby Ellin is the author of *Teenage Waistland: A Former Fat-Camper Weighs In On Living Large, Losing Weight, and How Parents Can (and Can't) Help*. A former *New York Times* business columnist, her work regularly appears in the Health and Style sections of that newspaper. She has also been published in *Time, Newsweek, Marie Claire, More,* and *Glamour,* among others. She has an MFA in creative writing from Emerson College and an MIPP from Johns Hopkins University. But her greatest achievement is naming "Karamel Sutra" ice cream for Ben and Jerry's. This story first appeared in *SMITH Magazine*'s Memoirville project (smithmag.net).

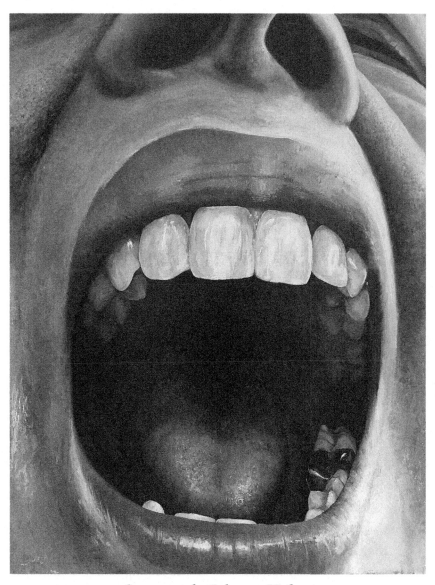

Scream 10, by Johanna Uribes

Artist Statement:

The Terrain Project is a series of paintings and interviews focusing on the skin wisdom we acquire as we travel life's highway. This work encourages the viewer to take a close look at the simple beauty of mid-life women.

I began by photographing myself in the bathroom mirror after noticing the changes that were happening on my own face. Seeing my skin up close, I realized it looked like a vast alien terrain. I quickly shot several intense close-ups. Looking at the reference photos, I saw aesthetic possibilities in every line and shadow, a kind of "skin wisdom." I decided to create large-scale paintings, enlarging these life-scored changes.

Next, I expanded my exploration of "skin wisdom" to other women between the ages of thirty-five and seventy-five. These are not individual portraits but instead represent the "everywoman." The project continued to expand into emotional terrain as I saw the range of emotions reflected in the faces of my subjects. While I took source photos, I began to ask my subjects questions that developed into a ten-question interview. The interviews enhance the images of *The Terrain Project*, offering a variety of individual, reflective viewpoints from midlife women at a range of ages.

The experience of making these paintings has been exciting for me. These luminous pieces focus on skin textures to show the quiet, self-composed magnificence of these women. Layering the color with loose finger-painting and rough brushwork creates the effect of translucence and depth in layers of skin. The bold compositions highlight all lines and irregularities, showing them as elegant colors and shapes rather than camouflaging these so called "imperfections." The big blowups of small facial sections create the feeling of larger-than-life imagery.

Looking at the paintings of these women, I began to see the natural process of aging. We live in a time that is obsessed with the dewy glow of youth, yet this obsession makes an inevitable part of life unacceptable—aging. The blossoms are lovely on a fruit tree, but we are anticipating the fruit. As we watch the blossoms fall away, we are undisturbed by this naturally occurring process. It is important to let youth find its way without having to face the additional self-consciousness of being a cultural fixation.

We live in a time of synthetic beauty. Models are airbrushed and women are encouraged to pursue a wide array of cosmetic procedures and enhancements. As the population demographic shifts and the 40+ age group grows to dominant numbers, *The Terrain Project* is a reminder of midlife's exquisite splendor. This body of work redefines the narrow boundary we use to measure beauty in American culture.

Scream 10

Female, age fifty-three: Some days, yes, I still do want to scream, but those days are far less frequent now that both adolescence and menopause are over. Now I usually feel pretty even-keeled; you develop an interior world where you can live for just a bit when you realize all your dreams may not come true quite as you had planned. But there's still a strong drive to succeed and have joy in your life.

Johanna Uribes

Johanna Uribes' creative body of artwork, *The Terrain Project*, provides a view of contemporary midlife women. This series of paintings with accompanying interviews shows the vitality and amazing resilience of these women. Born in rural Upstate New York, Johanna showed an interest in art at an early age. She attended the Otis College of Art and Design in Los Angeles and worked as a graphic artist. Eventually, she moved to the San Francisco Bay Area and completed her BFA at the San Francisco Art Institute.

Section Three

What Doesn't Kill You . . .

Freedom at the End of a Gun

Laurel Hilton

"So, how does it feel?" she said.

"How does what feel?" I replied.

"You know," she paused for effect, "to have a gun pointed dead-on in your face."

My boyfriend, Charlie, and I arrived in Alajuela midday after a noneventful red-eye from San Francisco. I slept the entire way and arrived in Costa Rica refreshed and excited. Alajuela is the second-largest city in Costa Rica, after the capital, San Jose, and though Alajuela enjoys renown as the birthplace of the country's national hero, Juan Santamaría, parts of it are really, really dirty and seedy, even by developing-country standards.

It didn't matter, as we planned to catapult out of there soon after we landed and head four hours directly east to a little surfing village called Puerto Viejo de Talamunca on the beautiful and remote east coast of the country. Ironically, neither of us surfed, but we craved the simple quietude of the beachside village, heavily populated by French, German, and Australian expat artists and wave-hunters, and the escape it promised from our ultrawired lives in the Bay Area.

We picked up a rental car just outside the airport, and not two miles and five minutes into our vacation, our lovely rental car blew a tire. Pulling onto the dusty shoulder of the two-lane road, we scanned the immediate horizon for a gas station that proved nonexistent. Then, from the shimmer of the morning heat already rising from the asphalt, a nondescript four-door red car emerged. Two local men approached us, speaking heavily accented English. They wanted to help us. What luck and what timing! Charlie and I nodded with a well-placed look between us. The two men busied themselves unloading our luggage from the truck to reveal a jack. Hoping to be useful, I shuffled our bags from the roadside to the back seat of our car.

To this day, I have no idea what compelled me to move the luggage inside, but I am glad that I did. So distracted were we by the task at hand, we did not notice the red car creep slowly up to align itself with the driver's side of our car. A third man jumped from the red car's passenger side and in a flash poked his arm through our driver's side door, plucked my knapsack off the passenger seat, and dashed back to the red car. Reflexively, I chased him, single-minded in my purpose to retrieve my knapsack, loaded with vacation-ready valuables: driver's license, passport, plane ticket back to the States, a credit card, and cash. As I reached toward him for the sack, blurting "that's mine" in crystal-clear English, he responded with a gun in my face, a gesture that needs no translation. My possessions mattered no more. I dropped my arms to my sides and backed up a step. He lowered the gun and jumped into the red car. Our two "Samaritans" were already smirking from behind the back-seat window, and then they were all gone. The whole process, from breakdown to breakaway, felt like ten minutes but was probably only two.

Shocked and angry, we finally flagged down a Fuerza Publica policeman and learned grim news. A red car full of Costa Ricans, or "Ticos," means nothing; taxis are red in Costa Rica. It was a weekend; the embassies and police stations were closed. Crimes like these, he said in broken English, happen to foreigners several times a day, especially by the airport. What choice did we have but to return like schmucks to the car rental station, cancel my cards, and get a new rental. While apologetic, the rental agents weren't surprised. No one deters street crime in Central America. I tasted the bitter futility of being a gringa in an unfamiliar land, but the gritty lump forming in my throat was pure and steely pride. I'd be damned if I'd let a few young punks ruin my vacation.

Having never been robbed before, and at gunpoint no less, I

expected to feel completely violated and trembling with vulnerability, yet I did not. As we cruised east and then south to the coast in our second rental car over bumpy, unpaved roads, counting the roadside churches fronted by soccer fields, I began to relish the loss of what I thought was important and embrace the feeling of being untethered and truly anonymous.

The first night, we settled in nicely to our Puerto Viejo de Telemunca bungalow despite the day's events. There was no electricity after 8:00 p.m. and no hot water—ever—but we didn't care. The next morning, keen to check out the area, we walked down to the beach for a swim. Instead of approaching the beach from the road, we cut through the jungle, stumbling over exposed tree roots the size of a man's thigh, and under leafy canopies to cross the quarter mile to the water. If we had entered the beach from the road, we would have seen the signs warning of dangerous rip currents.

The ocean was the deepest blue with occasional lacy, white-crested waves. Surfers bobbed like buoys in the water down the beach to the far right. But the expanse in front of us was immaculate and unpeopled, so we headed that way. We're both good swimmers and soon found ourselves splashing far from the shore. The water was warm and peaceful. My guard was down; maybe this would be the best vacation ever. The mild water turned suddenly surly, especially the further left I drifted. By the time we figured out what was going on, it was too late; I was caught in a rip current. Charlie tried to get to me, but with no success. He barked desperate instructions, but I could hear none of them against the soundtrack of my labored and panicked breathing. I did everything wrong—swimming straight into and against the current, when I should have swum sideways to escape it. Exhaustion weighted me down. I transitioned into hyperawareness, feeling the stinging droplets of saltwater in my eyes and nose and the soft yet unyielding pressure of the current propelling my body backward. Again, I experienced the unraveling of my cares and the desire to possess my body melt away.

Strong, brown arms suddenly hugged me roughly under my ribcage and began pulling me backward towards the shore. I stared straight into the glaring sun and wondered if I would get sun blindness, but that thought was quickly suppressed as I turned my head to the sand and gushed up a stomach full of seawater. My rescuer—a member of the local Red Cross—held out a machete-cut green coconut to rehydrate my beaten body and mind.

"And it was a great vacation," I said. "Really, everything smoothed out from there and we had a wonderful time."

"But how did it feel," she asked again, "to have a gun pointed dead-on in your face?"

My answer lingered for a bit on my tongue, though I'd known for sure since the moment it happened.

"Mom, it felt OK. Actually, it released something in me. I just felt . . . free."

Laurel Hilton

Laurel Hilton is an obsessed eco-traveler who can be found immersed in a great travel-inspired tale by Sarah Vowell, Paul Theroux, or Mark Twain when she's not on the road. Laurel authors a green parenting column for Examiner.com and writes on family-friendly expeditions for Uptake.com. She is a featured essayist on KQED's *Perspectives* radio program, a finalist in the 2013 Notes & Words contest, and a founding member of Write On, Mamas! She resides in Marin County, California, with her husband, two little girls, and a very loyal Australian cattle dog.

Shedding My Skin

Stephanie Hosford

D*on't trust anyone.* This was probably my dad's most common piece
of advice growing up. Well, *don't trust anyone* and *change the oil in your
car on a consistent basis.* And while I'm sure these admonishments
stemmed from concern for my wellbeing (I can only imagine the auto-
motive mishaps that were averted), the seed containing the words *don't
trust anyone* effectively implanted itself in my brain and blossomed over
the years into a overwhelming need to shield myself from being duped.
Admittedly, I have become essentially faithless, rather than simply the
cautious person I believe my dad was attempting to foster. My skepticism is like a full bodysuit, offering me some degree of protection from
the outside world, but it is also rather constrictive. Today, though, I am
hoping for a change.

As I lay in the dimly lit room, partially reclined on the smooth,
white paper that has been freshly rolled out over the examination table,
I am fidgeting with my thin cotton robe: untying and retying it, trying to pull it tighter around me. Why are these robes always so difficult? You'd think I'd be used to them by now and know how to quickly
adjust the closures for maximum comfort. The paper crinkles beneath
me as I sit up and scoot my hips forward to put my feet into the stirrups.
I lay back down, my head on the small pillow.

"This is it," I say, looking over at my husband, Alex, who is sitting
in what has become his usual chair, on the left side of the table near my
head. "This is the big one. The moment of truth," I add.

"I know, Bug," Alex responds, smiling and reaching for my hand.
He gives it a squeeze and keeps holding it. "It's going to be fine," he
adds. Why can't I be more like that? Confident and secure that this will
turn out OK.

The ultrasound machine is quietly whirring near my right shoulder across from him. I look at its black screen, lit slightly at the top by the glowing green LED letters that spell out my name (last name, then first, followed by my middle initial, as always) and the date. Can it be May already? Will I really be meeting my daughter in less than a week? I want so much to believe that my team of doctors was right, that the toxic wasteland of my body did not affect Reese, that the chemotherapy drugs coursing through my veins for the past four months have taken their toll only on me and not her. Please, not her.

This is certainly not the first ultrasound for Reese and me. Oh, no. We have had several. I think the stock market is the only entity monitored more closely than we have been. Mind you, the decision that brought us to this point was not made on a whim. I am not the type to throw caution to the wind. In fact, I am quite the opposite. I over-analyze and research decisions consistently, decisions that take far less thought than whether or not to keep an embryo inside my body following a cancer diagnosis.

Eight months ago, when we were told that I could receive chemotherapy while pregnant, I was naturally incredulous, despite my doctors' assurances that the baby would be unharmed. Soon thereafter, though, my maternal instinct trumped my misgiving and I opted to go ahead with the dual plan. Within a few weeks, however, I could sense my resolve wavering. How could this all possibly turn out well? Alex's continuous words of encouragement were barely enough to keep me on track, and by the time we first walked down the hallway of the hospital toward the infusion center, it was all I could do not to turn around and bolt for the exit. As I watched the garish orange drugs snake their way through the IV tube and into my veins via the needle in my hand, that familiar bodysuit of skepticism I'd known since childhood nearly strangled me.

The following week, I had an ultrasound. There she was: my daughter's black-and-white image on the screen, moving around just as she should and developing exactly as a five-month-old fetus is supposed to. Emotion and relief overwhelmed me, and I sobbed there on the exam table.

The ultrasound following my second round of chemo proved equally positive. By the third and fourth ultrasounds, my confidence had increased enough to give Reese her name. The final test was yet to come.

Alex is still holding my hand when Dr. Holder enters the room, the nurse close behind him.

"Good morning," he says, with his friendly smile and soft Nigerian accent.

"Good morning," Alex and I respond together.

"So this is our last meeting, eh? Your baby will be born Saturday?" he asks while the nurse retrieves the ultrasound gel from the warming machine. (As a "high risk" patient, I am treated to the warm gel rather than the usual cold matter, which should not be discounted as a perk.)

"I believe so," I answer.

"Alright, let's have a look at Reese," Dr. Holder proposes as he squeezes the gel onto the transducer probe. I let go of Alex's hand to slide the bottom of my cotton gown up enough to allow Dr. Holder to place the probe on my prominent belly. I feel its gentle pressure, the gel warm and smooth on my skin. We are all watching the screen as he begins to glide the probe slowly, stopping every so often to adjust its angle. I hear Dr. Holder's fingers tapping at the computer keyboard, entering Reese's most current data. He and Alex are focused only on the screen as I glance nervously from Reese's image to Dr. Holder, trying to read his expression. I realize I am now holding my breath as the bodysuit of doubt tightens around me.

"Well, Stephanie," Dr. Holder breaks the verbal silence, "Reese looks wonderful. Everything looks very nice." I exhale. I look over at Alex, who is smiling at the screen, and I start to cry. Taking a long look at Reese's image, I think about my daughter miraculously thriving inside me after all we've been through.

My daughter will be born in five days. She will be fine. I will be fine. I believe this with every fiber of my being. As I stand up to take off the hospital gown and change back into my clothes, the bodysuit falls off me completely and crumples around my feet. I step forward and leave it behind on the floor.

Stephanie Hosford

Stephanie Hosford is a happily married mother of three living in Los Angeles. She holds a master's degree in occupational therapy from Tufts University as well as a black belt in Taekwondo from a dojang down the street. She is a new member of the Speaker's Bureau for the City of Hope Medical Center. When not shuttling her children about town in her minivan, she can be found writing, at the gym, helping out in her kids' classrooms, or dashing around Trader Joe's.

Last Call

Dolores Coleman

This is why I drank. When I was fourteen years old, my grandmother slid her glass of E&J Brandy on the rocks to me where I was sitting at the other end of the dining room table and said, "Try this."

I took a sip and shook my head.

"Go and get Daddy's Bacardi behind the door and try that," she said.

I went into my grandparents' bedroom and retrieved the bottle of Bacardi. I was excited because I thought if you drank, you were an adult. I went to the kitchen and prepared my first drink. Ice in the glass, four fingers of Bacardi, and a splash of coke. I sat back at the table with my grandmother and experienced a warm, burning feeling in my chest as the alcohol ran down my throat.

I liked it. I knew I had arrived.

That night, I drank the entire bottle. I drank enough to not feel a thing. I drank enough to not remember anything. I drank enough to forget that my mother had had me at sixteen, too young to properly show up for me in my life when I needed her, leaving my grandmother and great-grandmother to raise me. I drank to forget that one of my adult relatives had been molesting me for the past seven years, from the time I was seven years old and he climbed into the bed that I shared with my baby brother one late night. I drank to forget. And it worked.

I don't know why my grandmother passed me my first drink. Maybe she knew the pain I was living in. It was definitely never discussed, but here was my family, seven people living in the same small house . . . how could my molestation have gone totally unnoticed? Maybe she was trying to help me? What I do know is that from that first drink, I drank to get drunk, and I drank to forget.

Unfortunately, being an active alcoholic did not make my life any easier. There was the boyfriend who beat me when I was only sixteen. There was the neighbor who raped me when I was twenty-one, coming upstairs to my apartment to borrow a knife and turning it on me instead. Does it matter that I was drinking all day? Would it have made a difference? Would I have been able to fight him off? Who knows? Like an insidious cycle, each incident drove me deeper, gave me more to forget, continued the spiral of shame and remorse and guilt and yet another excuse to drink again.

At twenty-six, I was in a relationship with another alcoholic. Our lives were surrounded by violence and addiction and no intention of doing a damn thing to change any of it. His family surprised him one weekend with an intervention and shipped him off to treatment. I felt like my world had imploded. He and drinking were my everything, and I didn't know how to deal without both. My chest absolutely ached with the loss of him. Except it wasn't heartbreak. It was pancreatitis, from long-term alcohol abuse. Hospitalized, my now-sober, now-ex-boyfriend came to visit me and said the words that changed my life forever: "If you get sober, we will get back together."

And thus, my journey into sobriety began.

I first landed in an all-women's treatment center for ninety days. In a word, it sucked. I missed drinking the way a mother misses her baby. I was angry; I hated being around other women because I couldn't bring myself to trust them. In my head, women were the ones who stole the boyfriend, or lied and manipulated you. All along though, it was me I didn't like, because that's the type of woman I had become. The first time I realized that sobriety was going to stick and become my new life was when I spoke to the ex-boyfriend, now off the wagon, and thought, for me, there would be no going back. Maybe it was my story in Group of hugging my toilet bowl and praying to God to give me the strength to stop drinking. Maybe it was my friend, Janine, who said to me in Group, "Perhaps he just came into your life so you would get sober."

Or it could have been Tina, who had been urging me to simply find the willingness to be willing.

Or maybe it was just time.

I have been sober for 13.44 years, which is 161.28 months, 4,905.6 days, or 117,929 hours. My life could not be more amazing. With the grace of my higher power and my willingness, I am living a good life. The sober me chose a husband who is kind and loving and does not drink and does not hit. He knows every step of the journey I have taken to become the woman I am today. The sober me is a great employee, because I had to show up for myself, and it has translated into every aspect of my life. The sober me has amazing friendships filled with love, compassion, honesty, and so much fun. In learning how to love myself, I learned how to be a good friend to women. And then there is the most important relationship in my life, which I cherish the most, because it never would have happened if I had not gotten sober. Four years ago, I became a mother. I have been blessed with a little boy who thinks the world of me, who has no judgment of me, who thinks I'm the funniest person in the world, and who loves me unconditionally. Michael is a smart, amazing, funny, lovable little boy and has brought me the utmost joy. I get to be his sober mom.

Even thirteen years sober, I can still suffer from self-doubt. I will find myself looking at my beautiful child and my loving husband and ask myself, "Is this it?"

The wounds don't heal easily. My past will always be part of my journey, but it no longer defines the woman I am.

Dolores Coleman

Dolores Coleman, as of the publication of this collection, will be celebrating fourteen years of sobriety. As founder and head chef of the newly launched Dee's Soul Food, Dolores is ecstatic to be realizing a lifelong dream of running her own business. She continues to aid and mentor others on the road to sobriety, following the path she began while working at Reflections. Although Dolores is many things to many people, from mentor to advisor to counselor to wife to cherished friend, her favorite role in life is Michael's Mommy.

Age of Consent

Kim Festa

Eleanor Roosevelt was sadly mistaken. "No one can make you feel inferior without your consent," she said. With all due respect, Mrs. Roosevelt, I never really consented to anything. At age five, I never knew that I even had a choice. There were only the taut, puppeteering strings of intimidation and coercion, and the inherent inferiority that dwells inside those who endure the silent shame and denigration of sexual abuse.

I never dared ask *why* he did it. I just assumed it was because I was less.

Less worthy, less deserving, less human.

Inferior.

Irrespective of consent.

By the time I reached third grade, I had already buried that reality deep and prayed that no one would ever detect its sickening, decomposing existence. Like those molded plastic sand-art creations I made at school, I submerged that abominable cement block of a truth under alternating layers of artificially rainbow-colored granules.

I knew nothing about being powerful, being beautiful, or being hopeful.

Until she called me over to her desk that morning.

Miss Daniela beckoned me—calling my name as if it held some dignitarial importance. "Kim, please come to my desk when you finish your work."

My body stiffened in my cold metal desk chair, preparing for the onslaught of criticism that I had come to expect. The inventory of my faults continually rotated in my mind like the cards of a Rolodex: sloppy, ugly, irresponsible, impure, less. A steel, unbuckling infrastructure of septic messages constructed the empty shell in which I resided—an abandoned carcass that hid any vestiges of innocence.

At age eight, unblemished promises of childhood lay in tatters at my feet. During this time, I fried chicken cutlets for my siblings and folded mountains of underwear and towels. I tried to protect my family from being swallowed whole by his unrelenting, scotch-fueled rage. At eight, I had been thrust into the innermost edges of his maelstrom—the place where his most punishing winds persisted. As a recipient of sexual, emotional, and verbal abuse, I learned to just hold on tight. No questions, no reflection, and no consent. Just survival.

I couldn't tell anyone (and didn't want to tell anyone) because I subsisted in a spiral of terror and filthy shame—the kind that permeates the very fabric of your essence.

What could my teacher possibly want to talk to me about? Did she know? Her tone was different that day. Children always know. *I always knew.*

Tugging at my plaid Catholic school jumper, I shuffled over to Miss Daniela's desk. *Hang on. Brace. Weather.*

Her sky-blue eyes were a welcome invitation, assuring me that I was not in trouble, that I had done something right.

"I have something to give you, Kim. Something that I have been meaning to give you for a while now," she remarked.

I watched as her portly hand delved into her metal desk drawer. What emerged was a little red journal with a floral gold design on its hardbound cover.

"I bought this for you." She placed the hardcover book into my unfurled hands. I loved how newly stiff it felt: untarnished and unsullied.

I clung to the solace of every gentle syllable she directed at me. They were a momentary relief from the soul-breaking winds to which I had grown accustomed.

"What is this for?" I asked.

"Read the first page."

She must have sensed my reluctance and nodded for me to pull back the cover. Her words were delivered in red ink, but bore none of the usual punitive intent: *"My dear Kim, You are a good writer. Maybe to the Earth you are a dot, but you can think and write and the Earth cannot. Write down some of your thoughts and feelings and maybe someday, you just might be a poet."*

I peeled my eyes from the sharp peaks of each handwritten word and looked directly at her face. *Maybe she knew, maybe not. It didn't matter.* What mattered most in that moment was that someone understood, someone reached out, and someone dared to cajole the bunkered voice out of a little girl who never even knew she was entitled to one. In that framed moment, I began my lifelong transition from the embalmer of a terrible secret to someone who uncovered the galvanizing power of words and voice. When Miss Daniela handed me that journal, she gave me the courage to speak. And to heal. And to forgive.

As years passed, I clung to that journal and to the notion that Miss Daniela thought that I, despite being poor, abused, and neglected, could change my life with an education and unfetter myself from ill-fated statistics with my own transformative thoughts.

I recalled that notion when I won a scholarship to a private all-girls high school. And when I sat in an adult survivors group in New York when I was fifteen years old. And when I left home (and never returned) for Boston University and Universita di Padova. And graduated magna cum laude. And when I walked onstage to accept my master's degree from Harvard. And when I was featured in a magazine for helping my own student, a teenage mother, discover the power of her own words too.

In such moments, I remember Miss Daniela's face, hear her voice, and see the gold-flecked cover of that little red journal.

In other moments, I remember those who manipulate, desecrate, and undermine beautiful and burgeoning spirits to make others feel less worthy and inferior.

At age forty-one, I now understand that.

But I no longer give my consent.

Kim Festa

Kim Festa—mother, teacher, and high-heel aficionado—is the author of mamaheels.com, a blog about walking tall through life's challenges. A Teach for America alumna, Kim has helped many students discover the power of their voices through writing in many urban schools, including Newark's North Star Academy. Since 2000, Kim has embraced every ounce of joy and chaos in raising her three spirited sons, Gregg, Marco, and Luke. A graduate of Boston University (BS, 1993) and Harvard (EdM, 1998), Kim is married to internationally recognized educator Gregg Festa and lives in the wonderful community of Oakland, New Jersey.

What Am I Supposed to Eat?

Christie Tate

I stared at the ceiling of my dorm room. I was panicking, but didn't want to wake my roommate.

I thought about my schedule for the next day. Sundays were usually relaxing, but finals were about to start, so we'd be camped out in the library with half the school. I had been relying on a steady diet of hot tamales, Diet Coke, and purging to get me through for months. Now all of that was off the table.

No one knew I had gone to the meeting. I was scared to tell anyone *just in case it didn't do any good.* My parents and best friend had figured out that I was getting really weird about food; they suspected the worst, and they were right.

For years I had summoned every ounce of willpower to control the bingeing and purging, but my reserves could no longer bring full twenty-four-hour periods of relief from the cycle. The week before I went to my first meeting, I fainted in the shower after trying to throw up a chocolate muffin. I believed that if those twelve-step meetings didn't work, I would probably die like a junkie, except instead of heroin and needles I would be surrounded by salty snacks and candy wrappers.

I turned on my side and stared at the wall. In the darkened room I could just make out the picture hanging there. I could see an outline of myself with my sorority sisters—my silver hoop earrings and the letter shirt I wore on the day we pledged. It was supposed to be a happy day. I'd been invited in—my name was on the stationary, engraved in gold-and-blue letters. That was just over a year before, and even though I couldn't see in the dark, I remembered how my eyes looked that day. I passed as a normal college girl, but my eyes betrayed me to anyone looking closely. They were puffy around the edges, and there was a sadness that was usually mistaken for shyness.

Right after I got my invitation to join the sorority, we were assigned "big sisters" from the class above us. It was a tradition to spend the night all together at the house. My big sis, a sweet girl from the same all-girls high school in Dallas I had attended, drove me to my dorm to grab what I needed for the overnight.

"I'll be right back," I said, leaving her to idle in the parking lot while I ran up to my room. I was supposed to be packing a bag with a contact lens case, some deodorant, and something to sleep in. But first I stuffed my mouth full of as many pretzels and crackers as I could. I thought about going for the popcorn, but the kernels hurt my throat when they came back up.

As that picture was snapped later that afternoon, I was obsessing about how many calories I had digested during the binge. *Did I get it all out?* Now, in the dark, I wondered how different I would have looked if I had started going to twelve-step meetings years before.

I flipped again and stared at the ceiling. Had I really introduced myself to everyone as "Christie, a bulimic"? The details of the meeting swirled in my head. It had seemed like an utterly unremarkable way to spend an hour until the woman next to me started talking. "I used to drive around at night eating until I was sick," she explained, "but I don't do that anymore." As I heard her tell her story, I realized that I had actually gone a few minutes without thinking about food for the first time in *years*. I was listening, and I was fully present in the room.

For years my bulimia had been gaining strength, like a hurricane that starts as a colored smudge on the radar way off in Atlantic Ocean but eventually gains speed and destroys entire coastal cities. Areas of my life were slowly being picked off by bulimia's high winds. There was no dating, very few friends—all of that replaced by piles of secrets about food. My energy was devoted to food—where to get it, how to eat it secretly, and how to throw it up. I knew every bathroom on campus.

But some part of me—brain, soul, spirit—came to a standstill during the meeting.

"Do you have any questions?" A young woman with kind eyes asked me when the meeting was over. I was overwhelmed and afraid that the buzzing would start again as soon as I got in my car alone.

"I'm just wondering what I should eat . . ." I sputtered out what sounded like half-statement and half-question. I'd betrayed my biggest secret: a devastating ignorance about the most basic of human functions.

"We suggest that you eat three meals a day," she said simply, handing me her number on a piece of notebook paper. "Call me before you throw up again."

"That's it?" I asked, feeling the panic rise, wondering what I would do when the obsession started again.

"Come to meetings."

After the meeting, I shocked myself by not bingeing even though I was alone and my food stash was *right there*. I didn't let myself hope that my newfound freedom would last or that I would never find myself again on my knees before the toilet, coaxing food from my gut to the bowl.

I felt sleep coming, at last. I reached my hand up to the shelf above my bed and felt the piece of paper that had the nice lady's number on it. I planned to call if I wanted to throw up.

As for what to eat tomorrow, I decided to start with breakfast and then take it from there.

Christie Tate

Christie Tate is a lawyer, writer, and mother of two in Chicago. In 1992, while a freshman at a gigantic Texas university, she found her way into recovery from bulimia, a disease she thought would take her life. She blogs about body image, being a mother, and frequenting Costco and Ann Taylor Loft on her blog at outlawmama.com. She looks forward to the day when people suffering from eating disorders are as educated about Overeaters Anonymous as people suffering from alcoholism are about Alcoholics Anonymous.

Staring Down

Christine Beirne

I caught a woman looking down my shirt yesterday. It wasn't her fault. I was leaning over my bike, fiddling with the row of numbers on my lock. The top of my gray sweatshirt was gaping open, and since I had forgotten my reading glasses, the securing process was taking a while. She really had time to stare. When our eyes met, I wanted to tell her things, details that I had no business relating to a total stranger. I was almost grateful when she pretended to be suddenly absorbed by the zipper on her jacket. Otherwise I might have said something.

I had considered reconstruction. I was ignorant about the details and couldn't fathom a life without breasts. A friend who had been through a similar diagnosis a few years prior phoned me and said, "I'm really happy with my results. You can come over and look if you want." I spent hours online studying pictures and reading blogs. "Autologous tissue surgery"—the process through which doctors move fat and tissue from one part of the body to another—is an inaccurate term. The word should be "surgeries." As in, at least two surgeries. Possibly five.

Last week at my younger daughter's preschool, it was my turn to stare. Another mom and I were crawling around on the floor, and I could not avert my eyes. Her breasts, supported by lavender lace, were achingly beautiful, and my heart sank as I pictured the abandoned top drawer of my dresser. The intensity of my envy finally made me blush and look away.

Post chemotherapy, I was no longer a good candidate for flap surgery; implants were my only option. A friend came with me to the plastic surgeon's office, turning her chair sideways when it was time to open my gown. The doctor cupped my naked right breast casually, almost flippantly. He said if I decided to keep it, he could alter it to match the new one. His eyes narrowed as he examined me, his hands lifting my breast up an inch in order to demonstrate his vision of my future. "We can fix this droop pretty easily," he said. "By the time we're done, you'll match quite nicely." His words were meant to reassure me, maybe even cheer me up a bit. I was bald and weak and mourning my dead mother, but I would get a better body. I could still look good in clothes.

But even through the fog of chemo, the more I learned about reconstruction, the more deeply I understood that it would not aid my healing. Neither implants nor microsurgery would make me feel whole again. The surgeons, with all their talent and skill, would be operating on the wrong part of my body. It was my heart and mind that would need restructuring. And only I could do that.

As I slowly began to untangle from the barbed wire of treatment, the decision to decline both implants and prosthetics was, for me, the most authentic way to walk forward. I have friends who have chosen a different path, and I absolutely support their choices. I don't see myself as a radical flat activist. On the other hand, I don't feel compelled to appear as if everything is fine. Everything is *not* fine. Breast cancer took my mother in November, my hair in December, and my breasts in February. The sharp blade of my grief could shred all the world's pink ribbons into a million tiny pieces.

If you attend a Komen rally or an Avon walk, you might spot a T-shirt that reads: "Yes, they're fake. The real ones tried to kill me!" I understand why a woman would come to distrust and resent her breasts, but I never felt that way. My breasts were a beloved, power- ful part of my womanhood. They produced copious amounts of milk for my daughters and provided me intense sexual pleasure. I miss them terribly; my mourning process will be lengthy. As I try to reframe my concepts of femininity, attractiveness, and arousal, essential facts remain unchanged: I did not want this body. I did not ask for this loss. The truth of cancer's ferocity is a story worth telling—even if the narra- tive sometimes makes me cry.

My closet also has had its share of good-byes. Gone are the

turtleneck sweaters or anything with a V-neck; in their place hangs a growing collection of cardigans, scarves, and tops with busy patterns. My favorite sweatshirt is too big for me now, yet I continue to reach for it, soothed by its bulky silhouette. I can appear almost normal in its gray folds—so normal that I sometimes forget to be careful when bending over. The extra fabric shields me from the raised eyebrows of strangers in the supermarket or on the playground. It insulates me against unexpected gusts of melancholy when I catch a glimpse of my reflection in store windows.

This morning, my six-year-old daughter came into my room while I was getting dressed. Normally, these intrusions are quick round-trips from the playroom. She requests the hole punch or wants to know how to spell hammerhead shark, and then she's off again, legs and mind whirling. This time, she lingered, and I felt her gaze on my chest—a place she has seen thousands of times. I breastfed her past her second birthday; I was nursing her younger sister at the time of my diagnosis.

"Mom, are your scars always going to be there?"

"Yes, honey. They'll fade as time goes on," I tell her, "but they will always be visible. Do they bother you?"

"No," she replies. "I have a scar too. Remember that time I fell at Grandpa's house? It was a really big cut, remember? I needed three Band-Aids."

She sits down on the floor and pushes up one leg of her ladybug pants. Her hands cradle her knee as she squints at a thin, pink line I can barely discern. Her movements are curiously slow, her expression tender. My daughter has long since forgiven her body for its trespass.

"See it, Mommy? See it? Still there. That's OK, though. It doesn't hurt . . . and it reminds me of the time I was really brave."

She leaves and I am left alone, standing shirtless in front of my full-length mirror. I bring my hands up to my chest, trace the scalpel's path with wistful fingers. Legend tells of Amazon women who never had to weep over the terse syntax of a pathology report; they willingly sacrificed their breasts to improve their prowess with bow and arrow.

But when I finally meet my own gaze, no warrior looks back at me—just a pragmatic pacifist with a short haircut. I turn to face my closet. For weeks after the mastectomy, I could manage only shirts with buttons up the front; today the T-shirt slides down easily over straight arms. Out of habit, I look around for my gray sweatshirt, but after a few seconds, I give up searching. The day is bright and sunny, and my daughter is calling me from the next room. I decide to leave it behind.

Christine Beirne

Christine Beirne is a former English teacher, an aspiring writer, and a very current mother. When not immersed in the Zen of play dough or laundry, she can be found philosophizing with the neighborhood moms, indulging in the therapeutic properties of dark chocolate, or sipping good wine. And if the nap gods smile favorably, she has been known to manage all three simultaneously. She lives with her family on the San Francisco Peninsula.

The Whistle

Mary Susan Buhner

My three-year-old daughter, Savannah, stood on her tippy-toes to reach our silverware drawer and cautiously opened it to take out two spoons. She looked at me with silent determination. She gripped the spoons tightly as she walked across the hardwood floor of our kitchen in her plastic Cinderella shoes; one spoon held upright in each little hand, as if they were to be handled with great care.

The *clip-clop, clip-clop* from her plastic shoes was the only sound as I watched her bounce intently across the kitchen floor. She bent both knees, allowing herself to gently kneel, princess-like, in front of her newborn baby sister, who was strapped in her bouncy seat.

"Listen, baby sissy...listen," she said softly.

Ashlyn stared wide-eyed up at her big sister to wait patiently for what would happen next.

Clang, clang! Clang, clang! Savannah's soft blonde curls lay motionless as she stood like a soldier, straight as an arrow, banging the spoons together inches from her little sister's face. Disappointed that her baby sister was not startled by the noise, she looked at me for an answer.

"Mommy, why doesn't sissy cry when I bang the spoons?"

"Because she can't hear them." I stated simply. "She can't hear anything."

It was a cold and blustery November day. I could see the autumn leaves falling off the tree outside our kitchen window—one by one they fell to the ground. I watched them effortlessly glide through the air and delicately fall on the wet grass. I realized that I had finally said it aloud. I had choked the words in a series of sobs to family and friends before this moment, but not yet to my three-year-old daughter. Oddly calm, I took the spoons from her little hands and kissed her to confirm she understood. "Your sister was born deaf, honey," I whispered.

My guilt felt unforgivable. Had I eaten too much spicy food or drunk too much caffeine during my pregnancy? What had I done to take away the ability of my baby girl to hear the birds sing, hear my voice, hear her big sister giggle? What had I done wrong? My husband accepted her deafness and greeted it like a friend coming over for dinner. He surrendered to it. I grieved it.

I began to check out medical journals from the library (this was pre-Internet boom), meet with local support groups, and educate myself on deafness. I was told very quickly everything my baby would never experience: no appreciation for music, no dancing (because she wouldn't be able to hear the music), no playing of a musical instrument, no team sports, no mainstream school, no talking on the telephone, no hearing a smoke alarm if the house was on fire—no speaking, hearing, or listening. I was devastated.

I was consumed with reading medical journals because a few mentioned cases where a deaf child could learn to speak and hear with digital hearing aids or cochlear implants (ten years ago, neither were common in newborns). I felt a sense of control over my grief with this gathered information. I methodically carried around my three-ring binder, much as my oldest daughter had carried the two spoons— carefully and with determination. I was still grieving—not even close to surrendering. What was I missing? Hope. I needed hope to push forward.

Then, on a snowy February morning, I got it. It came quietly and by surprise. My oldest daughter said, "Mommy, you said you would take me to the library today. Remember?"

Had I made that promise to her? I couldn't remember.

"It's snowing today, honey. I think we will stay home." I said.

She looked down at her little princess shoes and said to herself, "But you promised." Reluctantly, I bundled all three of us up and headed to the library.

It was snowing hard, and I wondered how my three-year-old had talked me into this. We pulled into the library, and the parking lot was empty and covered with snow. Holding the pumpkin seat in one hand and my oldest daughter's mitten-covered hand in my other, we headed in and walked with purpose to the children's section. I sat at the small round table and took off everyone's coats, hats, and mittens. I sat the pumpkin seat in front of me on the small table. Ashlyn and I locked eyes, as we often did. Even though she could not hear me, I talked to her incessantly—all the time, about everything. She would look up at me with her deep blue eyes and ponder my face and my moving lips. I had graduated from her silence feeling like torture to it feeling like a timer keeping track of all the sounds she was missing all the time.

There I sat at the kiddie table in an empty library on a snowy February day. As my oldest began stacking her selection of books on the table, I saw another mom walk in out of the corner of my eye. She stood by the door and bent down to talk with her son as if giving specific directions and not wasting any time. He nodded and marched over to the selection of books near where I was sitting. As if in slow motion, there it was—hope—standing right in front of me. The young boy had short hair that only accentuated the hearing aids that fit over his ears. I studied him for a split second, wondering if he could talk, hear, and listen. He began to whistle, and I began to cry. He turned around, waved to his mom, and said, "Come here, Mom. I need your help." There it was: on a snowy February day in an empty library, hope walked up beside me and whistled.

I knew at that very moment that my newborn daughter would learn to hear, speak, and listen. I was given the courage to find my own voice to be her advocate. To fight the status quo, the norm, and to push past what was expected of her and of me.

Today, Ashlyn, my daughter born legally deaf, is ten years old and uses no sign language to communicate. She hears, speaks, and listens just like you and me. She plays the guitar, had a solo in the fourth-grade choir program, plays basketball, loves to talk on the phone and dance.

What is ordinary to her—like turning her head to hear a bird sing—is still extraordinary to me.

Hope . . . it's everything. It is the small thin thread that ties us from the life we know to the life we need to lead. Would we have the courage to cross over and transition into the new life without it? I don't think so. I think it gives us the courage to meet our potential. In my case, two spoons and a snowy day at the library gave me not only the courage to help my daughter, born deaf, find her voice but also the courage for me to find mine as well. For that, I am forever grateful.

Mary Susan Buhner

A writer at heart, Mary Susan Buhner is the author of the book *Mommy Magic: Tricks for Staying Sane in the Midst of Insanity.* She writes a monthly featured column for *Midwest Parenting Magazine* based on her popular blog, MommyMagic.com, and hosts a weekly TV segment on FOX. Before becoming an author, she had a rewarding career in nonprofit. She earned a degree in speech communication from Indiana University and a Management Certificate in fundraising from the International Center on Philanthropy. A true extrovert, Mary Susan enjoys traveling and adventure. Her favorite motto comes from Gandhi: "Be the change you want to see in the world."

Becoming Special

Jennifer Bush

About a week after my son was born, some friends came to meet the new baby. Cathy, who also had an infant, made herself comfortable in an armchair, threw a blanket over her shoulder, and started nursing. She looked at me, smiled blissfully, and said, "Wouldn't you just jump in front of a bus for him?"

I didn't want to admit how tired and frazzled I was. Everything, including that "natural" act of nursing, had been a challenge. While not exactly opposed to being a mother, I hadn't quite warmed up to the whole thing. I nodded my head and said something along the lines of, "uh-huh."

My transition into the joys of motherhood took a little while. But I did adjust. I learned how to click the infant carrier out of the car and into the stroller. I wore my baby to the grocery store and stocked the freezer with homemade organic purees. My son and I went to play dates and music classes, and at four months *to the day*, we began sleep training. And soon enough, I loved my chubby baby with jump-in-front-of-a-bus ferocity.

And then, just about the time that I was comfortable enough in my role as "mother" to have a second child—six weeks after that second child was born, in fact—a woman with a white coat and distinct Canadian accent looked at me and said, "Your son has autism."

Once again, I found myself not quite sure how to feel. Only this time, I had no time to get used to the idea of being a special-needs parent; there was no "transition" about it. While there was no denying the diagnosis—the signs had been building for months—I couldn't quite make sense of the words I had just heard.

There is an essay often given to parents of newly diagnosed

special-needs kids called "Welcome to Holland." In the essay, you prepare for a trip to Italy. You read up on the culture, pack the right clothes,
even learn some of the language. You board the plane. But when you
disembark . . . you are in Holland. Holland is a beautiful place, with
windmills and tulips and lovely people. But you were supposed to go to
Italy. Pasta! Gelato! *Buongiorno!* And now you see only wooden shoes
and salted herring.

After Wesley's diagnosis, my son seemed a stranger to me. Though
people told me, "He's the same child he was before the diagnosis," it
certainly didn't feel that way. In a single instant, he went from a happy,
mellow toddler with some speech delays to a kid whose entire future
was uncertain. Would he ever speak? Have friends? Go to prom? Yes, in
those first days, I thought about high school prom, that silly yet quint-
essential hallmark of adolescence.

Even the terminology sounded all wrong. How do I describe my
son? What reason do I give when I explain that we can't go to play dates
anymore because Wesley has twenty-five hours a week of therapy? I
practiced when I met new people. "He has special needs." "He is developmentally delayed." "He has autism." "He is autistic."

I started reading blogs by people who called themselves "autism
moms" or "special-needs moms." Was that me? I mean, *I* don't have the
special needs. "Mom to a child with special needs" was just unwieldy.
They were accurate, but nothing felt right. How could this possibly be
my life?

And all the things people said to make me feel better only made
me angry. *God only gives you what you can handle. Everything happens for
a reason. Special kids go to special parents.*

I resented all of it. They say that people with autism have difficulty
with transitions, but I was the one who couldn't accept this new role. I
didn't want special. I didn't want different. I just wanted my son back.

I spent hours looking for cures, researching diets or methodol-
ogies that would help my son "recover" from autism. I read blog after
blog about kids who accomplished so much more than experts said

they would. They graduated from college. They got married. Some of them even went to prom! And every so often, Wesley would do something so "normal" that I knew in the core of my being that he would be OK. That he, too, would be a success story.

In the four years since Wesley's diagnosis, I'd like to say that things have gotten easier for us. I want to share with you that story of amazing progress, of undiscovered talents or remarkable beauty. But that is not our story, at least not yet. In many ways, things have gotten harder. My son, who is approaching six years old, doesn't speak. He is not toilet trained, can be aggressive, and often goes for weeks without sleeping through the night. His disability and behaviors became so challenging last year that we pulled him out of school so he could return to a full-time in-home therapy program.

I'm not yet comfortable with the life my son is forced to lead, though I suppose he isn't forced any more than any of us are forced into our own neurologies. I'm not comfortable with the praise that is automatically given to parents of special-needs kids. I'm not comfortable with the scratches and bruises I've acquired when Wesley becomes frustrated at not being able to communicate his needs. I'm not comfortable with the uncertainty of his future, with the knowledge that my husband and I will never be empty-nesters, or with the ongoing fights with school districts, insurance companies, and therapy providers to make sure that my son is safe, educated, and treated with respect.

But some transitions happen no matter how hard we fight them. I am no longer a tourist in this foreign country. I know the terminology and am able to throw around acronyms with the best of them. I have learned to speak Dutch, as it were. I have become adept at advocating for Wesley's needs and have immersed myself in local and online communities of special-needs moms, some of whom have autism themselves.

I am no longer trying to cure my son or make him into the "normal" child I expected to have. I wear proudly the title of autism mom, just as I want Wesley to grow to be a proud autistic adult.

I am Wesley's mom. It is a special role indeed.

Jennifer Bush

Jennifer Bush is a blogger and autism advocate with degrees from UC Berkeley and the Yale School of Management. After earning her MBA, she spent several years in the high-tech trenches of Silicon Valley. Jennifer lives in San Jose, California, with her husband, three-year-old daughter, and five-year-old son, who is on the autism spectrum. You can read more about her family at her personal blog, Anybody Want a Peanut? (wantapeanut.com)

A Name for This Pain

Aubree Deimler

My eyes scanned over the array of magazines on the table in the waiting room—*Parents, Parenting, Family Fun . . . Why didn't I bring something to read?* I glanced at my watch, then shifted my eyes to the floor to avoid looking at the big, pregnant bellies to my left and right.

It was lunch hour on the day of my twenty-ninth birthday. My gynecologist had recommended I come in for an ultrasound since I had mentioned irregular bleeding and chronic pain in my pelvic area that was growing worse every day, along with feelings of sheer exhaustion. After spending time doing my own research, I had a sinking suspicion that my symptoms pointed to endometriosis.

With endometriosis, cells from the uterus are found in all parts of the body, especially in the pelvic region. For me, this meant excruciating periods that left me bedridden each month. My uterus went through contractions that I believe competed with labor pains, except at the end of it all, I had no baby . . . and I couldn't help but worry that I might never have one.

My research had taught me that endometriosis is the leading cause of infertility. The thought of not being able to bear a child spread severe sadness through me. As I sat in the waiting room, I felt like an outsider. I was the only nonpregnant woman. My mind played with a resounding thought: *that may never be me.*

My name was finally called, and I went back to an examination room where I waited again on a paper-lined table with the dreaded stirrups, cold and uncomfortable in my crinkling paper gown. The ultrasound technician greeted me, and after a little fiddling, she captured some images of the inside of my pelvic area. She did not find anything unusual but recommended I speak with the doctor.

When I saw the doctor, we talked again about my symptoms. My voice wavered when I told her I'd been off birth control for over three years and had not gotten pregnant. I watched the concerned look on her face.

"I think I have endometriosis," I said.

She agreed it could be a possibility, but the only way to know for sure was to have surgery. She gave me a small pat on the shoulder when my built-up emotions burst out in tears. These tears continued for the remainder of my twenty-ninth birthday and for many days thereafter.

I cried because I knew there was no cure for this disease, and I knew that it would only progress. I felt hopeless that the pain would never end, and I could not escape the thoughts of infinite infertility. These thoughts created an empty sort of pain deep in my belly, radiating to my heart. *Why me? Did I deserve this pain? Was I not worthy of a child?*

A few months later, laparoscopic surgery confirmed that I did indeed have endometriosis. I was relieved to finally have a name for the pain I had suffered for much of my life, but the realities of the diagnosis were depressing. The surgeon reminded me that endometriosis is a chronic condition and that it would spread, causing more pain and robbing my chances for conception.

I declined the hormonal drugs offered to me. I'd spent a decade on birth control, and while it helped with the pain, it brought with it side effects that I was tired of dealing with. And getting back on the pill seemed to me to be accepting defeat that I would not be able to get pregnant.

I returned to my everyday life of pain and exhaustion, coupled with a relentless feeling of sadness. I found myself spending a lot of time in bed, cuddled with my heating pad. The pain was unyielding and made me hate my body and the disease spreading through it. I fell into a dark place where my thoughts were impeded by suicidal considerations.

In spite of the negativity that easily spread with the physical pain, a part deep inside of me told me to not give up hope. I could not just lie and submit to pain and negative possibilities. There had to be another way.

So I started researching again. This time I came across a website that shared the story of a woman who essentially cured her endometriosis with diet. She suggested cutting out specific foods in order to cut inflammation from the body. Three big ones were gluten, dairy, and soy.

One day, as I sat down to a meal my husband had prepared, I decided that I was going to give this diet a try. I pushed away the buttered English muffin and explained my new dietary intentions. I could tell by the look on his face that the idea was pretty crazy.

Deciding what to eat became a touchy subject over the months that followed, escalating at points to frustrated outbursts. The restricted foods were abundant in the diet I was used to consuming. It became a challenge to eat, especially at restaurants or social events.

The hardest social events were baby showers. In the year following my diagnosis, I was invited to at least four of them. I went to one where there were five different pregnant ladies! The dreaded question was always asked of me—"So when are you going to have kids?"

I didn't want to bring up my newly named disease, which was wreaking havoc on my reproductive organs, amidst discussion of car seats and breast pumps, so I replied with a soft, "Someday," while my heart ached with doubt.

With my new dietary restrictions, I declined the snacks and cake at these showers, stating "stomach issues" as the cause. Again, I felt like an outsider—the last remaining "non mom," unable to obtain something that seemed to happen so easily for everyone around me.

I stuck with the diet, and lo and behold, I started to feel better. Seeds of hope grew inside of me. *I can beat this.* The improvements I felt prompted me to continue to research natural healing. I found a relevant connection with endometriosis and the liver, so I decided to cleanse mine.

In turn, my physical pain continued to decrease, allowing my mind to flourish again. I awoke to optimism unfelt for many years, and the hate for my body shifted. I dipped into new spiritual teachings and began living my life in a more mindful, positive manner.

I learned that the pelvic region is located in the second chakra and relates to suppressed emotions. I also learned that the liver tends to be the physical storage place for many of these emotions. As I went through various detoxification stages, these emotions were released, and as I spent more time in meditation, they were realized.

In an unexpected way, endometriosis taught me a vital lesson that I'd failed to capture for many, many years—I didn't love myself. This was evident in my actions. For years I fed myself poor foods, drugs, and alcohol and spent time in verbally abusive relationships. I was unhappy and, in my mind, unworthy. This toxicity spread, manifesting itself in physical pain, in the very part of me where new life was supposed to bloom.

The pain of endometriosis forced me to change and take better care of myself. It forced me to evaluate my own life's stress patterns and expectations. It forced me to dig deeper and release the pain I'd been holding inside for so long. I realized that with self-care and acceptance, I could heal it. And most important, I learned that I was worth it.

It's been a little over two years since my official diagnosis of endometriosis, and I feel better today than I ever have. This past month, my (hated) monthly friend came in a mild manner. I waited for the pain, but it did not show.

I will not miss it.

I look down at my un-pregnant belly, then down to my feet, where my two boxer pups curl against me, and smile in silent gratitude. I know now that there is no sense in worrying about the child I may or may not bear—I am perfect the way I am.

Right here. Right now.

Aubree Deimler

Since being diagnosed with a chronic and painful condition called endometriosis, Aubree Deimler has embarked on a journey to tackle this disease through natural methods. She is very passionate about women's health and wellness and blogs about her research and experiences at peacewithendo.com. She is enrolled at the Institute for Integrative Nutrition, and upon completion of the program in May 2014 she will be a certified holistic health coach. Aubree is a native of Colorado, where she lives with her husband and two boxer pups.

Rock Bottom

Shelly Guillory

"Dude, what were you thinking?" I interrupt Adam as he recounts his story of running away two days ago from the rehab where I work as a registered nurse.

"I don't know." He shrugs his shoulders and grins. Adam is new. Like most of the teens in the facility, he needs to prove he won't surrender easily to the rules of the place. I know this feeling.

Adam plops down on an old, lime-green examination table, swinging his dangling, restless legs. My brain flashes back four years ago to a time I can't forget no matter how hard I try.

For fifty-seven days, I followed twenty-six other patients into the group room for the nightly 6:45 p.m. Alcoholics Anonymous meeting. While someone read the introduction from the AA Big Book, I felt anxious. Heart racing, sweating, and hyperventilating, I had to get out. I had to run from some invisible, irrational fear that took over at the most inappropriate times. I was sick of rehab, tired of being told to get on my knees and pray to a god I didn't believe existed.

I walked out, ran through an overgrown field, and climbed over a nine-foot wooden fence. I trudged two miles through a heavily wooded area in the backwoods of Mississippi until I got to a small convenience store. The woman working the counter shot me a look that told me she knew what I was—a dirty, cut-up escapee, with a wild look in my eye and no destination. I asked to borrow her phone. While I tried to figure out whom to call, I knew I had made a mistake letting my faulty fight-or-flight system dictate my actions. I felt alone. And scared.

Debbie, a counselor who dressed in leopard heels and had a thick Southern accent, walked in and pried the phone out of my shaking hands. Without looking at her, I walked outside, sat on the curb, and lit a Camel menthol light. Rock bottom. I had always thought that when a person hit "rock bottom" it meant he was living on the streets, dumpster-diving for aluminum cans to exchange for drug money. "Rock bottom" meant a person had a pimp, pawned everything he owned or stole, and lived in crack house. After five trips to rehab, it finally hit me: I was at rock bottom.

A month after trying to flee, I left rehab. My husband, angry about wasting money on another rehab opportunity I had screwed up, flew down to pick me up. The road trip home was tense, with only a few words exchanged for 1,830 miles.

At home and sober, panic attacks trapped me in my house. I couldn't leave my house alone. I spent most of my time lying on the couch, huddled under blankets, fighting panic attacks that came eight times a day and resisting the strong urge to get wasted. Emotions returned with a vengeance, making up for eight years of being smothered by drugs.

Some think drug addiction is a choice, which isn't true. But it is a choice to recover, and I don't think people, especially family members who have had enough of the lies and deception, understand how hard it is ignore the call of drugs. I harbored guilt for the pain I caused my family, which I didn't know how to deal with without swallowing a bunch of pills.

Two days after I returned from rehab, I ransacked my room looking for a prescription for tranquilizers, the same drugs strung-out tweakers use to reverse the mania that results from days of smoking meth and snorting cocaine. I found a script shoved inside a shoe and drove an anxious mile to the pharmacy to get it filled.

But while I waited, I made a choice.

Slowly— and without drugs—I moved forward in life, making small progress, loosening the tight grip of agoraphobia. I carved out a new life, one that I was unsure about but that made me excited.

I swore I would never return to nursing. I blamed my addiction on my career choice. I told myself I was too sensitive, too inexperienced, and too incompetent. I had failed to emotionally separate myself from my patients. Tangled up in their emotions, I matched their fear and apprehension. At times, my anxiety made it impossible to work without the threat of a nervous breakdown. After pushing an IV medication, I peeked into a patient's room every two minutes to watch the rise and fall of his chest, feeling a sense of relief when I saw he was still alive. To deal with anxiety, I swallowed fewer of the drugs prescribed by my doctor and more tranquilizers I bought off the street from creepy men and Mormon moms who lived double lives.

I couldn't risk screwing up my sobriety, so after rehab, I took low-paying, less-stressful jobs, including a three-week stint at CURVES, where I chatted with older women about their relationship woes while helping them get physically fit. But I needed and craved something more meaningful, something more than serving coffee or bagging groceries could fulfill. Despite my apprehension, I applied for a job as a nurse at the rehab facility.

"You know you can totally do this," I tell Adam. He nods his head. He probably doesn't believe me, so I will keep telling him until he does.

Adam knows I'm not angry. His counselor already dropped him a level and placed restrictions on him. It's not my job to tell him to pick up trash for two hours or hand down some other punishment. I pour medication into the client's hands and examine every nook and cranny of their mouths, making sure they swallow their pills. But my job also requires me to listen, to help them pick out appropriate dress clothes for an interview, or to congratulate them on landing a job. I need this job to stay sober as much as these clients need the structure of the facility.

"This is probably the hardest thing you are going to do, but you can do this." And I mean it when I say this to Adam.

Adam doesn't say much about what he is feeling. But he doesn't have to. He might make it. He knows rock bottom, though he might not realize it. He hit it the night he ran.

"When I was out there, even just for the night, I didn't like it," Adam explains.

"I know. You don't have anything out there, not even a dollar. While you are here, we can help you stay clean and help you create the life you want and deserve."

"I had money that night," Adam quickly responds.

"OK, let me rephrase that: Have money to support yourself that you have obtained in a legal way." I cock my head to the side and give him look that warns not to throw any bull my way. Adam laughs, and I hand him medications that help him sleep, calm him down, and make him feel less depressed.

"Leave again, and I will find you and drag you back," I tell him.

And I mean it in the most loving and supportive way.

Shelly Guillory

Shelly Guillory earned a bachelor's degree in nursing and in journalism from the University of Utah. She lives in Salt Lake City, Utah, with her husband and boxer dog, Layla, and is the director of nursing at a nonprofit substance abuse treatment center. She enjoys writing, photography, repairing old furniture, and snowboarding. She is also working on her master's degree in the Family Nurse Practitioner Program at Westminster College. Her work has appeared in *The Salt Lake Tribune, Salt Lake City Weekly,* and *The West View.*

A Red Sports Car Stops.
A Door Swings Open.

Rita Henley Jensen

Columbus, Ohio, November 1971

My little one was in bed with me that morning, as usual. As she had done often in the two years since her birth, she slept in the warm cave created by the blankets and the space under my armpit and next to my belly. We usually spent the early hours of each day with her wakening me to breastfeed a bit and afterwards both of us dropping off to catch a bit more sleep.

This was no ordinary day, however. I awakened just past dawn with no prompting from my daughter. I dressed quickly, trying not to wake her, wanting a final few seconds to myself before the day started. Cold poured in from the cracks in the weathered sills and down from the uninsulated attic above, and a light rain began to smack the room's windows.

Damn, I thought. *The kids are going to get wet.*

I pulled on a pair of polyester slacks and a nylon sweater. I looked once again at the mold bubbling the bright-green paint in the upper corner of the room, the product of an insidious leak, and sighed. It was not in my power to make it disappear by repairing the roof and repainting the bedroom. I did not have sufficient cash to purchase plastic for covering the windows.

Worry filled me. I had to rush or I might be late for the beginning of my future. Scooping my little one up into my arms, I tiptoed down the hallway to my older daughter's room.

"Honey, it's time to get up. We got to go. You got to go to school today."

She rolled over toward me, and I took her hand. With the little one slung over my shoulder, I led my six-year-old down the steps and to a kitchen chair with stab wounds in its flowered plastic cushions—a keen reminder of their father's threats to kill us and why I had left in May and applied for welfare.

I laid the little one on the sofa and changed her diaper, a process she fought vigorously. I pawed through the clean laundry piled high on the daybed and found a pair of corduroy pants, a cotton T-shirt, and socks for each.

I placed her on my lap and shoved her legs into the pants.

"Come on," I said to my six-year-old. "Get dressed. Put on your pants. We got to go."

The winters in Columbus, Ohio, like much of life there, are endured, not enjoyed. The temperature hovers at around thirty degrees, not cold enough to represent a challenge, just cold enough to assure a constant chill. Built on a fertile plain just north of the Appalachian foothills and between two rivers, the city is cursed with air laden with a gray damp that promises rain or perhaps a bit of snow, but rarely delivers. The rivers themselves add no beauty to the city's landscape. Their waters are chocolate-brown from soil erosion and agricultural runoff and are generally avoided. Far from the dramatic winds and snow that pound the lake region 200 miles to the north, the city's sky is overcast with clouds that rarely darken or open to permit light to break through. The air and the sky merge with the gray concrete of the streets and sidewalks so that an aura of bitter colorlessness and cold pervade the city.

Or so it seemed to me when I was twenty-four in December 1971.

As an economy, we did not eat breakfast. Two months before, my welfare check had been reduced to $81 per month because I had earnings as a waitress. Two weeks after I had reported those earnings to the welfare department, I was fired for signing a card indicating I wished to have union representation. At the same time, the legislature and the governor were engaged in a fierce battle over the state budget, and all welfare benefits were frozen. I had not worked long enough to be eligible for unemployment benefits.

To get by, I sold most of my food stamps to pay my $85 rent and my electricity, gas, and telephone bills. I began relying on my children's daycare centers to feed them two meals and a snack. At home in the evenings, I would give them a bowl of soup or a peanut butter sandwich. I tried not to eat much myself.

When the little one's pink snowsuit was zipped and the older one's coat buttoned, I pulled on my army-green parka and out we went—the little one perched on my left arm and older at my side, holding my hand, down the wooden back steps, through the grassless, soggy backyard, down the alley, across the street, and up one block to the vacant Dairy Queen on the main thoroughfare, Indianola Avenue.

At the corner, I stood on the sidewalk and faced the direction of the oncoming traffic. I let go of the older one's hand and stuck my thumb out. No car even slowed down. It began to rain harder.

Damn, I thought. *I am going to be late, and the kids are getting wet.*

I noticed, for the first time, the telephone booth behind me. "Come on, kids. Get in here. You got to stay dry."

I shut the booth's door to shelter them from the wind as well and turned back to the business of hitchhiking. Soon, a bright-red sports car pulled over. The driver leaned over from the driver's seat and swung open the door. He looked several years younger than me and he was beautiful—slender, but with an athletic build, blue eyes and light-brown hair.

"Need a ride?" he asked with a smile.

"Yes," I said.

I made a quick assessment. The car was so small that it had no backseat, just something that looked like a shelf.

"Could you wait just one second?"

I turned around and opened the telephone booth. Then I flipped the bucket seat forward and helped the older one onto the shelf. I released it, climbed into the bucket seat, placed the little one on my lap, and pulled the door shut. His face conveyed his surprise, but having made the offer, he decided to stand by it.

"Where ya going?'" he asked.

"Today is my orientation day at Ohio State," I said. "And I am taking the kids to daycare first."

Ohio State University was a ten-minute ride away, down Indianola. Its campus was vast, covering 15,000 acres. It had its own hospital, mental health facility, farm, shuttle bus system, newspaper, television and radio stations, and a football stadium capable of seating 84,000 spectators. The only admission requirement was a high school diploma. I had a high school diploma, albeit from Columbus Evening High School, not a regular high school, but nevertheless it was a diploma, and I was eligible.

I had borrowed the $15 matriculation fee from my mother and mailed my application in September. A neighbor had told me about a state agency, the Bureau of Vocational Rehabilitation, that might pay my tuition. I applied and was given a battery of tests in October to determine whether I would benefit from attending college. Now in December, with the beginning of classes just weeks away, I still had not heard if the bureau was going to help me.

But I was going to Orientation Day regardless. This day was going to begin my new life. I was going to read books, including history, and write papers and one day be able to get a job good enough to support my kids.

The driver asked me where the daycare center was. Sensing his desire to be kind and to help me, I confessed there were actually two— one for each kid. He asked no explanation; he did not demand to know why I had not made it easier by placing them in the same center. The four of us fell silent in the damp, cold gloom.

I showed him the way to the first and asked him to wait while I dropped the little one off at the federally funded daycare center in the basement of the campus Unitarian church. I returned and led him to the campus Methodist church that permitted a parent-co-op to operate a center that cared for elementary school children before and after public school hours. I did not have to ask him to wait for me again while I took older one downstairs to the church basement—it was just understood that he would.

As we headed toward the student union, where my orientation was to begin, my eyes fell on the open pack of Marlboros lying between the seats, behind the stick shift.

I had not had a cigarette for weeks. I would not waste my money buying them. I rarely missed them, but now I wanted one, really wanted one. This man had been so extraordinarily kind, did I dare ask for a cigarette too? The red sports car was fast approaching the end of my ride. I was beginning college within five minutes. I closed my eyes and asked.

"Could I, I mean would it be OK, I mean . . . could I have a cigarette?"

"Sure," he said. I picked one out of the pack and, at a stoplight, he used his Zippo to light it. I inhaled deeply, ashamed that I had asked and delighted that the smoke calmed me a bit. When he let me out, I thanked him. He nodded, revved his engine and sped off.

Rita Henley Jensen

Rita Henley Jensen is the founder and editor-in-chief of Women's eNews. Launched in June 2000, the daily nonprofit Internet-based news service covers issues of particular concern to women. She is a graduate of Ohio State University and Columbia Graduate School of Journalism. Throughout her career, she has won prizes for public service journalism, most recently the Casey Medal for Meritorious Journalism. In 1994, she was fortunate enough to be awarded a year-long fellowship during which the need for Women's eNews became apparent.

Motherhood

Kelly Corrigan

It's clear to you immediately that you can have anything you want when you have cancer.

Your doctor called at 1 p.m., and since that moment, your husband has met your every need, even anticipating needs (proving that he had been capable of such all along).

Word spreads, and your doorstep shows it—a cheery bunch of Gerber daisies, a little tin of peanut butter cookies, a calla lily. The phone calls are endless. You think to yourself that your diagnosis is probably generating as much curiosity and awkwardness as winning the lottery would.

Everyone treats you like a saint—an elderly, disabled saint.

Except two people who still want you to find their bunny—not that one!—and fill up their sippy cup and read them a book. They never say "please" and they always interrupt and they lean into you even when you are so hot already. And their ignorant self-centeredness is proof that you are still managing to put your children first, even when you are in the crisis of your life.

Claire comes toward you with her bulging diaper, and her hair is stuck to her forehead with the musty sweat that builds up during her morning nap. She knocks over your tall pilsner glass of iced peppermint tea, the one that Edward made for you in a moment as romantic as the one in which he proposed. Claire doesn't say she's sorry; she just cries because her T-shirt is wet on the bottom part and she loves her Elmo and Rosita T-shirt. Georgia also cries, because the tea went onto her paper where she is scribbling. She is so close to three. Her party is in five days. You've been talking about it for months—when you push her in the swing, when you put her to bed, when you cut up her apple.

"Guess what's happening in two weeks from today?" you say. "Ooh, look! The mailman took the party invites!"

Then, between calls to medical centers, long sessions on breastcancer.org, and e-mails to work colleagues, Edward says, "We're not gonna do the party, right? It's too much." But you say, "No! She has to have it!" because you are feeling dramatic and magnanimous and like you can't possibly let cancer have its way with your daughter's first real birthday party.

"She'll never even remember it," he says.

"I will," you say.

On Wednesday you swing into the mammography center to pick up your films to take them over to the national expert you will wait three hours to see, making lists and pretending to sleep and reading old *People* magazines about Jen and Brad and that Angelina Jolie. On the way home, even though you've just been told you will do chemo for five months and then probably have a mastectomy after that, even though it's dinnertime, you pass Michael's craft store and you tell Edward to pull in—"real quick"—so you can get some decorations and order the helium balloons and he looks at you like you've just cut your own hair with a kitchen knife.

But then you're in there, at Michael's, and it's so exciting to be in line with the other people whose greatest concerns are finding three matching green photo mats and some extra-wide grosgrain ribbon for their fall door wreath. You're up, and the tired cashier says, "How are you tonight?" and you say, "Good!" and it's the biggest lie you ever told as well as the God's honest truth and you don't really know what you're doing but someone's gonna have a great birthday on Saturday and it'll all be because of you and you aren't irrelevant yet, even if you are defective and are messing everything up for your family.

You are perky coming out of the store, even holding the door for the woman behind you, who is having a bad day, you can tell. Edward is slumped over the steering wheel like he's been shot from behind, which he kinda has. He sits right up when he feels you coming towards the car. He is "fine, just tired."

Your kids are asleep when you get home and Sophie, the babysitter who breaks out every time she has a pop quiz, looks at you tragically but you divert her by saying, "Look! Look at these great party hats—they go with the plates—see?" You sound like Mrs. Dalloway. Edward hands Sophie a wad of twenties and says, "Thanks, Soph."

You unpack your shopping bag from Michael's and show Edward the candy decorations for the cake you haven't made but will and he says "good" and you can't bear to ask him how he is again because it might come out this time for real and so you just turn on the stereo and as he heads to the answering machine, you say, "Let's do that tomorrow" because the machine says fourteen people called and every one of them wants to tell you that you are in their prayers and that God doesn't give you anything you can't handle and what doesn't kill us makes us stronger but Edward is responsible and level-headed and says, "It could be about your bone scan." You realize you forgot something in the car, maybe, so you say "OK, I gotta go get something in the trunk anyway" and when you come back he says, "The scan is on Friday. I'll call Sophie."

The party is scheduled for Saturday afternoon and when you send out the e-mail about it—yes, it's happening, please no cancer talk—you realize you will have to have a conversation with your children before all these people come over. You Google "talking to children about cancer" and you start to worry that some kid will say, "My grandma died of cancer," and then you realize your daughters don't know what death is. Because why should they?

Then you find this line: "Cancer is like weeds in a garden." That's really good. You think you should send a thank-you card to the person who came up with that phrase. You think, "See how important words are?"

The bone scan makes you cry. "Stay still, please," says the technician, who has an Irish accent and looks like a guy who loves his pub. It's so big, the machine. It's so Willy Wonka/Mike Teavee and you can tell it is extremely expensive and you know very little but still enough to know that if they find it in your bones, you'll probably die before you turn forty. And that's why you cry and that's why the technician asks you again to "stay very still" but when he comes to your side to help you up off the table, he has tears in his eyes and you know that he does this every day so why would he cry?

Friday is a two-Ambien night. Sleep is deep and black and divine.

Saturday! The party. Georgia is at your feet in no time. "Mommy! I'm three! I'm three years old!"

"You are. Do you feel any different?"

"No."

"Are you sure?"

"No, I don't feel anything. Everything feels exactly the same." She looks concerned, as though maybe if she can't feel it, it didn't happen.

"Well, even if you can't feel it, it's real," you say, newly expert in the matter.

Edward comes in and lifts Georgia up and she is so happy and the party will be great.

Everyone will come with a bigger gift than they had planned—at the last minute they will tape something extra on the top: a recorder, a ponytail holder, a My Little Pony. Claire will also get a pile of gifts. In an hour, Georgia will blow out her candles and there will be wrapping paper everywhere and the goodie bags that complement the paper plates will be torn through and it'll all be on film and towards the end, after about half the people have left and the afternoon is drifting towards five o'clock, you will open a bottle of chardonnay and the remaining mothers will gather around and fill little polka-dot paper cups and you will all stand in the sun and look at each other and your children and shake your heads and make that little laugh sound you do when you don't know what else to say, the little sound that says, "Didn't see this coming," and you will lean into one of them and feel that tiny contraction in your throat that means you're going to cry and you will decide to let it come. It's really OK now, because Georgia is running in circles on the back deck with her new butterfly wings on and a hot-pink helium balloon tied to each wrist and needs absolutely not one more thing from you.

For now.

Kelly Corrigan

Kelly Corrigan is the author of *The Middle Place* and *Lift*, both of which topped out at No. 2 on the *New York Times* best-seller list. Kelly's third book, *Glitter and Glue*, comes out February 11, 2014, and is about her mother, who liked to remind her children: "Your father's the glitter, but I'm the glue." She is also the cofounder of Notes & Words, an annual event that puts writers and musicians on stage together for an evening of smart, satisfying entertainment to benefit Children's Hospital of Oakland.

Extra Inner, by Nancy Calef

Artist Statement:
Extra Inner

Comfort zone pushed out of range
As I grow, transition and change
My internal world must stay aground
to integrate what's all around
A map of the essential tools
To balance the in and the out
A key for coping and releasing stress
The heart radiating in the state of undress

I shoulder my karma while paying the toll
As commerce sets in the wave of my spine
the sex protected, my eye holds a jewel
That extra dose of inner is my fuel
—Nancy Calef
November 2013

Painting title and medium:
Extra Inner, oil and found objects on canvas, 36" x 36"

Nancy Calef
Nancy Calef creates "peoplescapes," oil, sculpture, and applied objects
on canvas, addressing cultural, political, and spiritual issues facing
society. By juxtaposing people in recognizable places and situations,
each painting weaves together a narrative about contemporary life,
filled with layers of detail, symbolism, and humor. Nancy has been
exhibiting around the world for thirty years. She is also a singer-
songwriter, a computer animator, and the author of *Peoplescapes—
My Story from Purging to Painting*, her new illustrated memoir (Babu
Books, 2014). nancycalefgallery.com

Section Four

Sex and Marriage

Staying the Course

Lisen Stromberg

I didn't think we would do it. We'd been blustering at each other all day, surfacing old wounds, adding a few new ones just for good measure. It might have seemed like a typical power struggle between a long-married couple, but somehow the cuts felt deeper this time, more definitive, more dangerous. So when my husband called out from the kitchen, "Time to kayak," my instinct was to say no. But perhaps old habits do die hard, because it can only have been habit that had me grabbing my oar and heading to the water; it certainly wasn't him.

For the past decade, we'd spent the month of July in a small summering community called Annisquam. It's about an hour north of Boston, far from our home in California. For the first half of the month, the children and I would settle into a hazy routine of sailing camp, tennis matches, and idle afternoons swimming and sunning at the beach. Then, during the last two weeks of July, my husband would come and stay. On those evenings when the tide was right, he and I kayaked together along the coves and inlets around the bay near our beloved summer home.

During the winters in soggy California, we longed for those seemingly innocuous excursions. The picturesque coastline, the stolen moments alone, the chance to talk through the deeper issues. While our oars dipped in and out, we discussed careers, money, children, family, friends, and life. It seemed, each year, big decisions were made out there on that generally placid water. Summer kayaking had become our own marital catharsis.

On this night, as we pulled our kayaks from their perches, the early evening air was thick and sticky. There was a breeze, but nothing we couldn't navigate or hadn't before. Silently, we eased the boats into the water and rode the tide out past the cove and around the point, down along the rocky shore. Black cormorants dipped their heads in and out of the water, matching the dance of our oars: in, out, in, out.

About a mile down, I turned my kayak towards my husband's and said, "We need to talk."

He'd heard this line before. These conversations showed up with some regularity, usually tied to important events: birthdays, anniversaries, or the news of yet another divorce from some seemingly happy marriage. This year we were celebrating a triple whammy: we each were turning fifty and our twenty-fifth wedding anniversary was only weeks away. All these years, and still I had lingering doubts about us, about him.

My husband shook his head and looked out across the water, watching as the sun fell below dark-purple clouds hanging above the horizon. "Enough talking already. Let's just appreciate right here, right now," he said and then glided his kayak on ahead, ignoring my calls for him to "wait" and "slow down." I was still ready for a fight, even if he wasn't.

As I raced to catch him, the sky suddenly grew darker. The purple clouds became various measures of gray and black. The once gentle breeze blustered across the ocean's surface, forcing the water to dance and roll.

"We'd better go back," my husband shouted above the rising storm. "It's getting too rough out here."

He kayaked fast ahead of me, pushing across the current, his sun-baked arms bulging with the effort. "Wait," I called to him again, this time more from fear than anger. But he kept his pace, putting more distance between us. So typical. Why did he always seem to abandon me just when I needed him most? I cursed at my husband, boiling over with long-held frustrations and simmering resentments.

"All these damn years, how is it I am still married to *you*?!" I yelled into the wind.

Back when we first met, in the mid-1980s, the headlines warned that, statistically speaking, a career woman was more likely to remain single than be killed by a terrorist. So when my boyfriend proposed, I took the cautious route and said, "Yes." My best friend asked if I was sure. I told her, "I'm not looking for perfect. He's good enough."

"Aren't you afraid you're just settling?" she asked.

"Don't worry," I told her, only half-jokingly. "This is my starter marriage. Think of him as my placeholder husband." Worst-case scenario: I'd make the requisite mistakes, fall down, get up, brush myself off, and try again with someone else, perhaps a better match.

"When the time comes," I assured her, "I'll move on."

But the time never came. Our jobs, the children, the busyness that is life kept me from focusing on my exit strategy. In my heart, though, I harbored the fantasy I could jump ship at any moment. Freedom would taste sweet.

As my kayak bounced back and forth, I cried out above the waves, "And so what if I haven't left yet? I could still go. I could!" I slumped over, tasting instead the salty water that ran in rivulets down my cheeks, tears and the sea.

A bitter slap of wind and rain pellets caused me to look up. As I had been scrutinizing our marriage, my stalwart husband had stayed the course, slowly making progress against the elements. He was like that, always had been. Driven. Reliable. Calm in a crisis. I am more prone to ups and downs, attracted to drama, occasionally even reckless. "You bring the excitement," he often told me. If opposites attract, we were the definition of that old cliché. I watched him in the distance moving farther and farther away and with sudden clarity realized my never-wavering husband was far more than a placeholder. He was, and always had been, home to me.

I began paddling hard, head down, trying to catch up. But each time I pushed ahead, the gale and rising waves forced me back. My arms strained; I couldn't make it. I was exhausted and defeated. It was time to give up; better to let the tide take me where it would than to fight the current that was forcing us farther apart.

And then my husband was there beside me—"Don't stop. We can do this," he shouted. He raised his oar high and plunged it in the swell. Raised it again and plunged it on the other side. Oar in, oar out, oar in, oar out. I began to follow his movements, and soon we were advancing toward the shore. It took all our effort, but we were winning this battle, together.

Eventually we rounded the point and managed to steer into the cove. The water calmed and the angry wind petered out to a manageable breeze. The rain softened as our kayaks beached feebly on land. My husband jumped out and dragged his to safety. I sat in mine, too exhausted to move.

"I didn't expect it to be so hard," I cried, my crimped fingers aching from the death grip they had molded around the oar. My husband reached down, gently eased my hands into his, and helped me get up.

"Sometimes it's like that," he said. Then he picked up my kayak and pulled it to safety too.

Lisen Stromberg

Sharon Olds once said, "I was a late bloomer. But anyone who blooms at all, ever, is very lucky." Lisen Stromberg, too, is a late bloomer. After twenty years in marketing and business strategy, she began a second career as a writer. Since then, her work has been published in a variety of magazines and newspapers and has won numerous awards. She recently completed her MFA in prose at Mills College and is now working on a book, *A Mother Is a Phoenix*, about the power of "opting in" to one's life. You can visit prismwork.com to learn more about her.

The Flip Side of Coming Out

Eva Schlesinger

I had just arrived at the coffeehouse when I ran into an old friend.

"What's new?" Kate said.

"I'm now partnered with a man," I said.

"You look more straight," she waved her hand the length of my body.

Is it because I'm standing straight? I wanted to say. But I didn't. I wasn't sure if I was standing straight.

I came out as a lesbian when I was nineteen. In high school, I had been so in love with my best friend that when she chose another girl over me, I was heartbroken. Being a lesbian made sense. I was certain a relationship with a woman would soon follow. Instead, I fell in love with a man. A friend wore a button that said, "I am a woman. I love women." I wanted a button that said, "I am a lesbian. I fell in love with a man. Now I'm confused."

Nathan and I broke up because I thought I was more attracted to women. While I did find a sense of camaraderie with the women's community, I also pined for him, wondering what my life would have been like had we stayed together. I had felt at home. With women I was trying out for the part of girlfriend and seeing how long I could last. I concealed my feelings, worrying that if my lesbian friends knew, they'd outlaw me. I dreaded losing that feeling of belonging. I had been an outsider in high school; in the lesbian community I loved how connected I felt reading at open mics, going on hikes, or at games night.

Being a lesbian was a case of mistaken identity. My new coming-out process began when I moved to San Francisco and my roommate told me she was bisexual. I said, "Last night I dreamed someone told me, 'Admit it, Eva. Admit that you're really bisexual.'"

I didn't admit it at that time, but I kept my dream in the back of my mind for many years. One day a friend e-mailed me for advice; she was dating a man, but her heart said otherwise. What should she do? "Follow your heart," I typed. And winced. I hesitated before pressing "send." How could I tell her to follow her heart when I wasn't following mine? I wrote, "I'm dating women, but *my* heart says otherwise." As I stared at the black letters on the computer screen, panic rose in my throat. I couldn't say that. I backspaced, deleting words. I was a lesbian. How could I tell her, or anyone, I preferred men?

I continued to mull over my sexual preference while working as an advisor to a middle school gay-straight alliance. At our weekly meetings, the advisors came out to the students. I admired the counselor who said "bisexual" in her strong, clear voice. I wished I, too, could reveal my identity with confidence.

A year later I fell in love with Eli. I wrestled with the idea of coming out to my community. I felt protected and safe, wrapped in the silence of my secret. I didn't know what would happen once I spoke the truth. Yet I had spent over twenty years in the closet. I hated hiding. I was making myself an outsider by leaving my real self out of the picture. Beyond sharing my poems and stories, I rarely volunteered information about myself. Tired of living in seclusion, I decided to be strong and clear, like the counselor.

Coming out taught me there is room for all. One woman told me I was still a member, since I had spent so much time in the community. Another, who identified as a separatist, said she couldn't wait to meet him. Everyone has congratulated me on finding true love. Perhaps, I mused, I had to come to terms with myself and be willing to share who I was to find the acceptance and respect I desired.

So many things passed through my mind when Kate said, "What's new?" I could have said that I had published two poetry collections or that my dad had died. Instead, I thought of how we became friends at a women's open mic. We used to talk about relationships—hers and mine. Mine had been the short-term variety. I wanted her to know I was at last in a long-term relationship. I also wanted to be true to myself, and to her.

As the music trilled to a close and people clapped, I tilted my head at her. "I don't identify as straight. I'm bisexual."

Her eyes widened. "Now I know."

I remembered running into another lesbian friend at the grocery store. She, too, had asked, "What's new?"

Glancing at the cashiers, I turned back to her warm gaze. "I'm now partnered with a man." I held my breath, wondering what would happen next.

I was surprised when she said, "I have felt that yearning myself."

Eva Schlesinger

Eva Schlesinger has been a contributor to *Chicken Soup for fhe Soul: Tough Times, Tough People* and *San Francisco Chronicle Magazine*. She is the author of the chapbooks *Ode 2 Codes & Codfish* (dancing girl press, 2013), *View from My Banilla Vanilla Villa* (dancing girl press, 2010), and *Remembering the Walker and Wheelchair: Poems of grief and healing* (Finishing Line Press, 2008). Eva lives in a banilla vanilla villa in Berkeley, California, where she reads voraciously, draws whimsical animals, plays magical flute melodies, and writes. Visit her online at redroom.com/member/eva-schlesinger.

The Chair to Somewhere

Gina Raith

The chair was cheap and anti-ergonomic. Probably Ikea. What brought me to it—one of 1,100 or so in the cavernous Oakland Convention Center occupied by hair-on-fire California bar exam applicants spending three quality days together—is not a fairy tale.

It's more like a fairy's fall.

The word "hurry" is my middle name, so it's not entirely surprising that I went from Budding Perfectionist to Student Athlete to Overachieving Chicago Litigator to Mother of Three Daughters/Yoga Instructor/Room Parent (I know, how annoying) to Adulterer to Occupant of Uninviting Chair without a lot of downtime.

Yeah, I buried the lede.

My reason for being amidst a sea of aspiring lawyers on their way to phase next, then, was undoubtedly distinct from, say, the superlatively organized astrophysicist from South Korea seated to my left. My best guess is that he didn't end up in his seat because he fell out of love with his spouse of fifteen years. He was likely there for another reason. Maybe he wants to sue astronauts. Or codify time, space, and matter. Or offer legal services to underfunded scientists.

Likewise, it's inconceivable that the twenty-something recent grad to my right, who approached diabolically conceived fact patterns with inappropriate perk and finished every session early because she didn't "seem to have a problem with time" (I considered stabbing her with one of my Dixon Ticonderoga No. 2 pencils when she said that), was subjecting herself to eighteen hours of intellectual trench warfare because she detonated her life by falling irreversibly in love with one of her best friend's brothers-in-law and acting on it.

(Did I mention it's complicated? My therapist refers to it in a clinical tone as "orchestrating a catastrophic exit.")

It goes without saying that the doctor from India, with whom I rode the hotel elevator after day two—the one taking the most extensive bar exam in the country with the lowest pass rate "for fun"—had not experienced shame and ignominy as I, Hester Prynne, have.

Had I not been sporting so much emotional armor, I might have shared with the Ivy Leaguer I ran into at 5:30 a.m. every day in the nearby Peet's that if I didn't pass, I might have to sell my daughters' family home, adding incalculable pain to their already diminished childhood. When she blithely confessed, sipping a triple-shot something, to having started studying "four days ago" because she just got married, I should have blurted that when the same husband tells her, a decade hence, that they don't need marriage counseling—that they only need more time together—she'd do well to withhold sex or stage a carpool boycott. Anything to get him to go to therapy.

My (former) best friend, Amanda, once presaged: "My biggest nightmare would be meeting the love of my life while I'm married to Mark."

The train had left the station when she made her cautionary proclamation. She knew me like a sister and was onto me when she said it.

"You're in love with Holden, aren't you?"

"Yes."

"Have you had sex with him?"

"No." This was not a Clintonesque parsing of language. At the time she asked, we'd only kissed once. But it was under a full moon, atop a mountain. It was the kiss of a lifetime. Lifetimes. I often wonder if I'd disclosed the kiss, whether Amanda, a staunch Catholic, would have convinced me to not take a single step further without leaving my husband. It's one of a catalog of regrets I carry in my chest.

Holden and I went from friendship to slow-burn frisson to torrid epistolary *affaire de coeur* over the course of several years. Had he just been a gifted writer, I would have been fine. The surfer/banjo player bits were also easy to pretend to ignore. That he was a disarming, unexpected romantic who made me laugh, read my words, and drew me out—and in—with his *mirada fuerte*, proved my downfall.

And fall I did. No rope. No fairy wings.

I'd been in a desert, you see, unappreciated, unseen *in that way*, for years. Holden's love became my water.

Smash cut to nine months later. We weren't caught *in flagrante delicto*. His teenage daughter read our e-mails, and that was that. Or, more specifically, it wasn't. The ensuing community conflagration in our NorCal hamlet, unparalleled in its staying power, persists almost two years later. Very few marrieds seem interested to know that when we couldn't stomp out our feelings for one another, we made a plan. He was going to leave his wife (and did), I was going to leave my husband (and would have), and then six months later we'd have a date. It didn't go as planned. Shocker.

I've learned much from the prostrate position.

I've learned that space is to healing as time is to forgiveness.

I've learned to repent, to lead with love, to breathe through the almost daily turbulence.

I've learned not to judge those who have judged me.

I've learned that before children of divorce, or in my case traumatic divorce, emerge as more resilient because mom and dad are OK, they are inexorably and justifiably angry. And that even when they are screaming *"It's all your fault!"* as my middle daughter did this morning when she remembered she had left her PE shorts at her dad's house, they still love you, deep down, under the pain. No matter what. Because there is a God.

I've learned how to cry my face off while running, while getting my teeth cleaned, while making love.

I've learned that seventy-five percent of affair partners, well-intentioned in their path to becoming life partners, don't last. And that although Holden is really good about walking my dog and taking out the compost without my asking, this reality scares the living hell out of me.

Which brings me back to the chair. Of the dozen or so people I met in Oakland during exam week, the only woman with whom I considered sharing the story of my spectacular fall from grace was the self-defined "professional repeater" seated directly in front of me. When she admitted this was her fourth attempt, I wanted to embrace her. When she copped to being a paralegal, conceding that her firm paid for the test every time and she was worried about her credibility at work, I had found my heroine.

Here's a woman who got back in the chair, again and again, chin up. Who courageously allowed herself to be human *and* fallible. Out loud!

I believe there are no coincidences, and that she ended up in front of me in my own chair to somewhere for a reason: to remind me that the most challenging transition of my life was not what had come before. Dismantling a marriage by succumbing to unprecedented desire— to, yes, true love—was, in fact, the easy part.

The real work lies ahead, in creating the life I gave myself permission to envision with the person I was destined to meet.

But first, I think I'll sit here a little longer.

Gina Raith

Gina Raith has been many things to many people, including former board member of the Chicago Chapter of the National Organization for Women, civil litigator (she went after, among others, Big Pharma, Big Tobacco, and credit card conglomerates), court-appointed special advocate for abused and neglected children, certified yoga instructor and wellness coach, producer/director of a short documentary, blogger, and published writer. Mostly, though, she's a mother of three daughters who light up her days, a slower runner than she used to be, and someone who aspires to improve the world for women, whether through legislation, precedent, the written word, or perseverance. You can find her at ginaraith.com

A True Love Story

Christi Levannier

For as long as I can remember, I have always said I did not want to get married. My role models all had troubled marriages, so I decided that it was not for me. I enjoyed dating a lot, but although I was having fun, I wasn't really being honest with myself.

At one point, I started to date a beautiful man who was very fun and mysterious. He would disappear for weeks at a time, then show up ready to play again. He wouldn't commit to boyfriend status, so I dated other men on the side. Still, I found myself developing deeper feelings for him; in hindsight, I see that he was simply reflecting back to me exactly where I was within myself.

After a while I confronted him, telling him that I wanted a committed relationship and needed to know if he could be faithful. He avoided answering until I threatened to leave, then caved in and agreed. However, it wasn't long before I began to feel that something still wasn't quite right. The phone would ring at 3:00 a.m. and he would fly out of bed, grab the phone, and dash out of the room. When he returned, he would say it was a wrong number, but I knew he was lying. Still, I remained in denial because I so badly wanted love.

The turning point came one day when his roommate told me to trust myself, that if I felt he wasn't being faithful, then he probably wasn't. That's when it hit me that I was not being true to myself by staying in this relationship. I confronted him again, telling him that I needed a relationship that I could trust, and when he said he couldn't give me that, it was time to walk away. I was in so much pain—I knew that I would never find another man as gorgeous as he was who was also truly right for me.

In the months that followed, I went to therapy and did yoga to help me move the stuck energy out of my body and mind. As I gained clarity, I realized that if I wanted to attract my ideal man, I needed to embody the qualities I sought in him. I prayed each night to my angels, ancestors, and God, asking them to help me develop the qualities I wanted in a partner and call in my True Love.

Halfway through that year, I received an e-mail from my brother, who was traveling around the world. He said that he had met a man named François in the Malaysian jungle, and he thought the two of us would get along; he included this man's e-mail address in case I wanted to contact him. I was not interested in dating at this time, but my brother had never recommended I date anyone before, so I decided that I had nothing to lose. Whoever he was, this man was safely on the other side of the world, so I sent him an e-mail along the lines of, "Hi, my name is Christi, I'm a Leo, I'm into meditation and yoga and live in California . . ." What do you say to someone you have never met and probably never will?

Despite my doubts, something extraordinary happened after I sent this e-mail. That night, I dreamt that someone was knocking on my front door. I opened the door and saw a brilliant, shining light— it was divine love or God's light. I stepped forward into the light and became one with it as my physical body disappeared; I felt complete bliss and pure love radiating through my entire being. After I had been absorbed for a while in this amazing state, a man walked out of the light towards me. I knew who he was on all levels, he had beautiful blue eyes, and I felt I could trust him completely. I said, "Hello, François!" and he smiled, came toward me, and took my hand. Then we made love in the dream, and it was not like any experience I had had before. After we finished, he said, "I have to go for now." I didn't feel sad as he left, because I knew he was from the light and that I could trust him.

I awoke the next morning knowing that he must have e-mailed me, because that kind of vivid dream does not happen without a real connection. I also knew that my life would never be the same, because from now on, I would compare all other experiences with men to the light and trust I had felt in the dream. I ran to the computer, and sure enough, there was his email. He said, "Hi, I am François and I am an Aries, I'm into meditation and yoga and have been traveling around the world on a quest for deeper connection to God. I'm looking for my princess."

After that, we e-mailed about once every three months and kept it very platonic. I jokingly referred to him as "François, my future fiancé" with my friends, since they all knew I did not ever want to get married. After about a year, I decided to invite him to visit me in California, thinking that he would most likely not come. He responded right away and said he was coming for a month! Needless to say, I was a little freaked out, especially since my brother had requested we not exchange pictures. But then I remembered the dream and how deeply I trusted him, and this calmed me down.

We were to meet at the airport for the first time. I e-mailed him a vague description of what I would be wearing, and his mother called me and told me he would be wearing a gray cap and glasses. I waited at the arrivals gate, scanning the passengers as they filed off the plane. I saw several men with gray caps and glasses, but none were the man I had seen in my dream. However, one of the last passengers to emerge was a man with his hair standing on end, no hat, no glasses, a guitar case strapped to his back, and a spring in his step as he walked towards me with a big grin on his face. He radiated positive energy, and I knew this was François!

We greeted each other, gathered his bags, and headed home. We were so comfortable together, and he was hot! It was as if we had known each other forever. He stayed two months and we fell madly in love and were married five months later.

Now I could see why all my other relationships had not worked out. I had needed to become the person I wanted to attract and let go of patterns that were not serving me. It was my commitment to my own growth and clarity that allowed him to miraculously find me from across the world.

Now my True Love and I are approaching our tenth wedding anniversary—we have been happily married since 2003.

Christi Levannier

Christi Levannier lives in Mill Valley, California, with her hot husband François. She is a master-certified Spirit Coach® and trained intuitive. She enjoys helping people all over the world find True Love within themselves, thus co-creating magical, fulfilling, and flourishing lives. She and François co-lead workshops entitled "How to Become a Magnet for Your True Love," and have developed a True Love Magnet program. You can learn more about it at TrueLoveMagnet.com. Christi also enjoys volunteering with the homeless youth of Marin County through the nonprofit organization Ambassadors of Hope and Opportunity.

Game On

Nora Feeley

I had no idea how much game-playing existed in the world of post-divorce dating—all kinds of games and all kinds of playing. Some of the games I read about in the many books on how to get a man. If you want one, apparently you need to play games. Despite the advice, I vowed not to engage in game-playing of the mental variety. Now, when it comes to the other types of "play," which seem to be part of the divorce curriculum, I discovered that I'm more open-minded than I thought.

On Super Bowl Sunday, my post-divorce dating adventure began. It was my first solo "holiday" and one for which, normally, I would have invited all my husband's friends and their wives over for upscale sports snacks (crab nachos, anyone?), football (them), and commercials (us). But here I was once again, alone. And bored.

A few of my single-mom friends invited me to a Super Bowl party, so I decided to rally. The can't-sit-still overplanner that I am, I also decided to squeeze in a four-hour hike with another friend. And what is a hike without a glass of wine or two afterwards? I figured I could skip the shower and the primping and still be at the yacht club in time for the start of the game. So, my jeans, T-shirt, and ponytail would do just fine.

Since we were on Pacific Time, the game started early, and so did the wine. The party was not the singles scene we had expected. There was one guy I couldn't take my eyes off—he was tan with thick, wavy, slicked-back hair, a metrosexual shirt, great shoes (no socks), a body that clearly took a lot of effort, and a dangerously big grin. He was gorgeous, but so was the blonde with him. Striking out, my girl posse moved to Balboa Cafe. Now, if you have ever been there, you understand. You can't throw a breathalyzer in the Balboa without finding a hookup. But I am not a meet-a-guy-in-a-bar kind of girl, and besides, in my jeans and ponytail, I was safe in a sea of sexy, well-enhanced women.

Then I saw him again. He walked in, literally with bent arm and linen blazer over his shoulder. As he passed our table, Super Bowl Superman recognized one of my sassy mom friends, pulled up a chair, and sat down. With nothing to lose, I joined in the conversation, and was just—well, me. Sweaty, smart-ass, unsexy, not-sassy me. He was not only hot but funny as hell and, it turned out, not dating the hot blonde. The drinks kept flowing and so, as wine-induced judgment usually dictates, Sassy invited us back to her house for a nightcap. So we went back to her house and liberated all her wine, champagne, and tequila. Super Bowl Superman and I ended up on the couch, with Sassy in between us.

If my foggy memory serves me correctly, Sassy leaned over and said to me, "What do you think? You like?"

I responded with an intelligent and articulate answer. "Duh, yeah."

She looked at me with a semi-scary smile. "OK, I can make that happen."

With that, she artfully lifted her left leg and threw it over Superman, who was sitting on her right. All of a sudden, she was straddling him. Then she was kissing him. Really kissing him. It was more like a lap dance, even. His arms (and only his arms) were limp by his sides. He was so stunned that his mouth was hanging open, but not empty. While entertaining and disturbingly hot to watch, I didn't really understand how this would in fact "make it happen" for me. And then I did.

As quickly as her left leg had landed astride his, she spun back around to her original spot for a fleeting second. Then, with one continuous motion, her right leg in the air, and . . . uh oh. Oh no. Oh yes. She was straddling *me*.

I probably should have closed my mouth at that point. But I didn't. I should have gently pushed her away. But I didn't. Whoa. Yes, her tongue was in my mouth. Hmm. Although I could taste cigarettes, her teeth were smooth. Her hair was in my face. It was soft. Her arms were around my neck. And then I was kissing her back. It was strange and surreal, but what the hell. Then she was gone. Back to him. Sassy toggled between Superman and me for a while and then, without warning, she got up, cheerfully said, "Good night," and went to bed.

Akin to a National Geographic scene with a lion eyeing an injured but delicious zebra in the wild, helpless—he literally pounced on me. Fortunately, the rest is a blur (or at least that is the story I am sticking to). When I woke up on Sassy's couch the next morning, he was gone (what was his name?). As I walked into the kitchen—groggy and mortified—Sassy looked up from reading the paper.

"Good morning. You're a good kisser." And we both burst out laughing.

We remain great friends—but nothing more. As for Super Bowl Superman, a brief but passionate and exciting adventure ensued. But at that moment, with the sting still fresh from the sunburn of divorce, neither of us were ready for love or a long-term relationship. We were seeking lust and laughter. We had a blast, and once it had run its course, we both moved on. And so, as is the case with many games, Super Bowl was a bit of a heartbreaker, but a memorable upset that I'll never forget.

Nora Feeley

Nora began her career in writing in high school, when classmates would pay her to write their love letters and edit their school reports. After achieving degrees in communications and marketing and earning her MBA, Nora held various in-house consulting, copywriting, and communications roles across a number of industries. Her twenty-five years of writing experience spans from corporate communications and public relations to web copy, articles, speeches, headlines, and blogging. She is a divorced mother of one who lives in Marin County, California, and still helps her friends write their online dating profiles.

Falling

Jenny C. Mosley

The first time I met my mother-in-law, she handed me a baby blanket. It was quilted, with rocking horses and teddy bears, pastel cotton squares edged in pink satin.

J.D. and I had been together for only a couple weeks. He must have indicated that I was someone special, or maybe Odessa just really wanted a granddaughter. But I was in no frame of mind for a serious relationship, particularly not with a Hollywood stuntman who lived 400 miles away. I'd recently shaken loose from a failed marriage and I wasn't looking to marry a guy who threw himself in front of moving vehicles for a living.

That first day I met her, we dropped by on our way to dinner as she was rinsing dishes at the kitchen sink. She was delighted to see her son, flushed and flirtatious.

"There's my terrible boy," she started, batting her eyelashes coyly at J.D. while she dried her hands on a worn dishtowel.

"Mom, this is Jen," he said, gesturing toward me.

"Hello," she greeted me, reaching out a boney hand. "Isn't he awful?" she asked conspiratorially. "He never comes to see his mother anymore."

"Oh yes, he's horrible," I agreed. "That is actually the first thing I noticed about him."

J.D. leaned down to kiss her on the cheek. "Mama-san, you are the queen!" he cried, dancing her around the kitchen before she smacked him playfully with a wooden spoon. As we talked, I saw that this was a solid guy; how a man treats his mother is illuminating, and he was funny and sweet with her.

"Go say hello to your grandmother," she told him, shooing him away with the spoon.

I was surprised by her Spanish accent. J.D.'s all-American radio voice hadn't clued me in. He was born and raised in the city, and I'd most likely heard him on KFRC or KGO in the eighties, but I wasn't sure. His voice was warm and smooth, as if his vocal cords were wrapped around a permanent grin.

I stayed behind in the kitchen while J.D. went to the back. His grandma was living in the house's master bedroom; Odessa had recently taken early retirement to care for her. I followed her into the nearby sewing room, where a long, high table occupied most of the space. Pale-blue fabric pieces were pinned to tissue-paper patterns, and a tall dress mannequin stood inert in one corner, waiting to be clothed.

"How did you like teaching high school?" I asked, hoping to learn something about this stranger. "I'd think high school would be a hard age to teach."

That's when she pulled the baby blanket from a narrow closet. "The students respected me," she said, handing me the quilt. "This is what they made me when I left. It's a shame I have no one to give this to," she added.

"That *is* a shame," I answered, unsure if I was reading her right. "You must have friends with grandbabies . . ."

"No, it really should stay with the family," she replied, shaking her head sadly.

"Uh-huh."

"See the nice stitching here?" she continued, tracing a dark finger over a gingham elephant.

I laughed nervously.

"J.D., your mother is showing me baby blankets!" I called out, half joking, half hoping to be rescued. He didn't hear or was busy with his grandma. Odessa giggled as I tried to return her keepsake.

My romance with J.D. started abruptly when I invited him to my divorce party on the day we met in October 1994. His résumé and headshot had secured him a job on an industrial film I was producing, and so he'd driven up from Los Angeles to San Francisco. I invited the whole cast and crew to join my friends in a celebration of my changed marital status that evening. We partied in the private back room at Julie's Supper Club, a lively bar south of Market Street in an area where homeless entrepreneurs scare you into accepting two-dollar windshield washes.

I had pre-ordered a small chocolate cake and snapped the head off a cheap plastic cake-topper groom, embedding it in the frosting at the bride's feet. The party was well underway when J.D. arrived, looking handsome in a letterman-style jacket with a Stuntman's Association logo stitched in royal blue on his chest. He brought a new light into the dim back room. His dark eyes sparkled when he saw me, but I was skeptical. I'd worked with enough actors to know they can light up on cue. Plus, he was too tall, too striking. I was leery of beautiful men. My taste leaned more toward hooked noses, bushy eyebrows, mysterious scars, and asymmetrical faces. But J.D. was true to his headshot—an unusual occurrence in the film world, where performers often show up for auditions looking like older, frumpier versions of their photos. I was struck by the ease of his smile, his long, angular chin and closely shaved head.

When he had arrived at the studio that morning, instead of shaking my hand, J.D. had spread his long arms and wrapped me up in a giant hug. It was an unusual gesture in my experience as a producer. Too friendly. Overly familiar. I was perplexed by his warmth. The rest of the afternoon he spent falling down the Pacific Stock Exchange steps for my video, a stunt that was timed closely with an on-camera narrator who kept botching his lines. By the time he got to the party, J.D. had already fallen for me twenty-one times that day and still seemed game for more.

Finally, Odessa took the quilt back, carefully wrapping it in a plastic bag and placing it deep inside the closet. As we crossed back to the kitchen, I noticed older headshots of J.D. tacked to the wall above a small desk. A calendar from a neighborhood insurance agent hung askew with the weight of a formalwear advertisement showing J.D. posing in a black tuxedo.

At the divorce party, I raffled off my wedding mementos: a single silver toasting goblet, my satin bridal shoes, and the engraved cake cutter. I wore a homemade campaign button proclaiming, "You may *now* kiss the bride."

J.D. effortlessly blended in with my friends, helping cut the divorce cake and calling out the raffle winners. When it was time for him to go, I walked him out to the sidewalk, past the swing band, through the grooving crowd. Alone in the damp night, he asked if he could take me up on my button's promise. When presented with an opportunity to kiss a handsome stuntman, I figured I should take it. The warmth of his grin extended to his kiss. I hoped my blushing was obscured by the yellow-green glow of the neon Supper Club sign.

"I'm just here for the weekend, so we should go out tomorrow," he said. I'm sure etiquette books would instruct me to politely decline, but I scrawled my number inside a Julie's matchbook and returned to my friends inside the party.

From the bay window of my Oakland hilltop apartment the next afternoon, I watched J.D.'s van turn onto my block and ease into a space on the crowded street. He jumped out and ran to my building. He ran. *Who is this guy?* I wondered. A hugger, a stuntman, a boy full of spirit who isn't the least bit concerned with looking cool.

We went to Jack London Square for dinner, where we talked naturally. I was relieved to discover he wasn't a name-dropper, though I knew from his résumé that he had worked on movies like *The Right Stuff* and *Angels in the Outfield*. We walked along the water holding hands and laughing. The boat lights glittered in the harbor and salty waves lapped at the pier in the cool autumn wind. Playfully we pushed and pulled at each other, finding our mooring.

Four years later, I received a shower gift that I'd been expecting. Odessa gave me the baby blanket, but this time I was ready for it.

Jenny C. Mosley

Jenny C. Mosley is a freelance writer and editor living in Northern California. She writes essays and fiction as well as marketing communications for corporate clients. She has a son in middle school and a daughter in high school who are very glad she took a chance and fell for their father.

For What It's Worth

Katie Clarke

"Why do we need a prenup anyway?" I asked one night through heaps of despair.

"It's for the far-off chance I meet and fall in love with someone else. And I decide to leave you," he said. "And you try to take me, and my life, for all it's worth."

He moved out the next day. He took the ring and all my insides with him.

I collapsed on the floor of my closet for the next two days or two months. It's impossible to know which. Long after standard apartment carpet texture was firmly embedded into each side of my face, I rose to ensure my outside world matched my inside one. I started with engagement gifts and bridal vision boards, but I couldn't stop. Like a fire through a forest I raged to empty the biography of my possessions from age twenty-six down. *Everything had* to go.

"Memory box" trash piles make for an addictive kind of pain. I gutted old journals, ripping page after page of my history from their spines until they'd succumbed, naked and weak. One high school journal entry stopped me in my masochistic tracks.

"I bargained with life for a penny," a poem propagated by my tenth grade English teacher, Mrs. Scott, was folded into the journal, with the line "For life's a just employer / He gives you what you ask" priggishly underlined three times. On the journal pages that pressed the poem, I'd gone so far as to create a life list:

1. Marry a doctor so we can take our family on third-world medical missions (like Jennifer Reese's family).

2. Live in a Colorado ski town and jump on the trampoline with our happy kids.

3. Teach at a college.

Seeing the list made me want to puke. I could hear Mr. "Far Off Chance" filling my mind like a migraine. He was wringing my dreams dry from the rooftop of his Upper East Side apartment—where, four years prior, under the intoxication of new love in New York, I'd revealed my "someday" suppositions. I'd even left out the doctor part (because he wasn't one).

"Yeah!" he retorted through a splay of incredulity and bottled, imported beer. "And I had sophomoric visions of having babies on a tropical island. There they go! Running through the surf in their diapers! Grow up. You can't live in a ski town *and* expect to make a living. You *vacation* in a ski town. Why would you spend your *vacation* in a third world country? And how are *you* qualified to teach college? I love you."

Love me? Flooded with the memory of that toxic moment and all the ones following it, I *hated* me.

What was I thinking? Why did I stay with him for *four years*? Why did I turn down the promotion in New York to move back to Colorado with *him*? Why hadn't I *ever* even *considered* becoming a doctor *myself*?

"Because I am a moron," I said aloud. And then I traded in all those ridiculous dreams for one: kindness.

I cried in front of my class the day one of my students asked, "Are you OK?" Our office secretary found me under my desk in the fetal position during planning period. After school I watched my jeans dry in front of the electric fireplace and stared out the window. My brother dropped a "don't kill yourself" book by my apartment. I painted the walls of my bedroom a sage-green color because it felt gentle and kind. My teaching mentor pulled me aside to mention I looked like an X-ray. My mom took me to the doctor. I started going to a therapist once a week and taking purple happy pills twice a day.

Near the end of the school year, my friend Beth and I were sitting on the stairs outside the school cafeteria. "I feel the sunshine," I said. Beth gave me a hug. Later that afternoon, Beth stood on her chair and announced to our office, "Everyone: Katie felt the sunshine today!" They all stood up and cheered, especially the secretary who'd found me under the desk.

Because every song I'd ever owned reminded me of him, I started buying new music. I bought Joan Jett's "I Hate Myself for Loving You." He sent me an e-mail saying our iTunes account was still linked and he didn't appreciate the title of the song I'd purchased, and asking me to create my own account. I did, but not before buying Carly Simon's "You're So Vain." Then I changed my e-mail.

By the end of the summer, all songs had ceased to be about him. Whitney Houston was asking "How Will I Know?" through the headphones in my bicycle helmet as a guy driving a Honda civic with multicolored panels waved me across the street.

The traffic signal was mine. My pace was strong. His foot hit the gas. Not the brake. His car accelerated. The world slowed.

In stop-motion effect I watched my foot break against the bumper one frame at a time. The horizon slowly tilted as I careened through the windshield.

I don't remember much after that. Except for this one medical student. He made me laugh so hard. He had kind, sage-green eyes—the same color I'd painted my bedroom. He checked on me every day, even after I'd fully recovered.

Our favorite wedding gift is from my brothers, a trampoline. We took it with us to Hawaii, where our babies ran through the surf in their diapers.

He just interviewed for a position in a Colorado ski town. The position involves medical missions in third world countries for physicians and their family members.

Guess what else? It's in a college town. Turns out I really do love teaching college classes.

I don't know if he'll get the job. And it's worth noting that our modern day-to-day fairy tale isn't all sunshine. We've lived in far less desirable locations, like the arctic. And I've spent an evening or two crying in the closet over one thing or another. And that's OK.

Because when I look back at myself in the fetal position under my desk, all those years spent wading through shards of shattered dreams, hollowing out the heartache of a broken engagement, the "accidents" are all worth it. They're all part of the gestational process in becoming the person, and living the life, we dream of.

For some reason, I ended up not throwing my dreams away that day. Instead, the tenth grade journal entry hangs on the wall in our bathroom with a quote from another piece Mrs. Scott shared with us sophomore year, Max Ehrmann's *Desiderata*: "Whether or not it is clear to you, no doubt the universe is unfolding as it should."

My near-miss Mr. *was* right. We did need that prenup. We needed it for the far-off chance that I met and fell in love with someone else. And I left him. And now? I try to take myself, and my life, for all it's worth.

Katie Clarke

Hot-dogging across America via Weinermobile, ad-agency hopping from New York to Amsterdam, reporting for duty as "army wife" in far-flung places most would rather just visit: Katie Clarke is on a story-collecting adventure. She's a teacher, writer, speaker, coach, mother, wife, friend, and experienced trampoline jumper.

A Not So Sure Bet

Valerie Singer

I bet him five dollars that he wouldn't marry me. But he did, and I lost. Marrying was something he did causally, I discovered, and he was much married: once in Connecticut, once in Massachusetts, and once in Rhode Island, possibly concurrently. I don't know about Vermont or New Hampshire. The New England states do not share vital records.

We married in the wilds of Maine. A justice of the peace nervously pronounced us man and wife. His wife and a flock of wooden duck decoys served as witnesses. I wore a dress shoplifted from Bloomingdale's. He wore khaki pants, a gray sweatshirt, and a leather jacket, as he had done every day I'd known him.

It started with a falsehood. My boundaries were so porous at twenty-three that my inner self, like the liquid center in a melting candy shell, had leaked out. I'd been stuffing cigarettes, marijuana, boys, fiction, and sex into the hole for years. Such emptiness made it easy to become the French exchange student I pretended to be that December night the Charles River nearly froze over.

That I couldn't speak French didn't seem like an obstacle. I divined a passable accent and an improbable backstory on the spot. I found him so handsome, canny, and wildly exciting that I assumed he would not be interested in the genuine version and created an improved model. We were drinking bourbon in a strange, covert bar in Cambridge's gritty Central Square. Had I headed to Harvard Square instead, I might have gone home alone—university boys would have called me on the accent.

That accent was tragic in the harsh, hungover light of the next day. I actually offered him French toast. This detail makes my face burn with embarrassment even now, even in the face of what followed.

He asked for my number. I'd taken it for granted that he was a one-night stand when I became French. I had no follow-up plan.

What were the chances that he'd be conning me as much as I had tried to con him?

By the time I came clean as a middle-class girl from New Jersey, it was too late. I was in love. And like the talented con man he was, he'd had me figured out from "bonjour." I was a textbook mark. I saw myself as both tough and rebellious, even street-smart. As a flawed by-product of unpredictable artists, I didn't require the standard features of a suitable boyfriend: a fixed address, a discernable job, or even a working phone number. I was as vulnerable as a snail without a shell, and he offered everything I craved.

He was both hyperelusive and attentive. He was impossible to pin down but could turn into a hot flame of ardor when it served him. He kept me at arm's length and then, in a wink, became jealous and intensely possessive. I understood that as love. That felt familiar.

I kept him away from the house I shared with my sister as much as possible. She saw the miles of red flags and was concerned for me. He was older, with no fixed point, and he claimed a barely believable résumé of ex-jockey (at six foot two), ex–Navy SEAL, ex-SDS member, and ex-Wesleyan University student. He told us that he worked nights as a marine diver: a literal dream job that took him out of accountability for weeks. I saw him as impossibly cool and mysterious.

I painted him as a brilliant radical who had the world's number, in part because he was black. And because he was a black man, I conveniently and dishonestly blamed my sister's distrust on his skin color.

Having left college, I was lost and anchorless. I was a stranger to myself in the most profound sense. With no compass or rudder, his dream to retreat from the world seemed the ideal course of action. He spun tales of travel, of getting back to the land, of living in a teepee or buying a farm—and of taking me along. He offered me the idealism of the sixties I'd been too young for and repackaged it as a big, red

Valentine. He was my Jack Kerouac, my Ken Kesey, and my handsome Huey Newton, all in one.

If I dressed our hot and heavy relationship in the cloak of independence, I could accept the deep crazy that followed. He held no passport, no driver's license, and no social security number. All these were trappings of "the man": a stirring phrase you didn't hear often in the suburbs.

"Your family and friends can't stand the idea of me," he whispered in my ear. And knowing what I did of my father's racial proclivities, this man convinced me that what I needed was him and no one else. My Romeo.

Six months later, I dared him—I bet him five dollars he wouldn't marry me, and he took me up on it. I thought it was the seal on the deal that he loved me for who I was, even if I wasn't Parisian. From that three-day jaunt to Maine, from matrimony to the funky motel where we honeymooned with a drunk's pint and a lobster dinner, I left no crumb trail.

We went underground, or I did at least. He'd been gone from his (now ironic) suburban family for years. His mother, a high school principal, knew his true character. In those days before cell phones, he used her phone number as a contact point for his conquests and con games. She took my messages without comment, even after I explained that I had married her son and was now her daughter-in-law. She'd heard that before. When I called, frantic, to complain that I hadn't seen him for weeks, she would kindly tell me to take up solitaire to take my mind off him. His brother, a Secret Service agent—deliciously ironic in the light of things—had warned me to run far and fast. Of course, I didn't listen.

We had many exciting adventures. Crisscrossing the country without a goal, we'd drive twelve hours a day in rented cars, stopping only for a sandwich or a nap in a string of shoddy motels. In Nevada, an old cowboy took one look at us and smiled toothlessly, whispering that

I was the prettiest negress he'd ever seen. We picked wild marijuana in Nebraska, tracking down the fields by the fancy loop-de-loops of intoxicated birds. Although it was useless hemp, he packed it into fancy wooden boxes and sold it for a profit in Boston and Berkeley. Sell the sizzle, not the steak, he tutored, more ad man than con man. He had a great brain but for the cracks.

There were endless schemes and plots, some more injurious than others. There were fake luxury goods and forgeries, stolen goods and false promises. And there were the lies. Miles of candy-floss tales to justify everything from long absences to a bloom of love-bites on his neck. He lied about lying. He lied for no reason.

Inevitably, the ardor began to pale. A steady diet of change grows wearying. Fights outnumbered kisses and endless, insane arguments turned to exhaustion as the gilt flaked and I glimpsed the man behind the curtain. He was shorter than I remembered. Promises grew rusty. I wanted sheets on my bed. I wanted a bed, not a sleeping bag.

Motherhood provided the impetus to leave. My daughter filled the hole inside me, and I grew strong around her. I never had money that he could cheat me of, no jewelry nor cars. So what would a con man want of me? In the end, it was an intact heart he was searching for, I think.

It has taken me thirty years to understand how lost he was in his own sociopathic reality. When once I asked if he didn't feel guilty for leaving his newborn baby and me in a motel with insufficient money, he gave me the strangest look. What does guilt *feel* like? he asked. He didn't know what love felt like either. Heartbreaking.

I have found true love, and our daughter will marry her true love soon too. Her stepfather, true and solid as a tree, will walk her down the aisle.

My daughter's father once warned me, his hands around my neck, that nobody would ever love me like he did. And thankfully, no one has.

Valerie Singer

Valerie Singer's work as a freelance writer and copywriter has allowed her to write for everyone from Apple to Levis Strauss to Warner Bros., and, in between, scripts for the original CD-ROM games of *Where in the World Is Carmen Sandiego?* and *Mario Bros.* Her work can be seen in *Creativity Magazine, The Pacific Sun, Yoga Journal,* and the "For Dummies" series. She was the owner of a vintage clothing shop, whatpoppywants. At present she lives in an empty nest with her husband and philosopher dog. She is writing a fictional memoir based on this essay.

Oral Sex

Claire Hennessy

By the time the tenth pretty push-up bra in a row didn't fit, the sweat was running down my back like Niagara Falls, and the skinny sales assistant at the expensive lingerie store was giving me snooty looks, I decided it was time to stop. Never mind push-up, I needed hoist-up!

What was I thinking?

Was I completely mad?

Why would somebody I had not set eyes on since high school want to go to bed with me anyway? My body was certainly not the same as the lithe teenage one he had known back when we first met. In the intervening period, I had not only added thirty years but gained well over thirty pounds and painfully ejected two large, wriggling ankle-biters by natural childbirth to boot. Added to this, my son had rather thoughtlessly stuck an elbow out and ripped me to shreds on the way out. My nether regions were a bit like a mismatched jigsaw puzzle, with the pieces not exactly in the right places.

I had rediscovered Bug, my first love, on an English school reunion website and had rashly e-mailed him, not thinking it would develop into anything as he was living on the opposite side of the world in California. Much to my surprise, a few tentative early e-mails had ignited a passionate rekindling of the old flames.

From the very start, Bug wooed me with an intensity I had never before experienced, sending romantic e-mails sizzling across the waves and straight into my heart. I would awaken each morning to lyrics from love songs, outpourings of how much he had missed me over the years, and bouquets of flowers delivered to my door at vast expense. It was intoxicating and made me feel more loved and special than I had in my entire life.

Finally, after a few months of long-distance communication, we had nervously agreed to meet to see if the physical chemistry was still there.

In the weeks leading up to Bug's inaugural visit to the UK, he began talking about sex rather more than I had been used to or was comfortable with, giving new meaning to the term "oral sex."

In fact, let's be honest: talking about sex was not something I ever did, except with girlfriends with much wine and hilarity. But intimately discussing sex with a man, even my ex-husband, had been taboo. I just didn't do it, even to let him know what I did or didn't like. Expecting men to be mind-readers, I would just moan a bit louder here or wiggle a bit to the left there, which is probably why I had not had a supremely rewarding sex life. It had literally been hit or miss.

But there was something about Bug's unconditional love and his complete lack of any inhibitions that enabled me to open up a part of myself that I had previously kept tightly locked.

During our four- or five-hour nightly Skype marathons, the topic of sex kept rearing its bulbous, purple head. Bug would tell me how much he was looking forward to bedding me, precisely what he wanted to do and what he liked. At first I was overwhelmed with embarrassment, blushing madly and awkwardly, changing the subject. But Bug was not one to be easily put off. He became obsessed with the female G-spot, having read about it extensively. He was aroused at the prospect of foraging for it, he told me. I didn't know whether to be excited or terrified!

Bug was so boldly open himself, however, that it somehow gave me permission to be vulnerable too. I trusted him not to laugh at me as he encouraged my initial, stumbling attempts at talking dirty.

Why are the official anatomical words for our most female parts of the body so unpleasant? *Vagina. Clitoris. Vulva.* So cold and clinical, so *unsexy.* I tried other words and fell a long way short of erotic. *Front-bottom*: no, that sounded too childlike. *Minge*: hmmm, not very enticing. *Beaver*: well, that just made me laugh. *Lady garden*: lovely, but didn't make me feel sexy. *Pussy*: yikes, now I felt like a porn star. And of course, there was always the forbidden "C" word lurking behind the beef curtains, ready to pounce at any moment. Ultimately, the word I felt most comfortable using was *fanny*, but that led to some jolly strange conversations, because now that Bug lived in America, one of us was referring to my bottom and the other to my vagina!

As the date of our first meeting approached, rushing at me full speed like a sex-starved nymphomaniac on the way to an orgy, the prospect of revealing my menopausal, out-of-shape, postkids body in all its nakedness was horrifying. I cringed when I shyly peeked in the mirror at my flabby tummy and cellulite bottom, my large white thighs and my bat-wing arms. Which is why, after opening my underwear drawer and finding only hideous, Bridget Jones–sized big pants, I was now subjecting myself to the exhausting ordeal of venturing out into the terrifying world of "intimate ladies' apparel." I was determined to purchase sexy new lingerie, my thought process being that if I could distract his eyes by wearing something lacy and provocative, he might think me merely voluptuous rather than voluminous.

When I eventually found something suitably gorgeous, I realized I had never actively shopped for something sensual to entice a prospective mate; I'd never planned a seduction so openly before. I felt promiscuous, maybe even a little slutty, but I also felt magnificent, feminine, and powerful. He wasn't going to know what hit him!

Ironically, the first time we made love was full of such high expectation that, although extremely enjoyable, it was not the earth-shattering, mountain-moving, firework-exploding experience I had been anticipating with bated breath and brand-new underwear. Thankfully, because we had talked so openly, we were both mature enough to appreciate the situation for what it was and know that true intimacy comes with time. I was also able to tell him verbally, albeit haltingly, what felt good to me, rather than just shifting around as if I had ants in my pants.

In the years since, I have opened up and become much more uninhibited. Bug likens me to a beautiful blossoming flower, the petals peeling back and revealing more of me, one by one. But then, he does have a penchant for overly romantic gestures. It would probably be more accurate to say I was like a rather sturdy onion: each layer wrenched away leaving a nasty, sticky mess in its wake.

The result of this exposure, however, has been the amazing, deep level of intimacy Bug and I now share. By breaking down my barriers to this most forbidden of subjects, we can now talk about anything; nothing is off-limits. Our marriage is stronger and more open than I could ever have imagined. Now, walking gloriously naked in front of Bug, I feel more in touch with who I am as a woman and have more self-confidence than at any time in my life, oblivious to the fact that my bottom is wibbly-wobbly and my nipples are pointing down to the floor.

Claire Hennessy

British-born Claire Hennessy is writing a humorous memoir about reuniting with her childhood sweetheart after a thirty-year separation. She also writes a blog, Crazy California Claire. She has had work published in the *Marin IJ*, a charity fund-raising anthology, and has gained more than 94,000 reads on Scribd.com, where she was awarded Scribd Favorite Funny Story. She has performed her work alongside Anne Lamott, Kelly Corrigan, and Ayelet Waldman. She and her two kids now live in Marin County, California, in a blended family. Claire is a founding member and website editor of the Write On, Mamas!

Dorothy

Ginny Graves

"We can't just sit around and watch her die in the living room," I hissed at my husband, Gordon. We were huddled in the kitchen, next to the sink, still filled with grease-smeared pans from our Christmas dinner several hours before; his seventy-eight-year-old mother, Dorothy—"Gramma Dee" to our two teenage sons, "Hurricane Dorothy" when Gordon and I were venting privately—was in the next room in front of our eight-foot Douglas fir, propped up against pillows on the distressed leather sofa I'd bought at Crate & Barrel years before. ("I was picturing something more classic," Dorothy had sniffed when she saw it.)

Two days before, we'd picked her up at the hospital, a routine we'd grown wearily accustomed to. Over the past six years, she'd had major strokes and ministrokes, had lost dozens of pints of blood for reasons no one could fully explain, suffered a small heart attack, and had an asthma spell so severe she'd flatlined by the time the paramedics reached her apartment. Her doctor had warned us one sunny September day that she wouldn't last until Christmas. That was three years before. "The unsinkable Dorothy Wright," her favorite nurse, Pam, called her. Now, on December 25, she appeared to finally be going down.

Before we'd bundled her into our SUV and pulled out of the Kaiser parking lot forty-eight hours prior, we'd met with her doctor and nurses. "I'm done with hospitals. *Done*," she'd said, slamming her bony fist on the bedside table for emphasis. "I'm not coming back here, ever." For once, we'd all agreed, and we scheduled the first available appointment with hospice—for December 26. Then, an hour earlier, she'd called out for help, and the instant we saw her droopy right eyelid and lopsided posture, we knew. She'd had another stroke—bad, from the looks of it. We called Gordon's sister, Susan, in Los Angeles—"I love you, honey," Dorothy had managed to mutter when we held the phone to her ear—then pulled out the number for hospice.

"We can't send anyone, because you haven't signed the paperwork," the hospice employee informed me, sounding sympathetic but firm.

"Wait, what?" I said, not getting it. "What are we supposed to do?"

"I'm not allowed to offer advice," he said, then lowered his voice, "but if it were me, I'd get her to the hospital."

I hung up, stifling a sob, feeling angry and abandoned, not so much by hospice, I realized, but by *her*. The person I'd long turned to for advice in an emergency, who always had an answer, a solution, an opinion—right or wrong, solicited or not—was now slumped on our sofa, staring blankly ahead, mute and powerless. *So un-Dorothy*, I thought sadly, knowing she was already gone, no matter how long her indomitable heart held out.

When I met Dorothy Wright's son in 1991, I didn't fall in love, I tumbled headlong. Everything about Gordon appealed to me—his gregariousness, his sweetness, his passion for literature, cooking, rugby, and history. Everything, except his mother. Imperious, gorgeous, loving, foul-mouthed, hot-tempered, proud, and fiercely loyal, Dee, as he called her, bowled me over—and scared the shit out of me. If I married him, I'd be wedded to her as well. Could I learn to love a mom like that, when my own, whom I treasured but who lived 2,000 miles away, was so stable, supportive, and for the most part, agreeable?

For Dorothy, our bond was never in question. She was crazy about me from day one, her love like a spotlight—disorienting, exposing, and just hot enough to make me uncomfortable. She bragged about my work to anyone who would listen—the checker at Safeway, her hair stylist, her doctor, her bridge club. "My Ginny is so talented," she'd boast. "She writes important articles for magazines." She'd surprise me with little gifts—a necklace, some nice olive oil—when we had dinner at her house. At a cocktail party one evening, after she'd had a couple of martinis, she squeezed my butt and said loudly, "Look at that ass. It's perfect!" I blushed madly, mortified and delighted all at once. No one in my reserved Midwestern family had ever loved me so brazenly. I wanted to bask in it—and run for the door.

If she loved me, she adored Gordon, who in her eyes could do no wrong, except the one thing no one was allowed to do: disagree with her. He'd long ago begun moving purposefully away from her gravitational pull, but if we were going to be a family, I wanted her in our orbit. She was his mother, after all. "You have no idea what it's like being raised by someone so domineering," he said once, after they'd had a nasty argument over dinner. He was proud of her accomplishments; when his dad left during his adolescence, she started an interior design firm that helped put him through college. But he chafed at her bossiness—and her appalling lack of boundaries. She still bought him socks and underwear, as if he was a small child. And before our wedding she spent a chunk of her meager savings on matching Tumi luggage—for him and her.

While Gordon distanced himself as much as possible—and pounced on her when she crossed the line—I tried to keep our family interactions brief and steer conversations away from topics that could trigger a confrontation. Still, we sustained—and inflicted—wounds. When I mentioned one evening that I would be keeping my own name after I married her son, Dee drew her lips into a tight line and said, voice quivering with rage, *"That. Sucks."* She barely spoke to me for the rest of the night and for years addressed my birthday card to Mrs. Gordon Wright. Holidays were particularly fraught. The first time Gordon and I hosted Thanksgiving, Dorothy insisted on "helping" us in the kitchen. Fed up with her criticism, he finally demanded she mingle with the guests. Infuriated, she stormed into the living room, announcing loudly, "We're never having Thanksgiving at this house again!"

For a time, I bent to her furies, accommodated them, and even, improbably and imperceptibly, became the glue that held the family together. Her fiery flare-ups intimidated me; everything about her intimidated me. But as our infant sons grew into toddlers, then boys, I began losing patience with her audacity.

The turning point came when we were having dinner—it was Christmas, of course—at our home. We'd survived the cooking portion of the evening without any major blowups, but once we were at the table, the subject turned to the recent capture of Saddam Hussein. "It's good he's no longer in power," I agreed. "But it bothers me that we went in there under false pretenses. The whole weapons of mass destruction thing was a big lie." Dorothy glared at me. "How dare you!" she said, pointing a bony finger at me. "You sound like a traitor. You should be ashamed of yourself!" Both our sons' eyes grew wide and turned toward me, waiting for my response. My heart was pounding wildly, but I took a deep breath, looked at her calmly, and said, "You can't speak to me that way, Dee. You're in my home, and we're eating Christmas dinner. If you'd like to be civil, we'd love to have you stay. If not . . ."

I didn't finish the sentence. She threw her napkin on her plate, shoved her chair out behind her, grabbed her purse, and marched out the front door. It took me hours to calm down. She didn't speak to us for two months. But after that, something shifted. She became slightly less effusive, but far more respectful. The woman who had always offered her opinions now started seeking out mine. "What do you think about flu shots?" she asked me one day, and another, "Where do you stand on gun control?" She usually didn't agree with my point of view, but she was more willing to accept that I was entitled to one.

As the heat between us eased, I began to see that beyond Dorothy's volatility lay a kind heart and a resilient, optimistic spirit—qualities I grew to admire more with each passing year. The same woman who flipped the bird at her son, hung up on her daughter, and once famously said, "I don't apologize," also volunteered three days a week at Kaiser and reached out regularly to old high school classmates from Ohio, friends in Indonesia, and my mom, whom Dorothy called "her buddy." After Dee's first stroke, she had to move for months to an assisted-living facility—a move that inspired several memorable clashes. "I *hate* it here," she insisted. Even so, by the end of the first month, she knew everyone's names and had started helping out—making sure Marie had taken her medication and wheeling Jim to and from dinner. "We should put her on the payroll," joked one of the nurses.

As her health slowly deteriorated, I fell into the habit of calling her in the morning, mostly to make sure she was OK. During those conversations, I'd ask her advice about little things—carpet purchases, discipline issues, cooking techniques—not so much because I thought she'd have the right answer but because I knew she'd have an opinion, and I had finally realized that her rigid certainty was her bulwark in a scary, precarious world. And, galling as it could be, her staunchness often gave me comfort too.

Now, here we were, Gordon and me, nearly twenty years after we'd met, making a momentous decision on his mom's behalf, and she couldn't weigh in. "If this were a Hollywood movie," I said to my grieving husband, "we'd honor Dorothy's dying wish and she'd pass away peacefully in our home. But it's not. We don't know how to make her comfortable. We don't have morphine or bed pans. We don't even know if we can safely give her water. What if she chokes?" By now I was crying, and so was he. Worse, Dorothy had started making scary, gasping noises. The last words she'd uttered before drifting into what-ever oblivion she was now in had been, "Help me." So I did. I picked up the phone and called 911, then sat down on the sofa and held her hand while we waited for the ambulance.

Ginny Graves

Ginny Graves is an award-winning journalist who has been writing in-depth features and essays for national magazines for more than twenty years. Dubbed an "uber-freelancer" by *The Writer* magazine, her work appears regularly in *Vogue, More, Glamour, Self, O: The Oprah Magazine, Prevention, Health,* and *Ladies' Home Journal.* Known for her ability to research and distill complex ideas in psychology, health, and fitness, she has written several books, including *For Richer or Poorer: Keeping Your Marriage Happy When She's Making More Money.* She lives in Marin County, California, with her husband and two teenage sons.

Withdrawal, by Katherine Mariaca-Sullivan

Artist Statement:

Withdrawal is one of artist-author Katherine Mariaca-Sullivan's earliest works. She painted it in 2000 as she was transitioning out of a painful marriage. The central figure in the painting, a woman, is caught frozen just as her lover's hand reaches for her in what should have been a loving and intimate moment. Unfortunately, she finds herself pulling away rather than leaning into her lover's arms. It is this physical reaction that convinces her that the relationship is over.

Like many of Katherine's earlier works, the woman in this painting is nude. While Katherine believes that the female form is luscious and gorgeous, which is a good enough reason to paint female nudes, her reason for painting the woman in *Withdrawal* without clothing has more to do with stripping her subject of everything except the raw emotion that is attached to what is happening in the moment expressed by the painting.

Painting title and medium:

Withdrawal is a 40" x 40" acrylic on canvas. It remains in the artist's private collection.

Katherine Mariaca-Sullivan

Katherine Mariaca-Sullivan is both an artist and an author. She began showing her large-scale acrylic-on-canvas paintings in 2000. Her paintings have appeared in galleries in the United States, Puerto Rico, and Mexico and have been used as illustrations for a number of books. She has studied art in Puerto Rico, Mexico, Hawaii, North Carolina, and New Hampshire. Katherine's writing includes two novels, *Water from Stone* and *The Stages of Grace*, published by Madaket Lane Publishers, as well as book of collected stories and illustrations, *The Complication of Sisters*, and a number of nonfiction works, including *When a Loved One Dies: The Complete Guide to Preparing a Dignified and Meaningful Goodbye*. She graduated with a BS in psychology from Tufts University and an MFA in creative writing from Lesley University.

Section Five

Life, Death, Religion, and Spirituality

What Remains

Christie Coombs

"Hello, is Christie there?"

"Uh, yes, this is she."

"This is the New York Medical Examiner's Office . . ."

For a swift second, my heart skipped a beat and then seemed to stop altogether before it began to race. My knees felt weak and wobbly. With one hand cupping a mug of tea and the other wrapped around the phone, I blindly sat down on the stool behind me. I knew instantly why the Medical Examiner must be calling.

It was three years after my husband died. Under "cause of death" on his death certificate, it read "Blunt trauma. Body not found." "Blunt trauma" was a gross understatement. He was a passenger on Flight 11, the first flight to be hijacked and careened into New York's World Trade Center on September 11, 2001. The "blunt object" was a massive steel building. The death certificate should have read "Cause of death: Murder by terrorism."

Up to this date, I hadn't received any notification from the Medical Examiner's office about my husband's remains. I was in the majority of the nearly 3,000 families who lost a loved one on 9/11. Only a very small percentage of victims had been identified, and even today, too many families have not received word of any remains being recovered. I figured because Jeff was toward the front of the plane, there was little expectation that any of his remains would be identified at all. The call came as a complete surprise.

I had just been at the Medical Examiner's office in New York with a group of 9/11 women from Massachusetts. We took a trip there to learn about the identification process—to be reassured that the hunt for remains and their commitment to identifying our loved ones would continue. Although I had recently submitted Jeff's electric razor for possible DNA match, they told me they had made no identification yet.

In the first year, I had spent my fair share of time wallowing in my home, my safe place. I had become a little antisocial at times, declining many invitations from friends, preferring to spend time alone with my thoughts and my pain. I immersed myself in my writing and into the foundation I established in memory of Jeff. But by 2004, I had come to accept the horrible hand of cards life had dealt me. I had peeked out of the black hole of grief and learned to have fun again. My kids had come a long way in their grief, too, and life was as close to normal as it could be. We were adapting to the "new normal." Jeff's physical absence in our lives was still very evident. His place at the dinner table was gaping, and his side of the bed remained unwrinkled, unless the girls snuck in for a late-night visit once in a while. I often thought I heard his car coming up the driveway around 6:00 p.m., but that was just my mind wishing it were so. We knew the void would be felt for the rest of our lives. In spite of thinking of him every day, we had become accustomed to life without him, and realizing we had no choice, we had learned to adjust.

We actually dared to hope that September 11 was behind us, and that we could move forward, as one does with any death of a loved one. Just when we felt ready to face another phase of grief, that call came.

"Christie, this is Steve," said the man on the other end of the phone. It was a familiar voice, and I was relieved to hear it was Steve calling. He was assigned to the September 11 ME team, and I had dealt with him a number of times to ask questions, set up our meeting, and connect him with other families. He had been kind, informative, helpful, and compassionate every time we had spoken. "I wanted to tell you myself that we have positively identified some of Jeff's remains."

My heart was still thumping as though I had just sprinted a 5K. As Steve explained that they had identified a six-inch piece of his left elbow, I felt a lump form in my throat. I took down the information and listened to his instruction. I would have to get a funeral director to sign off on all that was left of my six-foot-four husband. He would then transport the package home for cremation or burial, whichever I chose. If I preferred, the New York ME office could "store" the remains indefinitely. I told him I would let him know what I was going to do, but I knew immediately I wouldn't be leaving any part of my husband's physical body in New York. I thanked him and hung up the phone.

I began to cry. I shook. I felt sick to my stomach. I felt as if I had been told for the first time that my husband was dead. Again. I wondered aloud to myself why it hurt so much hearing this. Nothing would change. It didn't make Jeff any more dead than he was before the call. Obviously, I had no doubt in my mind that he was gone—I had seen the towers collapse in a massive plume of smoke. I had repeatedly watched the footage of Jeff's plane slamming into the South Tower like a deadly missile. But this call was confirmation, so I suppose in my grief-torn mind it did make him "more dead." My fantasy that he was off fulfilling his dream of hiking the Appalachian Trail was now snuffed.

After I calmed down a bit, I called my sister, then I called my friend Mary. She understood. She had been through it a couple of times already, having lost her own husband in the towers. That call was followed by a call to my grief counselor and a subsequent impromptu meeting to work through another stage of grief.

When suffering a loss, the pain never really goes away. You learn to adapt to it, to live life fully in spite of it, or because of it. There may be situations along the way that interfere with progress, but hopefully something in you keeps you focused on life and the potential for full happiness.

In my case, it is my kids. Whatever we go through, we go through together. They're old enough now to know even the most horrendous details of that day. We've grown together; we've developed from a happy pre-9/11 family of five to what felt like a broken family, to whole again, with a missing piece. But he's not really missing. He's here—I just look at my kids, and there he is.

Christie Coombs

Christie Coombs lives in Abington, MA. Christie first realized she would be a writer when she was ten years old and won an essay contest on ecology at school. She studied journalism at the University of Arizona and has worked as a freelance writer for local newspapers, including the *Patriot Ledger* and *The Boston Globe*. A single mom of three young adults, writing has become her release. Having lost her husband on 9/11, she poured her emotions onto the pages that will hopefully become a memoir about loss, strength, love, single parenting, and survival.

My Splendid, Blended Family

Marcia Sherman

Every time I see a magazine or newspaper or Internet article devoted
to the "new, blended" family, I think perhaps I should tell my story—
my blended-family story. Here it is. It may not seem like a happy story
at first, but it is a story about change, about transition. As so many
life-changing events do, it all started with a telephone call of bad news.
But first, some history . . .

More than twenty years ago, my marriage collapsed when I discovered my husband was seeing another woman. Unsurprisingly, it
was an unhappy and disruptive time. It took me a year to finally leave
him. There were children, and I was trying to save a home. But leave
him I did, after which we all endured a few years of unpleasantness,
both overt and covert. Not my shining hour. He married her, and they
began a family. I also married again, and we two raised my daughter.
Relations and conversations settled in frosty cordiality for several years.

And then, that worst nightmare for any parent. The spring before
she was to enter kindergarten, their daughter was diagnosed with leukemia. In the few minutes it took my ex to tell me on the telephone,
everything changed. Obviously, their lives were going to change in
ways I could not even imagine. My daughter's life was also going to
change—this was her sister, her only sister. And my life changed . . .
how could you possibly stay angry with those who may be losing their
hearts? I cleared the decks of all animosity and determined to do whatever I could to help.

There followed days and weeks and months of illness and some
slight recovery and then more illness. Court-ordered visitation sched-
ules dissolved—my daughter was there anytime they wanted her. I

arranged a trip to an ice show, and the meet-and-greet with characters beforehand. I got my hair trimmed at a pediatric leukemia cut-a-thon. I participated in a walk-a-thon for all cancer victims. I took my daughter to see her sister in the hospital, and hung around in the lobby while she visited. We—me, my daughter, and her stepfather—were all prepared to find out if we could be bone marrow donors. The second Thanksgiving after the diagnosis, I put my just-barely-teenage daughter on a flight from Philadelphia to Minnesota. In only her second time on an airplane, and her first time without me, she flew to a clinic and celebrated the holiday with her father and his family while her sister underwent treatment. The next month was an abundant Christmas. It was a hopeful time. Plans moved forward for the bone marrow testing and transplant.

You have possibly guessed where this is going . . . remission was not to be. This cancer proved to be a particularly aggressive form of pediatric leukemia. Shortly after the New Year, her numbers were off again. After two rounds of treatments over almost twenty months, the question was put to the patient: "What do *you* want to do?" The way I understand it, what she wanted to do was stop feeling sick. She wanted to finally go to school, she wanted to have her First Holy Communion, and she wanted to go to Disney World. She wanted to go home and rest. So, with no more of the chemo coursing through her—and feeling better than she had in a long, long time—she got to do most of those things. She slept in her own bed again. She went to school for a few days. She enjoyed Disney with a few dozen members of her extended family. She received her First Holy Communion and was Confirmed. Then, she rested. The day before Valentine's Day, 2001, she rested for good, and wore her Communion dress for the second and last time. It was and is all so very sad. It happens far more than it should. We all grieved, and we still grieve. However, this is not the end of the story. This is a story of what came from all that pain. And what came from all that pain is love.

The day I discovered my husband, my daughter's father, was in love with another woman, I would never have believed I would one day love that woman too. Yet when faced with the reality of *my* daughter being *her* only daughter—how could I say no to whatever was asked of me? What was asked of me was to listen. During her daughter's illness, and passing, it became harshly apparent that there was almost no one to whom this woman could speak about her grief. After all, everyone in her family had also lost a child, a sibling, a grandchild, or a niece. Fortunately, I was slightly removed. Sure, there were others slightly removed. Sure, I was hurting, too, but certainly not in the same way. And so I found myself on the phone, just letting her talk, and cry. What was asked of me was to share my daughter. All those stressful discussions and decisions about where my daughter spent which holiday? Never again. I found myself taking her over there more often. I found myself planning outings for us as one big, blended family: me and my husband and my daughter, my ex and his wife and their boys. A baseball game, a holiday church service, a birthday party. My daughter is as attentive to her stepmother on Mother's Day as she is to me—and I applaud it. What was asked of me was to love. I opened my heart over ten years ago and continue to keep it open still today. The three of us sat together and proudly watched our daughter graduate from high school and college. We are social media friends. We say we are one another's "step-wives." We have made good memories and have a bright future. The celebratory meal after that college graduation was the first time our extended families had ever been together. It certainly looked like a dry run for a wedding to me. Someday, some little baby can expect to be completely spoiled by two maternal grandmothers.

I believe that a broken heart is an open heart: to receive and give more love. I believe within every tragedy is an opportunity for transcendence. In this particular family tragedy, we indeed transcended. Our broken hearts opened for more love, and we transitioned from a splintered to a blended family. A splendid, blended family.

Marcia Sherman

Marcia Sherman resides in a two-generation, two-cat household in southern New Jersey. Employed full-time in the public sector, her pastime and passion is writing. Her body of work includes a newspaper column, essays, poetry, and flash fiction. And of course, she is writing the Great American Novel. Other interests include gardening, home repair, crafts, and reading—especially fairy tales. With help from her blended and extended family, Marcia has raised one perfect Rose.

Finding Me

Shannon Weisleder

I will never forget the sadness that hung over me on a Friday morning last January. I had been shopping for my brother's new rental house. I was excited to plant spring pansies to boost his spirits as he was starting over. Recently having gone through "the perfect storm," as we called it, he had lost his marriage, his career, and a public election for local office, and was diagnosed with a mood disorder—a mental illness—bipolar disorder.

I stood in Home Depot fretting over just which pots would bring him the most cheer, and I recall being a bit disappointed in the color selection of wintertime pansies. Would Pat care that they were burgundy with a little yellow center? Nah.

I left Home Depot and ran to get my garden tools along with the chairs and small table I had to assemble for Pat's small deck. I thought to myself, *He can have his iced tea here or have a sandwich with the sunshine warming his face.*

Later, I was standing with a group of ladies at school and was a little put off when someone asked me why I was not invited on a trip that a bunch of my neighbors had just left to go on. It actually hadn't crossed my mind, but it put me in a foul mood, souring the morning of kindness I had set out to enjoy.

I had also recently pulled a muscle in my neck and had been on prednisone all week. Well, that alone can make a person wild and bitchy! Still, I plowed forward, heading to meet my mom and her best friend to finish unpacking, organize my brother's new kitchen, and set up the "garden" on his deck.

I had one last stop at the Greenhouse to pick up a plant for my brother's kitchen. I walked around agonizing for some silly reason over what kind of plant to get, when finally one of the sales girls came up to see if I needed help. "Yes, I need something my brother can't kill," I told her. We choose a great, green, stalky beauty—perfect, I thought!

I drove up to the "rental" with my music playing, happy to see my mom and her friend, and we laughed about having to assemble this tiny table with a million pieces. They knew I was in a bit of a funk, and I told them why.

"I feel so silly," I said, "but my friends went away and I was not invited . . . why do I feel so left out?"

My mom's friend came over to my car window later when I was leaving and said, "Shannon, let me tell you a similar story. Many years ago I was in a tennis group. I was left out of some lunch or dinner, I cannot even recall now. The next week, my mother died, and it put everything into perspective."

"Thanks, you're right," I said. "I need to buck up." We laughed, and I suggested the three of us go into business together: Decorating for the Downtrodden. We loved to decorate, no matter who or what for.

The next day, I lay on the sofa at my house while my brother was moving. My neck hurt, I was in a terrible mood, and really, I was exhausted: I had been to the consignment stores for furniture, Goodwill for kids' books, Dollar General, Target, and Crate & Barrel as well as through my own attic trying to prepare a "home is where the heart is" kind of place where my brother could heal and start his life over again.

When my mom called to check in, she was at my brother's apartment with him. She had just finished cleaning it and having lunch with him and a couple of his kids.

"Why are you cleaning his apartment, Mom?" I was a little perturbed at everyone and everything. It was just like a sister to be a bit jealous of a brother whose mama does everything for him.

"Say hi to your brother," she told me.

I started to tell my Mom that I didn't need to talk to him, and as

I was saying this, he was saying hello. I told him I did not feel well and was sorry I could not be there to move him. He told me not to worry.

"I'll be over tomorrow to sort through your clothes with you and bring you the rest of the drawers to the yellow dresser for the kids' room. We need to put the rug down first—I'll bring that too."

"OK," he answered.

Then we said, "Love you."

The next morning, my mom called and asked if I'd talked to my brother.

"No," I said. "Remember, you told him to sleep in and then we would be over."

"You're right," she said. She hung up only to call me right back again. "He is not answering his phone, and his car is there," she added.

"Mom," I said, "give the guy some space. He has probably gone for a run."

But my stomach was starting to hurt. Something didn't feel right. I asked my husband to hurry up and take the dresser drawers and rug over to my brother. "In a few minutes," he said. By then, I was pacing and getting worried . . .

"Hurry up," I said, "before you find him hanging from the rafters." I did not mean that, of course, but for some reason those words spilled out of my mouth. "Forget it, I'll go. My mom is on the way over there anyway."

Sensing my panic, my husband insisted, "No, I'll go."

I will never forget how slowly time passed once I left my brother a voicemail. "Pat, pick up, it's Shannon. Travis is on the way. He is bringing the dresser drawers and the rug. Are you there? Call me."

Twenty minutes must have passed. *Why* was my husband not answering his phone? *Why* was my mother not answering her phone?? Panic. Sweating. *Please, God*, let my brother be OK.

What time is it?? I checked my watch and it had stopped. Strange.

When my mom finally answered her phone, she was screaming. "He is dead, Shannon!"

Pause.

I cannot even explain the feeling of the world coming out from under my feet. I ran out of my house, up the street, past my friends' empty homes with tears streaming down my face . . . *No, this is not real, not possible. They are wrong.*

The blue police lights are something I will never forget.

My brother, at age forty-one, died on January 29, 2012. Gunshot wound to the head. My mother found him. My husband was right behind her. She pushed everyone out of the way and locked herself in the house with him and held his hand until the police arrived.

They say that you go through five stages of grief when you lose a loved one: Denial, anger, bargaining, depression, and acceptance.

I have been through, over, under, back around, and through the five stages again, and again. What I can tell you is this: I hated the author of the book that told me I would find a "gift" in all of this. *What?* How is that possible?

The gift I have been given is my voice. After facing something as traumatic as the suicide death of your brother, after setting up a home for him and then packing it up piece by piece, throwing things away, deciding what to keep, donating what would help others, I have found that if I can do that, I can do anything. What would I do if I were not afraid? Suddenly I was afraid of everything, though. Trauma will do that to you.

This is the first time I have taken a chance to talk about my brother's stigmatized illness and his public death. And what I know is that the truth will set you free. Love always wins. Good intentions, good will, compassion, and empathy will get you further than ill will, anger, and hate.

I think about Pat when he decided to depart this life—struggling because he felt broken and ashamed because he let others define his character. I wonder what his thoughts were and I wonder what answers he has now.

It has taken me all of this time, over 400 days, to work on my voice, with pain, tears, hope, and courage, to transition into an advocate.

I hope my brother would be proud.

Shannon Weisleder

Shannon Weisleder is a mom, a wife, a daughter, a friend, and a suicide survivor. Since losing her only brother to suicide in January 2012, Shannon has launched a website, trytomatter.com, to educate and inform people about mental illness and advocate suicide prevention. A Southerner from Richmond, VA, and a graduate of the College of Charleston, Shannon enjoys watching her three boys play baseball and her husband race sailboats. In her spare time, Shannon loves reading, gardening, and traveling, and one day hopes to write a book for suicide survivors.

The Unthinkable

Tanya Strauss

Wednesday, June 22, 1994

I arrived at San Francisco airport completely changed, but about
to further evolve in a very different direction. In that moment, I was
a college student, bursting with nineteen-year-old piss and vinegar. I
was a fluent French speaker and foreign traveler. I was also weary from
my journey but eager to show off all the maturity I'd earned during my
absence. The awkward, too tall, curvy-in-all-the-wrong-places teenager who'd left in March was gone. The new Tanya was curvy in *all* the
places (after three months of French food), a determined sophisticate,
and impatient to move on from that other girl.

As I emerged from the jet way, my heart swelled when I spotted
him, my touchstone . . . my dad's face towered above the crowd. After
three months in France punctuated by two interminable travel days,
the sight of my father cured the homesickness I didn't want to admit
I'd had. My parents and I celebrated our reunion with joyful tears
and rib-crushing hugs in the midst of the airport chaos. One whiff of
my mom's soft Ralph Lauren perfume and I knew I was home. I felt
conflicted by soaking them in so deeply . . . I had yearned for them
throughout my absence but I also wanted to retain some distance.
After three months of living abroad, I was better than the girl who'd
left them months before. I had a new edge, a coolness factor that they
couldn't understand.

Friday, June 24, 1994

My parents took the day off and we drove their brand-new con-
vertible Jeep Wrangler to Silver Lake. The heat felt delicious, and the
fresh pine smell reminded me of campouts, fishing trips, and hikes

on my dad's shoulders. We ate beautiful June strawberries and looked at photos. While living with my host family in Nîmes, I'd often stare at the family photos on the walls of their home and ache, longing for my own family, so I had asked my mom to bring along some old albums. Sitting on a huge granite boulder next to that ice-cold lake, we reviewed our life together, the life they'd had before I was born, and the journey from which I'd just returned. The old photos included my sweetest memories and a lot of retro fashions. Laughing at my dad's old knee-high socks and aviator sunglasses, my aches unraveled, and I didn't need to miss them anymore. For those three hours, I was their nineteen-year-old college student and we were exactly enough for each other, exactly where we belonged. It was one of the most wonderful and horrific days of my life.

The newly paved road rolled steeply downhill, long and straight, like a slash through the forest. I imagined that from above, the road must have looked like a seam in the lush carpet of forest. The sun was low in the sky, beaming at us full in the face. When I blinked my eyes, I saw green dots where the sun had burned itself into my gaze.

I saw the squirrel coming across the road, crossing from left to right. Not having seen another car for miles, I pulled the wheel left, into the oncoming traffic lane, to allow the squirrel to cross. That plan worked perfectly—we did not hit the squirrel—but still my father screamed, "Tanya, *don't do that!*" He knew I'd miscalculated the effect of such a sudden movement, given our speed and the Jeep's top-heavy design.

Once I lost control of the wheel, I thought of an old cartoon where a car went teetering down the road, swerving back and forth on two wheels at a time. The Jeep carved its own path—I was no longer driving.

The span of time from my realization that I'd lost control to opening my eyes was probably milliseconds. In that time, the Jeep had left the road and we were hanging, suspended. The left-front grill was deep in the forest floor; the left-back bumper of the car was digging into the side of the roadbed. The car formed the top line of a triangle between the roadbed and the uphill-slanted forest floor. We would have been buried in the forest floor under the car if the backseat hadn't been leaning against the trunk of a 100-foot pine tree. When I opened the door, my body sank a little. I was held by my seatbelt.

Getting oriented, I looked at my mother next to me. She was screaming, *"Jim, Jim!"* Her voice was full of a real panic I'd never heard before. My dad's body was crushed between the tree and the backseat.

Early Saturday morning, June 25, 1994

It's foggy and I can hardly see three feet in front of me. I'm holding an umbrella full of holes. My mom, my sister, and I are following my father, walking as fast as we can across the Golden Gate Bridge. It's cold, but I can smell my own sweat. My mother shoos her hand ahead—run and catch your father. Sandy and I hold hands and start running. Wearing khaki belted pants and a short-sleeved polo shirt and carrying a windbreaker, Dad's stride is long, harsh, and determined. He will not turn to look at us. Running our fastest, we call to him, "Dad, wait! Please!" He cannot hear us—or he doesn't want to. Suddenly, the fog overtakes him, and we cannot see him anymore. I drop the umbrella. I'm exhausted from running and weary with grief.

Slowly awakening from the dream, I can smell them in the bed—a perfect balance of dad's musky man scent and mom's warm Ralph Lauren perfume. The cotton sheets are soft from years of sleep and laundry. I feel peaceful and deeply at home.

"Oh my God, it really happened." As cruel consciousness invades, those words scream through my mind. As the dreadful morning light breaks into my eyes, the weight of my tragedy is nearly too much to bear. I killed my father yesterday.

Thursday, October 18, 2012

Before I'm even really awake, I instinctively slide my bare foot across the sheet to touch Jon's. He's still asleep, but his foot moves to meet mine. Our microfiber sheets are silky and my pillow is too warm from my face heating it all night. I flip my pillow to the cold side as Jon turns toward me. Silently, we flip in unison, completing our wake-up routine, his arms around me, his nose in my hair. The room smells sweet and stale, like sleepy bodies.

"Gooooood moooorrrrrning, Mommy! Can I watch a show?" the little voice squeaks.

Inhaling and exhaling, I calculate the hour, running through the day's schedule: nurse the baby, breakfast, preschool, naptime, play date, dinner, baths, bedtime, repeat.

"Sure, Babe, climb in. But first, I have an important question for you and Daddy."

"What, Mommy?"

"What's your favorite kind of cupcake? We're celebrating a birthday today!"

Today I will not consider the cruel, unnatural circumstances of his death. I will not wallow in memories of soul-crushing guilt, suicide attempts, psychiatric hospitals, or a painful divorce. Today, I will celebrate my father.

Tanya Strauss

Tanya Strauss lives in the suburbs and drives a family-size car but is anything but boring. Her deeply honest writing is inspired, often sad, and sometimes wickedly funny. She has a passion for words, which she indulges regularly by letting her husband beat her at Words with Friends. A wife, mother, and writer, Tanya lives in the San Francisco Bay Area with her husband and two awesome children. In addition to writing and parenting, Tanya can often be found in the back of the pack in local road races and is presently training for a half-marathon.

The World, the Flesh, and the Devil

Rose Gordy

My high school boyfriend begged me not to enter. He said over and over again that he needed me and that I could save my soul in the real world. But I couldn't listen to his pleas; I wouldn't let myself even hear them. I knew what I wanted. Three weeks after I turned eighteen, on September 7, 1957, I left home forever. On this momentous day I put my past life behind me (or so I believed then in the heady idealism of my youth). I became a lamb to the slaughter. A seed dying to be born again. I became a willing victim to a holy guillotine to be purportedly cut off from "the world, the flesh, and the devil" by entering a convent in western Pennsylvania.

I died to the world as a daughter and a girlfriend and a silly teenage girl, but was reborn into a new life as a nun under vows of poverty, chastity, and obedience. Everything was done on a schedule by bell or chime or clock—from waking to praying to eating to recreating to sleeping.

Without much effort I can still smell the Novitiate, the third floor of the Motherhouse where we young nuns lived. On certain Saturday mornings we Postulants and Novices waxed and polished the enormous pieces of old-fashioned furniture in the community room. I remember being crouched on my hands and knees scrubbing the white lines in the hallway floor with old toothbrushes. One afternoon during Lent, the inviting aroma of homemade bread wafted up from the kitchen to the Chapel too temptingly, especially since we had been dutifully fasting, even though mere teenagers.

If I imagine a little harder, I can even feel my new self inside my "Possie" outfit that first year: the extended black pleated skirt, long-sleeved black cotton blouse, flared black waist-length cape, short black veil, old-lady Cuban-heeled shoes, and heavy stockings, black of course.

After that, we all worked and prayed and studied for receiving the "Holy Habit of Religion," which consisted of many parts. First, there was a white, heavily-starched headpiece, called a coif, that covered all except the edges of the back of my head; the swooping forehead part dug into my skin and rubbed and chaffed. There was a white circular bodice piece called a guimpe, also heavily starched, and a floor-length black veil with the small waist-length opaque veil underneath. There was the black serge habit, unpleated to the top of my breast and from there following the form of my body to my waist, then flowing to the floor in multiple one-inch pleats. Lastly, a cincture: a two-inch black leather belt, and from that hung my oversized rosary beads, reaching to the floor.

All of these parts of our Holy Habit covered, protected, and enshrined us. I can still also feel my silver ring on the second finger of my right hand, engraved with the word I had chosen: *Maranatha*— Aramaic for "Come, Lord!" This modest ring came to symbolize the reasons why I had entered to "strive for perfection." Yes, I tried to accomplish the impossible and be perfect, so once I was professed, I believed I was at least closer to the day when I would actually be perfect—our main "raison d'etre."

As Religious Sisters, we followed "the Rule," which encompassed numerous and arcane directives. For example, the 9 p.m. Grand Silence, when at the toll of the large bell, everyone ceased talking—even midway through a word—and didn't speak again until after breakfast the next day. Another rule was keeping "Custody of the Eyes," which meant that we didn't look directly at anyone. We were not allowed to talk to laypeople unless there were extenuating circumstances. We could not use any object in any way except for its intended purpose. We couldn't visit our fellow nuns in their cells, as our bedrooms were

called, because there was a fear of "particular friendships," a euphe-
mism for a word never spoken, lesbianism. We didn't have any regular
clothes, or anything with color. We were not allowed to possess or wear
anything feminine. No scented soaps, no silk undergarments. We were
not permitted to seal our letters to our parents, so that our Superiors
could read them. No radio, no newspapers, no TV. We also had to perform a daily Particular Examen for sins, a weekly Confession, and a
monthly Chapter of Faults, where each of us announced to the rest of
the community some violation of the Rule, like talking at the wrong
time of day.

In those first few years, there were days I was so turned in upon
myself and always so serious about following the Rule that I felt guilty
for the ones who didn't. I embraced my new life completely, without
question.

In many ways, especially during those early years, I was relatively happy. But during the second six years, when I moved from the
Motherhouse to smaller local convents and taught English and French
in high school, I started to realize I wasn't meant for this life. Maybe
I'd been fooling myself for a long time. Despite my belief at eighteen
that I had a vocation to serve God, in some ways I entered for unconscious reasons. Years later, I realized that way of life was an escape from
a blossoming sexuality I had no way to honor and accept in my teens . . .
something I had only recently admitted to my frustrated high school
boyfriend.

In the final analysis, though, I don't regret those years I lived in
that hallowed, strange world. I entered when I wanted to and left when
I knew I couldn't be true to myself and stay. Significantly, the Mother
General understood that I knew my mind, so I didn't have to undergo
the usual psychological testing before I was permitted to leave. I did,
however, have to get a letter from Rome releasing me from my three
vows. Finally, I left at age thirty, with a BA, an MA, and eight years of
teaching experience, all leading to a promising future.

I continue searching today for the peace and perfection I tried to find in that other place and time, though it's now over a half century since those heady years when I first lived as a nun. Browning's question reverberates through my memory as I relive even these few experiences from so long ago: "Ah, but a man's reach should exceed his grasp, or what's a heaven for?"

Still today, having rejoined "the world, the flesh, and the devil" that I thought I had left in my youth, I struggle to come to terms with my convent experiences. I wrote the following poem, as Rilke said, to "live into the answer."

What is Life
But the living of it?
A Way of Awakening.
A Dawn.
We wander far from ourselves.
Only to find it there
In us all along.

Rose Gordy

Author and dream counselor Rose Gordy spent thirteen years of her early life as a nun, effectively cut off from the world. In spite of the conditions within the Church, she managed to leave and make a new life for herself, including getting happily married and having three sons. Through her experiences in the convent as well as decades of teaching in the classroom, she focuses on writing compelling stories and poems honoring lives changed forever by adversity.

The Sign

Tonja Steel

M̲y flight left Las Vegas at 2 p.m. and touched down a few hours later in Kearney, Nebraska. I was home, or at least close to it, but the thought of walking into the Kearney hospital ICU was unnerving me. I'd already been forewarned by my mother that my dad would likely not recognize me. Luckily, she was wrong.

"Hello, Tonja. How are you?" he said. I gave him my best big-girl smile. At thirty-nine, I felt so small and helpless. The next words out his mouth would cause me to laugh out loud.

"I'm so sorry your love life has been such a train wreck," he said, wincing at me.

"I'm married now. Just five months ago you walked me down that aisle, remember?" I said, waving my one-carat diamond near his face.

"Oh, that's right. What's his name?"

"Doug."

"Yes, Doug. I like that guy."

It was strange to see my father struggle to remember. He had always had such a great memory and was often lamenting life lessons and creating original quotes. Things like: *Pain is just a state of mind. . . . It's a great life if you don't weaken. . . . Don't sweat it, it all works out in the end.*

I glanced over at my mother. She looked as if she had aged ten years in just a few weeks. My father had woken up one January day in 2008 with a headache. Other than some blurred vision, everything had been fine. They were on their way to the doctor's office for a routine checkup when he'd had a seizure. It had been twenty-four days and still no diagnosis. The only thing they could figure out was that at age sixty-one, he was quickly losing his memory and control of his motor skills. I was absolutely terrified.

"He keeps asking for his mother," my mom told me in a hush.

"But Grandma has been dead nearly ten years," I say.

"I know, but he tells me she's in the room."

"You're just going to have to keep telling him to fight and hang on until we can figure out what this is," I said.

My mother and father had been together nearly four decades—high school sweethearts from Bird City, Kansas. The Bird City cardinals were their mascot, and a pair of cardinals had always adorned our home—in photographs, statues, and paintings.

At the hospital, nearly every day at 3 p.m., my father would start a discussion about who was watching the kids and ask if everyone had gotten their watermelon.

"I don't understand what he wants," said the nurse on call.

My mother smiled and explained that her husband had been an elementary school principal and his favorite day of the year was the all-school fun day, when he made sure every child had watermelon by 3 p.m. Apparently, every day is all-school fun day, she explained.

His personality was definitely changing. When asked by the doctor who my brother was, my father replied, "The postman."

Pointing to my mother, the doctor said, "Who is that?"

"The postman's assistant."

The next three weeks trickled by. I had to tell mom good-bye and fly back to Nevada. I received daily updates over the phone. On February 13, 2008, a diagnosis was finally made. My father had Creutzfeldt-Jakob disease, or CJD. Some of the first symptoms of CJD include dementia, personality changes, and blurred vision. In my father's case, his vision began to change several months before the other symptoms set in. He had additional symptoms, too, including seizures, hallucinations, gait changes, and memory loss. The doctor explained, much to our horror, that these symptoms were caused by the death of the brain's nerve cells from prions, or abnormal proteins. In most cases, death occurs within one year. We had only hours. My father died later that day, after my mother found the strength to whisper in his ear the diagnosis and tell him that she loved him and that if he wanted to cross over, she understood.

The funeral was gut-wrenching. Seven hundred people—many of them former students and colleagues—filled the tiny gym. Friends and family spoke about my father, the man who had led the school with joy and dedication for the past three decades. A small wooden box sat near the podium. It contained my father's ashes, as it was mandatory that all CJD patients be cremated; just one last cruel twist that CJD could play. After the service, family gathered at my parents' home. After forty-two years together, my mother would be alone again—something she hadn't experienced since she was a teenager. My eight-year-old niece would sneak away to my father's closet and re-emerge wearing his hat, tie, and shirt. The dress shirt hung on her small frame and dragged on the floor. In those first few hours and days, we were all just trying to cope.

My mother had been very clear when she whispered in my father's ear the day that he died, "You must give me a sign. If you are going to transition, I need to know you made it OK."

My brother and I held on to her optimism but realized that she was asking the impossible.

But then it happened. Just a few short days after the funeral, long before they should be showing up, two cardinals appeared in my mother's backyard.

"Look!" she exclaimed.

"Oh, Mom, it's a sign," I said. Then they flew away.

And then, just to prove his point, my mother's cell phone began to ring. She picked it up, and there was no answer. I suggested she look at the caller ID. We scrolled over to the caller ID screen, and there it was: the call had come from my father's cell phone.

"Who has dad's cell phone?" I asked her.

"I had it shut off three days ago," she answered with widened eyes.

I don't know how those birds ended up in Mom's backyard in the dead of winter, and I can't imagine how a turned-off cell phone could place a call, but I took these as a sign, a sign that wherever my father was going on his journey, he had made it safely. And although I can never prove it, I swear I could hear my father's voice ringing clear in my head: *Don't sweat it, it all works out in the end.*

Tonja Steel

Tonja Steel is a writer. Her most recent compilation is titled *Mother of the Year: She Said What?* published by Willow Creek Press (2013). She collaborates with Las Vegas artist Jodi Pedri, and they have developed 2,000 giftware products through their company, Working Girls Design. She lives in Las Vegas with her husband, Doug, and is working on her first novel, *Cancer Free Emily,* a book inspired by her mother and late father.

Initiation

Cristhal Bennett

E{arth}

My mother was a vibrant woman; she was my breath, my ground, a healer, seer, and holder of my spiritual lineage. No matter where I lived or traveled in the world, we had a bond that could not be broken by space or time. As a child I was called her shadow, because I was always standing beside or behind her. I am my mother's child.

At sixteen I began my search to know God, which culminated in a spiritual awakening experience at twenty-seven that totally infused me with Spirit. It was so profound, I called home to tell my mother that I was seeing into people and healing them. As if she had been waiting for the call, she said, "That is who you are, it is not what you do. It is also who I am." Years later I realized that with those words, my mother had begun the process of initiating me into the spiritual lineage of our family.

W{ater}

In November 1995 I was speaking with my mother, who lived in Alaska. She had been ill off-and-on since a trip to Chicago in August, and something in our connection that day felt different. As I spoke with her, I heard the quiet, still voice of Spirit whisper to me—loudly— *She has cancer throughout her body*. I still recall the distinct feeling of being frozen in time, as if standing between two worlds.

I pleaded with my mother to go to the doctor, but she refused. I finally understood, or rather I heard in her voice, that she intended to die, and from the quiet, still voice of Spirit I heard, *It is her life, it is her will, it is her decision that she will not give to another.*

With an unspoken understanding of what was before us, I hung up the phone and ran to my bed, crying uncontrollably. My husband

and nephew came to see what was wrong with me. They looked at me with blank faces, and I told them, "My mother is dying."

Fire

I wish I could say that I spent quality time with my mother in the months before she passed away, but life isn't always romantic like that. Between November and June, I was doing something else for her: I was taking care of her first-born grandchild, my nephew Andre, who had been diagnosed with HIV.

In the spring of 1993, Andre moved to California to be with me, as he said I was the one person he believed would support him on his journey with the disease. I married a year later, and that evening Andre had a severe allergic reaction and asthma attack after eating a cake made with nut flour. His immune system compromised, Andre's respiratory system never recovered, and within six months he was diagnosed with full-blown AIDS.

In September 1994, Andre was living in San Francisco, and I found him in his apartment alone, obviously near death, suffering from pneumocystis pneumonia. My beautiful "baby," whose skin was usually a radiant shade of cocoa, was now gray and without life. He was in bad shape, barely able to walk. I rushed him to the San Francisco General emergency room so he could be admitted to the AIDS ward.

To my surprise, I was coldly instructed to take a seat, and Andre, though almost lifeless, was placed on a gurney to wait beside people with blood-stained bandages and dirty clothing.

Shocked, I paced between Andre's gurney and the receptionist. Panicked as I was, I tried to comfort Andre, praying for guidance. I watched the hands on the clock: the time, like Andre's life, seemed to be slipping away.

Frustrated and feeling helpless, I told my nephew, "If you are going to die, then it will be with dignity. I'm taking you home to die." Weaker than when we arrived, I carried Andre to my car, we drove to my home in Marin, and I began nursing "my baby" myself.

Needless to say, it was a very intense and emotionally challenging year for our family. We lived in and out of the hospital, and hospice was called in twice. By December 1995, Andre's viral load was so high that he was given six months to live. In May 1996, Andre's death imminent, my husband and I took him to Maui.

On the third day of our stay, Andre began to perspire for the first time in six months. By the end of our trip, instead of death, life had returned to Andre, and instead was taken from my mother.

Air

My last conversation with my mother took place hours before I boarded the plane for Alaska. It was one of the most heartbreaking yet empowering talks that we ever had.

Her voice was weak yet held a strength that belied her condition. She asked, "Did I give you anything? Did my life have meaning?"

A voice that I did not recognize as my own replied, "Yes, not only for me, but for my sister as well. I watched as you said yes to others when you needed to say yes to yourself. Because of that, I know that when I am saying no to others, I am really saying yes to myself. In your selfless way, you taught me how to care for myself."

She responded, "Good, now I can rest."

Sitting on the plane in silence, I was aware of being connected to my mother by a thin cord through which I could feel the pulse of her life in me. Every breath held silent prayer that we could see and hold each other one last time. As the plane touched the ground, I felt something inside of me snap loose—the cord that held us together was broken. Without needing anyone to tell me, I knew my mother had taken her last breath.

Spirit

My mother was on life support for two days. In those two days, my nature changed, and those around me felt it. Although I was not yet ordained, my family seemed to recognize the spiritual legacy passed to me thirteen years earlier by my mother.

Now, my mother's Spirit called upon me to open the veils that would allow her to join our ancestors. A nod from my father—his blessing—and I began. With my mother's Spirit guiding me, I covered the mirrors in her hospital room and opened the window. It was a still summer day, yet we all saw a gentle breeze stir from within the room and part the curtains. I watched in awe as her Spirit took flight above the land of Alaska that she so dearly loved.

We stood in silent prayer. After twenty minutes, the curtain blew inward. I felt a gentle caress on my forehead; the Spirit of my mother had returned. Looking around, I could see that everyone was aware that she had returned. We were all transformed by the sacredness of the moment.

Suddenly, above and around my mother, I could see the veil between the worlds open. I could see my grandparents, my sister, and my mother's family standing above her with open arms. I exclaimed to everyone, "Can you see them? They are here! So many of our ancestors, calling her home." I watched in awe as my mother's Spirit rose from her still body into the arms of her own mother.

She turned to me, a gentle nod of her head an affirmation and blessing. No longer an initiate, I became the holder of our family legacy. I am a Spirit Walker, Healer, and Seer.

Cristhal Bennett

Rev. Cristhal Bennett, MDiv, is an interfaith minister and founding director of Silver Light Guidance. She comes from a long lineage of intuitive and clairvoyant healers, seers, midwives, and ministers. Cristhal is a radiant and inspirational spiritual teacher, intuitive, clairvoyant, psychic healer, and yoga and meditation teacher who supports individuals, couples, families, and businesses internationally. Her greatest joy in life is supporting her clients in awakening to their inherent divine nature and joyful, purpose-filled living. She can be found at silverlightguidance.com.

Love Wins

Gabrielle Bernstein

For more than twenty years I kept a journal. In it I wrote about heart-break, anxiety, and eating disorders. I wrote about trying to quit drugs while high on drugs. Pages and pages are filled with self-loathing, self-doubt, and a running calorie counter. I wrote the same romantic mini-drama with dozens of different names attached. My journal entries were my only outlets from the turmoil and deep-rooted pain I lived with every hour of every day. Through writing I'd release my fears onto the page and get honest about my sadness as I scribbled over my tears.

Today my journal entries are much different. They reflect an empowered woman who is happy and bleeds authenticity. Instead of dwelling on my diet or obsessing over romance, I use my journal to honor myself. The words on the page are tinged with pride and com-passion. I've overcome my addictions to love, drugs, food, work, fear—you name it, and I've recovered. I worked hard, and man, was it worth it. Today, each of my journal entries shows a deep desire to continue growing from the inside out.

My primary guide on my journey to self-love has been the meta-physical text *A Course in Miracles*. The *Course* is a self-study curriculum emphasizing practical applications for relinquishing fear in all areas of life. Its unique thought system uses forgiveness as the road to inner peace and as a guide to happiness. I was first introduced to the princi-ples of the *Course* through the spiritual teacher Marianne Williamson, known throughout the world for her best-selling books and her inter-national speaking circuit. Marianne is the leading teacher of *A Course in Miracles* and is a straight-up spiritual rock star.

The *Course*'s lessons taught me to view my life and how I experi-enced it in a totally new way. I learned that much of what I feared in my life was not frightening at all, or in many instances even real. I learned that fear is simply an illusion based on past experiences that we project into the present and onto the future. Making this realization was revelatory in that I'd awakened to the fact that if I stuck to the *Course*'s plan, I could truly relinquish my fearful patterns.

It was with that burning desire for change that I set out to purchase the *Course* to begin with. Upon entering my local bookstore, I noticed the sturdy-looking dark-blue hardback with the title *A Course in Miracles* scrawled in illuminating gold print across the cover. Instead of being daunted by it, I found the thickness of the volume inviting and reassuring, so much so that I smiled as if I had received a wink from the universe as I grabbed the book off the shelf.

Then the most auspicious thing happened. The book literally dragged me to the counter. No joke. I physically felt the book dragging me to the register. It felt strange and yet oddly comforting. Intuitively, I knew I was in for something good. I bought the book immediately and walked out of the store. As I stood on a busy New York City street corner, I flipped the book open to its introduction and read, "This is a course in miracles. It is a required course. Only the time you take is voluntary. The course does not aim at teaching the meaning of love, for that is beyond what can be taught. It does aim, however, at removing the blocks to the awareness of love's presence, which is your natural inheritance." This passage sent chills down my spine. I'd found what I was looking for, a guide to removing all the crap that had been blocking me from inner peace and love. In that moment I made a commitment to myself to become a student and a teacher of the *Course*—a sacred contract that would change my life.

Through reading the *Text* I was guided to understand the mission of the *Course*. Simply and succinctly, the *Course* states that "its goal for you is happiness and peace." The *Text* also gave me a deep understanding of the basis for my fear and guilt and how they could be overcome. Finally, the *Text* taught me the meaning of "the miracle." The miracle is simply defined as the shift in perception from fear to love.

Then I embarked on the *Workbook for Students,* which consists of 365 lessons, an exercise for each day of the year. This one-year training program began my process of transforming my own fears to love. The *Workbook* guided me to know a relationship with what I call my ~ing, an inner guide, or as the *Course* calls it, an Internal Teacher. This relationship with my ~ing became my primary tool for restoring my mind. Then, when I was ready, I began to practice the *Manual for Teachers.* This section of the *Course* prepared me to share its lessons in a way that was authentic to me. As a result of my dedication to the *Course,* I was blasted open to reconnect with my true inner spirit, which is love.

These days, I'm addicted to finding my happiness and love inside myself. My focus is no longer on *how to get happiness*; rather, my intention is to release the blocks to the happiness that already lives inside me. When you open your heart and mind to new perceptions, you are shown a whole new way to view your life. Your hang-ups will melt away, resentments will release, and a childlike faith in joy will be reignited.

Sounds like I've got the keys to heaven, doesn't it? That's right, I do! And I can testify to these tools because I work them like a full-time job. You too can have a miraculous life transition if you choose it. Just breathe and be willing to learn and grow. Your slight willingness is all you need to create powerful change in your life. *A Course in Miracles* teaches us, "Miracles arise out of conviction." Your commitment to change will be your guide to all the resources you need to move forward, just as it was in my transition. Remember you are not alone. Even if fear has you in a headlock, I'm here to remind you that love always wins.

Gabrielle Bernstein

Gabrielle Bernstein is the *New York Times* best-selling author of *May Cause Miracles.* She appears regularly as an expert on NBC's *Today Show,* has been featured on Oprah's *Super Soul Sunday* as a next-generation thought leader, and was named "a new role model" by the *New York Times*. She is also the author of the books *Add More ~ing to Your Life, Spirit Junkie,* and the forthcoming book *Miracles Now* (to be published in April 2014). Gabrielle is also the founder of HerFuture.com, a social networking site for women to inspire, empower, and connect.

My First Word Was The "F" Word

Siobhan Neilland

My first word was the F-word. By age five, I was shooting guns and driving getaway cars with sticks as pedals. At age six, I found myself at bars in Hollywood, getting on stage with John Lee Hooker, Jimmy Witherspoon, and The Drifters. By the time I was fifteen, I'd been told twice that I had only six months to live. Because of my lack of hygiene and social skills, I was labeled a "feral child." You're probably wondering, *Why? How?*

I was raised without electricity or running water, squatting on land at an impoverished California commune with my parents just outside Hollywood. I had to survive by any means necessary—and it was in this lifestyle that I was forced into unimaginable situations much too adult for my young years. Finally, I was taken away by the state of California due to overwhelming neglect and put first in juvenile detention and later, foster care.

Unfortunately, even in the state's custody, I was not safe. Not long after I entered foster care, I was kidnapped by a relative who had recently been released from jail. Thankfully, I was rescued and placed back into foster care, but not a year after that, I was kidnapped a second time by another relative who planned for us to flee across the Mexican border.

In this life, I was ravaged by addiction, subjected to abuse, suffered unspeakable suicidal depression, and bore witness to far too much death. You would almost certainly find some of the details of my story unbelievable. But looking back, I see that somehow, over time, I turned the shattered, scattered pieces of my life that were left in the wake of my upbringing into one vibrantly colorful mosaic. That long, painful transition—from broken to whole—began after a traumatic, heart-wrenching miscarriage.

Because of the extreme abuse I suffered as a child, a normal relationship never seemed possible, but, against all odds, I met him . . . a man who changed my life and who I desperately wanted to be with. For two years, we enjoyed a wild, intoxicating chemistry. I thought perhaps he would be my path to recovery from this harrowing childhood, and I became addicted to our seemingly indestructible connection. Then he broke up with me.

We had broken up before, but I had never been so devastated as I was this time, because I knew something was very different—I knew deep down that I was pregnant. I scheduled a doctor's visit for a pregnancy test, but before I could make the appointment, I found myself bleeding horrifically. The moment I saw the placenta, I realized I'd miscarried. I had experienced depression before, but nothing—nothing—could have prepared me for the tunnel of pitch-blackness that was about to engulf me.

I was diagnosed with postpartum depression. Dark and irrepressibly possessive thoughts of suicide controlled my mind. One day in particular, I was crying uncontrollably inside the pink car I had called home when I was younger. Parked on the edge of a cliff, I was only one little push of the pedal from infinite relief. And then something—*it*—hit me. I realized that I had to do something, anything, about whatever *it* was.

After the baby's father and I held a ceremony to bury her spirit, the emptiness that had overcome me didn't seem so empty anymore. Suddenly, my heartache felt purposeful, and I knew that in order to truly clear my mind and spirit, to stop viewing myself as a victim, I had to help those who were even more severely victimized than myself. I heard my baby—Sepulveda, we called her—whispering in my ear to go in her honor. "Go, mama." I decided my destination was Africa.

I planned my trip to travel the world without any extensive thought or research. I was simply following the voice in my heart that was urging me to heal through helping others. When I got to Uganda and began volunteering, I met Kirindi village's traditional midwife,

Mama J; our connection was immediate and intensely powerful. As she was showing me around her maternity clinic, the first thing I noticed were the totally insufficient conditions—many of us Westernized women wouldn't dream of giving birth this way. Still, hundreds of women had come to Mama J for support—oftentimes walking barefoot for miles—to deliver their children without medical supplies on a single twenty-year-old, blood-soaked pad. All of the sudden, the *it* hit me again, and I knew what *it* was. I experienced a clarity I hadn't felt in years . . . if ever.

I remembered my own miscarriage, and like a surging realization of one's calling, I knew my purpose was to help these women deliver their babies safely. It was as if in that moment, all the half-starts and unrequited dreams I'd ever had came together seamlessly to create one clear mission that glowed neon on the wall of my mind. I knew in my heart that I was divinely put through these trying situations in my past—abuse, addiction, poverty, heartache, grief, depression, the loss of my child—in order to find joy in this remote Ugandan village.

Two years later, I returned to Uganda bearing medical supplies and began the process of building what is now known as the OneMama Clinic with Mama J at its core. And it didn't stop there. OneMama aims to get birthing supplies to all the Mama J's of the world so they can help prevent HIV transmission by simply cutting the umbilical cord properly and having clean birthing grounds. OneMama is dedicated to making these clinics self-sustaining, so that their positive effects can be felt for generations. We even assist with family planning, as well as provide tradecraft and agricultural education for impoverished woman who live on less than $1 a day and must deliver babies with those limitations.

It didn't take long for me to realize, so gratefully, that OneMama *was* my child. If I could nurture it, give it a proper environment to grow based on its needs, and provide it useful knowledge, then I would be a mother to something the way I'd always wanted to be—and the way I thought I'd missed out on because of my miscarriage. OneMama made me a mother to thousands, and that has truly been the miracle of my life. I no longer define myself as a victim. I am a motivational speaker, a social entrepreneur, and a catalyst for change—with an annual income of *joy*!

The truth is, I have every excuse not to be a person who can function in the world. Studies show that children who come from backgrounds like mine overwhelmingly succumb to lives of addiction or resort to suicide. Have I failed at times? I sure have. The horrendous parts of my childhood are still parts of me. But they are only small pieces of the whole, beautiful, weathered mosaic that is my life. Up close, the pieces may not fit together seamlessly—there are jagged edges and holes to be sure. But when I take a step back, I see the substantive story I've woven—made of pain and pride. If I ever lose sight of that, I keep an image in my head of God moving me around like His chess piece—and though at times His actions may not make sense, I remember He has a plan.

Knowing that I have been able to transmute all the negativity in my past into a source of positivity is my constant motivation. Giving less fortunate women a way to heal has healed me too. Though at one time it felt impossible, I ultimately found a way to get my power back—and I emerged from a very dark hole into a place of profound love and light. The mental torment I endured ended up giving me an unshakeable inner peace. I created a way for women who have been silenced to use their voices, and that birthed a method of hope—one that is always fertile.

I gave birth to a baby that I never knew I could have.

Siobhan Neilland

Passionate about making a difference in the world, Siobhan Neilland founded OneMama to show those in need that they matter and are loved. Inspired by a Ugandan midwife, Mama J, Siobhan found her calling helping people in desperate conditions empower themselves to create change. Siobhan has taken her keen business sense and turned OneMama into a model that will create self-sustainability in each community it supports worldwide. Siobhan also founded ShaBoom Products & Cosmetics as a long-term funding venture for the OneMama organization and to show people you can look beautiful with natural products and change the world while you do it!

The Water Tower

Kelly Parichy Bennett

When my daughter Christy was four years old, she was convinced—without reservation—that there was a man living on top of the water tower we drove past to get to her preschool each day. The tower was easily 100 feet high and had been created before our eyes over the course of the school year. Teams of men had first fused the tower together along raw, rusty metal seams and then painted its base and giant bulbous tank white from the bottom up. We had been mesmerized each day by the men dangling from safety wires as they worked to erect the tower. I had even explained to Christy how the wires were kind of like seatbelts that kept the men safe from falling, as the job they were doing was quite a dangerous one. So, when the tower was finally completed, I was a bit surprised (to say the least) that Christy began to claim there was a man actually living up there.

The tower stood within view of the school's parking lot, and as we waited for our turn in the drop-off line, we used to have regular discussions about the man. "Look, you can see his bed—I wonder if he was cold last night," Christy would remark. Or, "I hope the man didn't get too wet when it rained this morning." Even when I would challenge her and question the feasibility of a man setting up a home on the tower considering its height and metal makeup, she remained firm. Tightly strapped in her car seat, straining to see movement from the tower, she'd declare, "Well, I hope he has a nice day." As we progressed closer to leaving her with her teachers, she would often go quiet, seemingly awaiting a wave or a glimpse of the man partaking in his daily routine, perhaps, I thought, in return for her determination to stand by his existence.

Those drop-off times were the worst times for me because I knew that after I left Christy, I'd have to drive home past the hospital next door to the preschool. The hospital where earlier in the school year, I had lost Christy's little sister, Hayley, when the umbilical cord got wrapped around her arm and she was stillborn. That was just five weeks before my mother passed away from pancreatic cancer. The road would wind away from the school and draw me past the parking place where I had left the car the night I thought Hayley would arrive, the night I found out the only heartbeat they could register on the monitor was mine. After each drop-off, I would have to avert my eyes and head the car towards home, juggling my thoughts and emotions between the sheer missing of my baby, the pining for my mother's soothing reassurances that it would all be all right, and the aching for my mom herself when I needed her most.

The mental gymnastics surrounding that time in my life felt like the training a real gymnast might endure for the Olympics. Anyone who has borne grief can imagine what a struggle it is to put these events into perspective. The double whammy of losing both a child and a parent in such a short amount of time really tried me and challenged my very faith in life. Added to that struggle, as a mother of a young child, I was wrenched with the worry of managing my sorrow within the confines of Christy's world, which I wanted unscathed, even as I shared with her the truth of what had happened and the impact it was having on our family. As it sometimes happens, however, in amongst the very thing I was worrying about, I found just what it was I needed to steer me clear of the precipice of dark thoughts and the melancholia of my losses. I discovered how the wonder, delight and sheer fun of the preposterous thinking of a four-year-old could lighten my way and lead me through to survive with my world intact.

Although I was at first perplexed and then bemused by it, I eventually found Christy's persistent, vivid conviction about something I could not see myself to be deeply heartening. I began to consider her unadulterated, unwavering faith in the man and the fact that he would make a home upon a steel water tower. With each reference to the man and the certainty with which Christy would elaborate on the details of his life, I got more and more drawn in. She would explain how he made fires to cook his food from breaking off the tips of the trees encircling the tower, and to clean up he would, of course, swim in the water tank for his bath. She even confirmed he did not have a television: he did not need one as he preferred to lie on his back to watch the stars, making wishes on the shooting ones. According to Christy, he never seemed to leave the tower, and his favorite activity was to watch over those below.

Her vivid descriptions and firm faith in the man were contagious. So much so that I began to truly contemplate his reality, asking myself, *Why not? Why shouldn't someone stake their claim on the curved mesa of a water tank plunk in the middle of Mooresville, North Carolina?* In fact, I reckoned that with Lake Norman lying nearby, the man must have found the sunsets over the water alone well worth the difficulty of setting up home so high.

With each school run, I discovered the easing of my heart as I eventually joined in on trying to catch a glimpse of the man from the corner of my eye. In the end, I did not challenge Christy anymore and instead rejoiced at the capacity of her faith—that it could be so strong as to make us believe in both the possibility of a man living on top of a water tower and the possibility of someone looking down, watching over us, and maybe even caring about us as much as we cared about him. Looking back, I find it no coincidence that where I thirsted most for faith, I discovered a way to quench my need through the innocence, imagination, and insight of my young daughter. I know some say that people can be vessels sent to guide us through the troubles of our lives. I believe children, our own and all those of the world, can be some of the best guides. Like the water tower, they can refresh us, cleanse us, sustain us, and inspire us to drink on.

Kelly Parichy Bennett

Kelly Parichy Bennett grew up in a family of five children, in which sharing was both a necessity and a way of life. She found the giving spirit woven not only through hand-me-downs but also in the way her family shared its love and stories. Her childhood and that of her own three children inspire her worldview and her writing. Kelly's commentary, *To Mother from Daughter*, aired on NPR (2005). She's currently collating her reflections from a year of chemo (*Chiquita Banana Lady Gets Cockapoo Curls*) from her home in Kent, England.

Grace

Shannon Lell

*G*race.

It was the word the yoga instructor asked us to think about moments before starting our ninety-minute practice on Thanksgiving morning. This annual Thanksgiving class is free, but donations are accepted to benefit a nonprofit organization, and this year it was Yoga Behind Bars. Yoga Behind Bars is a charity that teaches yoga and meditation to the incarcerated population. A representative spoke about the amazing work they do, and how teenage girls in particular are benefiting the most from their efforts.

I sat in the back of a police car twice when I was teenage girl. The first time was for underage drinking, and the second was for trespassing. Not my finest moments, but neither were most of my teenage years. The years from age fourteen to nineteen are my "lost years." Back then I struggled mightily with depression, anxiety, and impulsive, reckless behavior. I spent all those years hating myself for no particular reason, and at least that many *more* hating myself for the things I did while I was hating myself.

How I wish someone had taught me yoga as a teenager.

The word *grace* unfurled in my mind like my mat under my feet. The first thing I thought was *redemption*, followed closely by *forgiveness*. *There but for the grace of God go I.*

I met God for the first time when I was sixteen.

Early in life, religion was a concept no one told me to seek, and yet I found it anyway. Perhaps more accurately, *it* found *me*. I started going to Wednesday night youth group at a local Presbyterian church when I was nine, not because of my parents but because my best friend was going. For four years, the two of us attended weekly classes, sang in the children's choir once a month, and went to weeklong camps in the summer. But a Christian I was not.

In high school I attended Christian-based Young Life meetings. I even hosted one at my parent's house. This had less to do with Jesus and more to do with socializing. When I was sixteen, I raised enough money to attend a weeklong Young Life camp in Colorado—also for the socializing. It was at this camp, perched on a rooftop high above a blacked-out canyon under a starry Colorado sky, that I met God for the first time.

My modus operandi was to be where the party was—it was always my No. 1 objective. So too were the fun activities listed on the brochure, like rappelling, rafting, and horseback riding. Because that's the deal with these things—they attract you with fun and then slip in Jesus-talk at the end, which you must sit quietly and tolerate.

Each night after dinner the whole camp came together, and the main preacher dude stood up to tell us everything we needed to know about being saved. I was skeptical but also superstitious and naive, so I listened, restlessly. At sixteen I hadn't made up my mind on all things existential and I had yet to find proof of a God. But if you had asked me back then, I would have said, *"Of course* Jesus is my personal savior," you know, just in case the rapture was coming, lest I be perceived as a social opportunist with no intention of saving my soul from eternal damnation.

One night, the preacher dude said something that penetrated deep into my thick, self-assured adolescent brain. He said (paraphrased), "The only thing you have to do to have a relationship with God is ask. It's that simple. Ask, and thou shall receive." *Oh really?!* I replied to my snarky, skeptical, brooding sixteen-year-old-self.

That night, I took his bold assertion and made it my personal test of God. I'd ask him, all right. I'd ask as honestly and bravely as I knew how. I'd ask just as the preacher dude said I should ask, and God had better bring it or I was taking one step closer toward eternal damnation. That's what I remember thinking.

Each night after the Jesus-talk was over, we were sent out into the darkened camp to find a quiet place to reflect and/or pray on what we had heard. I usually headed for the small concrete slab in the middle of camp designated for the underage smokers—us sinners on the accelerated path to hell. But on that particular night, I chose to climb on top of a building that sat on the edge of a cliff. The cliff dropped off into a large gulch with mountains stretching up either side like sentinels to a cave. The stars dusted the sky like perfectly spilt glitter. I looked down into this deep, black, V-shaped gulch and up into this bright, celestial sky and I asked, quietly.

Then I listened, openly.

My whole body responded in a way that I have never forgotten. An abnormal peace washed over me—abnormal because at that time, I had no awareness of what peace felt like. It felt as if a tuning fork had struck the deepest part of me and resonated with the pitch-perfect sound of Universal Truth. I understood, without thinking, that this feeling was real, and it was a hint of the Truth I'd been seeking my whole young life. I also understood, without thinking, that on a deep, intuitive level I was loved—that I would always *be* loved and watched over—that even in my darkest hours, I would never be alone.

What I felt in that moment is what I call God.

It is only in hindsight that I can interpret what happened that night. Now I understand that it was the divine combination of my intention and the stillness of time and my mind, along with the openness of my listening heart, that allowed me to not only *hear* God speak—but to *understand* what God was saying. I sobbed. I knew I was changed forever. It would take years before I truly understood how, and years before I would feel it again.

I feel it now each time I go to yoga.

In this special Thanksgiving Day class, we sang "Amazing Grace." *Grace.* The one thing I have been offered so many times no matter how much I have failed. That thought and the cacophony of our voices together in that yoga studio overwhelmed me. The tears, just two of them, came so quickly that they did not linger on my lashes but leapt from each eye and fell straight to my mat. My mat. My church. My holy place. My rooftop perched high on a cliff side below a starry sky.

It has taken years to realize that I have been given, and forgiven, so much in my life not because I asked for it—but because I learned to open up and listen to what God was trying to teach me. I have come to realize that the answers to all my questions, the calming of all my fears, the peace I long for every day, lay there quietly in the silence of my open heart. It is that voice that I am still learning to follow. Always.

Silence: how sweet the sound, that saved a wretch like me.

Shannon Lell

Shannon Lell was ceremoniously pushed off a tall corporate ladder in 2010. Since then, she has become a writer, editor, and mother of two. She writes introspective essays on her blog, shannonlell.com, and studies literary fiction at the University of Washington. She is working on her first novel.

Ribbons, by Karen Young

Artist Statement:
Along a path of a thousand "what if"s lives transition. It is a bridge that takes us from one place to another. Some believe our transitions are meant to be, for a universal goal of goodness, light, love, learning, and teaching. On that path there can be anxiety, fear, and worry. We have all experienced this.

But as those feelings live there, there are others that may be hidden from plain view. The path of transition also holds wonder, curiosity, and positive anticipation. The level during change and transition can be a time to heal, to contemplate, to forgive, and to seek resolutions. If you believe that transition will lead to transformation, then you are already halfway there.

Let something inside of you rise. Let it bring reassurance in your stage of transition that there is something inexplicably meant to be for you, and it is within your reach.

It will come when you are ready for it to exist, and when others are ready for it to manifest. The other side of the bridge is your land but is shared by others as well. Sometimes it is not all within our complete control. But our perceptions during our personal journey in transition are ours to create. Your path is walked to take you where you know you belong.

You know where you belong. If it doesn't come to be, then there is another dream. The experience of transition can feel a bit longer at times, but change will come. Even when you get there, there will still then be another path to eventually take, but know that it will bring even more light. The path or bridge can be weak, jagged, or full of nothingness. We have all been in limbo at one point in our lives. The path can also be made of light ribbons that soar up and touch your next dream, and the ones after. They can connect you even when your next level has not arrived yet. Curiosity and positive anticipation are these ribbons that connect you from one land to another.

Karen Young

While attending the Rhode Island School of Design, Karen Young discovered the joy that the arts can bring children who suffer from illness. She earned a master's degree in art psychotherapy with a focus on pediatric medical art therapy, and she had the honor of working at the Children's Hospital of Philadelphia and the Hospital for Sick Children in Washington, DC. She was able to utilize her art therapy with children afflicted with serious illnesses to decrease the emotional trauma they experience when diagnosed with cancer, AIDS, cardiac problems, motor vehicle accident injuries, and physical abuse. The current chapter of her life is dedicated to her family, storytelling, creating art, and fundraising in Marin County, California.

Transition Point, by Susan Schneider

Artist Statement:

This piece—"Transition Point," an abstract spiritual landscape—was inspired by the idea that when we reach for spiritual help, the help comes. I tried to imagine visually what that might look like. The pink on the horizon represents heart, and the white represents an opening. Through our seeking and heartfelt gaze into the horizon of our world, when we need it most, I imagined a point of transition opening up to connect our space and time to a higher space and time. I saw this connection as a spiraling gold transition point where higher influences can connect more clearly with our world and then comfort and guide us. This transition point might look like a ripple or spiral in the fabric of our space and time—as if somebody touched a body of water that is perpendicular to our horizon. Thus the two perspective points are shown here: looking straight out to the horizon in our world and looking into the spiraling surface of a higher dimension—as if you are looking at the surface of a pond.

Susan Schneider

Susan Schneider is a native Californian and an artist who continually finds herself captivated by the natural beauty of the San Francisco Bay Area and beyond. After being introduced to oil painting at a young age, she went on to pursue studies at UCLA in their design program. She received her bachelor of arts in graphic design from California College of the Arts in 1989. After years of design work and only painting in her spare time, in 2010 she was able to transition to full-time painting. To see more of Susan's work, please go to schneiderartworks.com.

Section Six

Power and Independence

Cowboy Boots, Crawfish, and Courage

Katrina Anne Willis

Our sweet, worried server brought me a tissue.

"Ma'am?" she asked. "Are you OK, ma'am? Can I git you anything? Some sweet tea, maybe?" The buttery drawl of her Southern concern made me hiccup in distress.

And we hadn't even begun unpacking.

"She's fine," my twelve-year-old son said, while the other three kids rolled their eyes in embarrassment. "We just moved."

"It's a good place to live, right?" I asked, wiping my nose and trying to smile the way I imagined a mature and well-adjusted forty-one-year-old might.

"Yes, ma'am, I love it here," she said. "It's a real good place to raise kids."

But is it a real good place to raise adults? That's what I truly wanted to know. It seemed selfish to ask, though. More selfish, even, than unleashing my emotions in our new hometown burger joint while my kids bore reluctant witness.

In my four decades on this earth, the only permanent terrain I'd known was Indiana and her rolling cornfields. I was born and raised in Greenfield, met my husband at our small town high school, studied at IU and Ball State, and moved to Zionsville to raise a family. For ten years thereafter, we birthed babies and sent them to school and built houses and grew roots and made friends and played basketball and drank lots of wine with our neighbors.

And then.

Chris finished his doctorate, decided he no longer wanted to be— could, emotionally, no longer be—a high school principal, and was offered a professorship in Starkville, Mississippi. We'd never even set foot in the state. Most of those we surveyed hadn't, either.

But in a whirlwind of excitement and promise and adventure, we sold the house, sedated the dogs, kissed everyone good-bye, and headed South in true Clampett-esque fashion.

It was a big move, a colossal change. And when the newness began to wear off, I felt as if I'd ripped a bandage from a wound that was not yet healed. It was raw and weepy and in need of some Neosporin to combat the impending infection.

On their first day of school, my uniform-clad kids marched nervously past armed security guards like little Midwestern soldiers. They laughed and cried and giggled nervously and missed home and made new friends. I was amazed by the way they embraced their journey with strength and tenacity.

I wished their fortitude would rub off on me.

But instead, I ached for my Hoosier family and friends with such intensity, I thought my heart might actually split in two. It seemed easier, almost, to keep half a heart in Starkville and return the other half to Indy. I jumped in the Tahoe and drove ten hours home every time someone sneezed. My mom needed me, my tried and true friends needed me, my husband needed me, my kids needed me. There were months—long, wearying hours upon days upon weeks—that I straddled four states: one foot in Indiana, one in Mississippi. I tried to make a new home for my kids in the South while holding on to something that no longer existed up north. It was impossible and devastating and necessary.

Moving is hard. There is no way around it. It's physically and emotionally exhausting, it's mentally taxing. There are unknown roads to traverse, grocery store idiosyncrasies to navigate, new friendships to forge, school dynamics to figure out, social circles to build, trust to establish. For about a year, I didn't do any of it well.

"This is my two-year vacation," I told Chris. "We'll stay for twenty-four months, and then we'll reevaluate." There was no need to dip my toes very deeply into the Southern water when my mind landed safely on that halfway-in-between compromise.

So we tried all the BBQ joints and we traveled down to the Delta. We explored the Blues Trail and we sipped a bit of moonshine. We saw eagles and alligators and enough dead armadillos to last a lifetime. The kids learned to say "Yes, ma'am" and "No, sir," and every once in a while, a little "y'all" slipped from the tips of their tongues.

But living in perpetual limbo is not sustainable, not when you're growing kids and building characters and nurturing independence. You can't live half a life and expect to be whole.

Little by little, I reached out to some new friends—not to replace the old ones, but to stretch my heart and open my arms. I thought every day about a single sentence my friend Alexis had spoken when I first told her Chris had accepted the MSU position: "I'm so excited for all those Starkville women who get to be your friends now too!" That's what drove me, what motivated me, what made me get out of my pajamas every once in a while and make an effort.

This journey has most definitely been one step forward and two steps back the entire way. On a Sunday, I might feel brave and settled and ready to take on the world. Then Monday knocks at my window with its slow Southern pace and its smell of fried catfish, and I crawl under the covers and back into the fetal position.

But there is something that happens in the spaces in between. In Indiana, I was embraced by loud, loving, laughing friends and devoted family. Our Indy lives were big and bustling and full of noise. In Mississippi, we settled into a silence we'd not previously known. We played family games, rented movies together, read books side by side on the couch.

In Indiana, I'd defined myself by my family, my friends, my calendar, and my busyness. I'd expertly juggled jam-packed weeknights and overcommitted social calendars: basketball, softball, lacrosse, community theatre, book clubs, black-tie events, neighborhood gatherings, and birthday parties. In Mississippi, all that was stripped away and I was left with me, with my beautiful kids, with my beloved husband.

In Indiana, I was worried about how others saw me.

In Mississippi, I finally saw myself.

I began to appreciate the gifts I'd been given—my pen, my humor, my sensitivity, my ability to love wholeheartedly and with reckless abandon. And I let go of what I thought was important—my accomplishments, my social circles, my home decor, and the balance in my checkbook.

There is a method to our universe of madness. This I truly believe. I am here, sweating in the South, packing on deep-fried pounds, because there was something for me to discover in Starkville, some essential nugget of knowledge that had successfully eluded me in my Hoosier home.

Wherever our journey takes us next, another lesson awaits. This time, I'm ready to learn it, to lean into it, to appreciate its unique gifts.

This moment is the one in which I choose to live.

It is, after all, the only one that matters.

Katrina Anne Willis

Katrina Anne Willis is the author of *Table for Six: The Extraordinary Tales of an Ordinary Family*, based on her *Indy's Child Magazine* blog. In May 2013, she was selected as an essayist in Indianapolis's inaugural *Listen to Your Mother* show. She was named a 2011 Midwest Writers Fellow for her current novel, *Parting Gifts*; was a finalist in the 2012 Notes & Words Essay contest; was a 2012 "America's Next Author" short story contest finalist and anthology feature; and was named a 2012 Circle of Moms "Top 25 Book Author Mom." Katrina's favorite sound is the uninhibited laughter of friends over a shared bottle of red wine.

The Sound of Woof

Janice L. Green

Entering the World of Dog at age sixty-four—for the very first time—was a sign of something, but what? For two years I'd been turning the pages of dog books populating the best-seller lists and asking friends about their dog-owning experiences. I pondered, I imagined, I fretted—knowing that a rescued canine would be a totally different experience from my lifetime of feline companionship—that independent, aloof, self-assured, purring World of Cat I'd inhabited since I was a child. But none of that answered my question: Why a dog, now?

I treaded in that eddy of uncertainty and indecision until one midsummer evening when I was sipping a beer with my Colorado neighbor, Liz Andreas. Liz is not just an animal lover but possesses a special knack of intuitive communion with horses, dogs, and cats. She also works for the Humane Society in Pagosa Springs. That evening, a couple of weeks before I was to return to my Texas home after a writing sabbatical in my mountain cabin, Liz said rather matter-of-factly, but with lots of forethought, "Janice, I think I've found the perfect dog for you."

Uh-oh. 'Twas time for me to put up or shut up, a phrase echoing out of my East Texas childhood—an ultimatum issued by my parents decades earlier whenever I faced a challenge with equivocation.

My life was already full with winding down my career as a divorce attorney and tiptoeing into the life of a writer. It was a time of major identity shifts and percolating priorities. Yoga was keeping my mind and body agile, yet I hadn't escaped those creeping physical pangs that naturally accompany the stacking of years—more of which were behind me than ahead of me. Nevertheless, I believed those facts were not a deterrent but an invitation to dance with the new and adventurous. My sentiment was shared and researched by Sara Lawrence-Lightfoot, author of *The Third Chapter*, Eric Erikson's moniker for the stage of development between ages fifty and seventy-five. She described this period as one of enrichment, characterized by wisdom and reflection.

Pasha was about two when a gentleman dropped him off at the Humane Society—he had been found frantically wandering around a mountain community, emaciated and covered in burrs. When Liz first laid eyes on Pasha, she intuited his specialness, which was why she kept him in her office rather than in the kennels with the other rescued dogs. For three months she nurtured him, trained him, and revived his spirit, until that evening of her casual quip to me. A few days later, Pasha and I met, fell in love, and immediately became inseparable.

Pasha is known as a "mixed breed," formerly identified as a mutt. He has a yellow and cream-colored short coat, a suggestion of white angel wings striping down and around his shoulders, brown eyes, and blond lashes that look as though they're encircled with dark brown eyeliner. His ears, flopping every which way, belong to an undetermined breed. Pasha modeled adaptability: first to his new summer Colorado home, then on the two-day drive to Texas, and finally settling into his Austin residence that he shares with Modi (short for Modigliani), the black cat I had inherited from my deceased lover, who was an artist.

As I continued trying to find an answer to my "why now?" question, a lunch conversation thirty years before with a wise and dear friend, Helen Graham Park, resurfaced from my long-term memory. It was Helen's eightieth birthday, and I was presumptuous enough to ask her what it felt like to be that age.

"One of the joys of my birthdays is being able to look back on more years past and discern new patterns in my life," she said. I've never forgotten her positive take on aging.

My new era of life with Pasha has been marked by incremental changes:

~ I'm now tethered to a leash one and a half hours a day.

~ I look for the moon's phases, or its shadowy spot, around 10:00 p.m. every night.

~ I easily ignore the myriad of squeaky toys that litter my home.

~ I've rediscovered my old and comfy cotton turtleneck sweaters, which are perfect for walking Pasha on chilly mornings. Those rarely worn sweaters have inhabited my closet for years, defying my annual Goodwill purge.

~ At night, I willingly step over a stack of dog bedding to climb into bed.

~ I've met neighbors who have lived in my 'hood longer than my 20+ years and have enjoyed seeing their seasonal gardens bloom, all with Pasha by my side.

~ I no longer lose my balance when Pasha dances and pirouettes in my path.

~ When a trembling dog awakens me during a thunderstorm, I gladly pet his furrowed brow and console his fears, like a parent calming a frightened child who races into the parent's bed when thunder claps.

~ Tending to Pasha's dietary needs reminds me to down my daily C, B, calcium, and baby aspirin. After all, I want to stay healthy for him.

~ My home is alive with the Sound of Woof when strangers approach or the deer appear with newborn fawns on my front deck.

From these incremental changes, a pattern began to emerge in my rearview mirror. For the first time, I realized that love had been a constant theme through all the significant stages and phases of my life—romantic love, love of career, loving friendships, even love that encompassed endings and loss. A new variety of love was defining my life with Pasha—a trans-species love that bonds woman and dog.

Every morning as I try to find the right word for the daily crossword, Pasha jumps on my sofa next to me, flips on his back with his head in my lap, and grins. He's really too big to be a lap dog, but he lives within the joy of habit and eagerly awaits my neck scratches, tummy rubs, and adoring murmurs into his cute, floppy ears. A love-fest starts my days.

Why a dog now, at my age? That illusive answer was now so obvious, so simple. I was receptive and trusting. Perhaps that is the best way to greet change. Adopting Pasha was my way of embracing my Third Chapter and a forty-five-pound mutt all in the same outstretched reach of arms and heart.

Janice L. Green

Janice L. Green, a resident of Austin, Texas, is a nationally recognized family law attorney specializing in late-life divorce. She is the author of *Divorce After 50* (Nolo 2013, 2nd Ed.). After almost four decades in the divorce trenches as a litigator and collaborator, Janice now spends her summers writing in her mountain cabin west of Pagosa Springs, Colorado. She focuses her writing on many experiences later in life, including a love-story memoir. For more information about Janice, go to JaniceLGreen.com.

Word Mountain

Terry Sue Harms

Crossing over from functional illiteracy to the land of the literate has been, for me, like going from the lowest desert to the highest mountaintop—each word a step, each book a mile. My inability to read and write beyond the most elementary levels was a secret shame that I carried until I was in my early twenties—when I read my first book cover to cover. Learning to read has been anything but a straight path, but I've gone from a wrenching dread of reading to holding books as cherished treasures. My bookcase isn't filled with books—they're trophies. I look at them and think, "Wow, I read that."

In my youth, I would declare with great passion, "I hate to read." It was an unapologetic assertion that I flung in the face of anyone who asked. My mind was closed on the subject; I couldn't stand reading, I wasn't ever going to do it, and nobody could make me. I arrived at this position by way of a number of factors. First, I've come to understand that my brain struggles with all of the white space on a page, sometimes referred to as figure-ground assignment or perception. Unlike the majority of readers, I perceive the white background as the foreground, and since we are not taught to read the white shapes, I was lost from the start. Some children use reading to escape, but I was hypervigilant of my surroundings and never felt relaxed enough to slip into a storybook.

I'm often asked, "How did you ever get through school?" The truth is that I did a lot of cheating—plagiarizing every book report, sneaking peeks at others' tests, scribbling minuscule notes wherever I could hide them. Reading-aloud exercises were humiliating. I'd attempt to phonetically puzzle out the words or I'd guess, but more often than not, the display ended with my head on my desk and me in tears. I began kindergarten in 1965—the No Child Left Behind Act was thirty-five years away. I would stagger and lurch to the end of a sentence, but by the time I got there, I would have forgotten the beginning. I never enjoyed the internal payoff that good readers get when their imaginations are engaged and they visualize an author's intention. Despite my failings, I was quiet, polite, and never disruptive; therefore I was passed from grade to grade with very little, if any, mention of my subpar performance. I didn't care terribly about my grades, and anything over an F was satisfactory. One asset I had going for me was that I was a keen observer, and that helped. I wasn't unintelligent; I just couldn't and wouldn't read.

When I was sixteen, my mother died. I needed to get a real job, not the babysitting and house cleaning that I had been doing. This was before California's Proposition 13 passed in 1978, changing the way public schools were financed, so I was able to enroll in beauty college free of charge. I dropped out of high school, lied about my age, and had a friend with adult-looking penmanship forge my admission papers. I tried to get a GED, but failed twice due to my poor reading skills.

Hairdressing was an excellent choice because it's primarily intuitive, not academic. It's learned by watching, not reading. The cosmetology school I attended drilled us daily on what would be expected by the state board in the written portion of the licensing exam; nevertheless, I very nearly failed it when I misread a card that outlined a procedure I was to perform in the hands-on portion of the test. When the proctor suggested that I reread my assignment, I thought it was a trick to see if I would lose confidence. Confused and panicked, I couldn't see my mistake and continued with the wrong application. The second time she came around, she was annoyed. She read the card to me, and in that instant I understood my error, but by then the allotted time was up; all I could do was tell her what I was supposed to be doing. At the end of the day, when the proctor granted me my California State Cosmetology License, she paused before releasing it into my hand and gave me an encouraging wink.

I began working in a very popular salon on College Avenue in Berkeley, California. As my clientele of highly educated people grew—I saw doctors, lawyers, artists, writers, university professors, and students—I began to feel ashamed of my own lack of education. I had gotten a high school diploma through a night school program where good attendance alone gave me passing grades, but I still couldn't and wouldn't read. One day, a customer my age used the word "pathology," and I didn't know what it meant. He was floored when I asked him to explain it to me. He didn't understand how I could not know such a common word. My pride was wounded, and that was the turning point that got me to secretly vow to take a new course.

I went to the library and searched the stacks. With no preferences or understanding of literary genres, I hunted for the biggest book I could find. I wanted a mountain to climb. I checked out *My Many Years*, the autobiography of Arthur Rubinstein—a classical pianist. The book must have been more than two inches thick. Before I got it home, I promised myself that I wasn't going to cheat or pretend. I would read every word, and I wouldn't go on to the next sentence until I was sure I understood the one I'd just finished. It took me months, but I did it. Over time, focusing on the print got easier, and the story became more entertaining.

Next, I went for another fatty, *The Mists of Avalon*—one I could buy and keep. Soon, with pluck and determination, I registered at Contra Costa Junior College. I took remedial English classes and did poorly. My word processor was a godsend for its spelling and punctuation checker, but still, my papers were atrocious. I was so ashamed of all the professor's corrections and red ink that when those early essays came back, I destroyed them. Today, I'm so sorry I did that. I have a world of compassion for the young lady I was back then, struggling so mightily though the mountain of words and reading that is required in college.

It took me eleven years, but today I have a bachelor's degree in English from Mills College in Oakland, California. Furthermore, and a crowning achievement for this hairdresser who hated to read, I wrote and published a novel of my own. Writing *Pearls My Mother Wore*, in many ways, helped me put my dark, illiterate past into the proud light of transformation. My novel is the prettiest trophy in my bookcase.

Terry Sue Harms
Terry Sue Harms lives in Sonoma, California, and has been a practicing hairdresser since 1977. In 1992, at age thirty-two, she received a bachelor's degree in English from Mills College in Oakland, California. In 2005 the writing bug bit her, and for the next four years she, with the help of many, crafted a novel. *Pearls My Mother Wore*, published in 2009, interweaves family dysfunction with forgiveness. When not hairdressing or writing, Terry Sue enjoys hiking and mountain biking with her husband and friends.

Float

Camille Hayes

I learned to swim when I was forty years old. I really don't recommend it. There's a reason why mastering complex motor skills like swimming and bike riding are tasks we assign to children: not only is your body more agile when you're young, you're more flexible psychologically too. You haven't had time yet for thoughts and feelings about yourself to crystallize into anything as brittle as an "ego" or so unyielding as a "self-concept." A self-concept which, if you're a forty-year-old professional, probably doesn't include an image of yourself standing in the shallow end of a pool, surrounded by toddlers in floaties and waiting to be taught something most people learn by age six. Yet there I was. In that moment, I felt my own strangeness so acutely I nearly cried, humiliation mingling with chlorine fumes to sting my throat and shock tears to my eyes.

I'd worked so hard to prevent that moment from ever happening. A lifetime of fibs and evasions—and the strenuous avoidance of pool parties—had all been designed to spare me this reckoning, this instant when I was forced to feel the full weight of my deficiency, of everything I'd failed to do and all that had been denied me. I glared at the colorful decals of smiling baby ducks and fish adorning the walls, inwardly cursing my parents. How had they let this happen? What unholy combination of youth, careerism, and benign neglect had produced this . . . *spectacle* of a grown woman splashing around in a kids' pool? I tallied the childhood moments lost to adult inattention, and they added up to inadvertent recklessness. The world is full of latent menace that only a vigilant love can anticipate; mishap brooks no distraction. Feeling too weighted down with memory to attempt swimming, I moved to leave, just as my swim teacher glided over from the deep end and introduced herself as Lynne.

"How are you?" she asked in a way that said she already knew.

"I'm fine!" I chirped, which was as good an answer as any, because at the time I couldn't have told you how I felt.

To my surprise, swimming came easily. For all my self-consciousness, and despite my conviction that if anyone could drown in three feet of water with a certified lifeguard on hand it would be me, I was doing a serviceable freestyle by the third lesson. Even more surprising was realizing I was fast, skimming so quickly from end to end that Lynne commented on it. "I'm just eager to get out of the pool," I said, but secretly I felt proud. The shoulder muscles I'd sculpted at the gym were finally useful for something besides looking good in tank tops: they were for pulling me through water. It was a revelation.

Things progressed smoothly until the fourth week, when Lynne announced, "Today we'll learn to rest." I smiled and said that resting had never been my strong suit, and I thought I was joking, until she rolled me over onto my back and we discovered I couldn't float.

Everyone has different proportions of fat, muscle, and bone that combine to make them either more or less buoyant. All we could figure is that I must have iron deposits instead of bone marrow, because just lying flat in the pool, limbs suspended, was uncommonly hard for me; I simply went under. You know that game kids play where they cross their legs and sink below the surface and pretend they're having an underwater tea party? We tried that once. Like most people, Lynne sank partway and bobbed a foot or two above the bottom, her natural buoyancy holding her up. But I descended all the way down until I touched the pool floor and there I sat, unbudging, drinking my imaginary tea alone. When I pushed up to the surface, Lynne and I marveled at my body's dense gravity, joking that at least I'd never have to worry about osteoporosis. We laughed, but I could tell she was slightly shocked. "I've never seen anyone sink like that," she said.

Trying to float uncovered a layer of fear that swimming hadn't exposed. The few times I actually managed it, I found that I loathed the *sensation* of floating. I hated drifting haphazardly rather than controlling where I went; I felt disoriented from staring at the ceiling, losing track of where I was in the pool. Was I about to hit the wall? Had I floated into the deep end? Time and again I'd stand up after just a few seconds, frantically insisting I couldn't bear not knowing what was happening around me. I didn't understand what caused my terror of drifting, but I knew that it ran deep. I felt I'd rather sink than stay afloat without a rudder, vulnerable to invisible dangers. Once Lynne observed, "It seems like you're very protective of your body, like you're on guard." That insight, that I was *protecting my body*, impaled me like a knife point, sliced me open to reveal a jumble of images and perceptions that my mind had, wisely, kept hidden. I broke down and sobbed for twenty minutes. The lesson was over for that day.

All kinds of unpleasant things happen to us when we're kids, mostly without our permission: vaccinations, scary swim classes, weird vegetables—unwanted things, which are imposed on us by grownups whether we will them or not. Mostly, we pass through such trials with no lasting harm done. But there are some impositions for which there is no precedent, and no way for a child to understand. If, like me, you were unlucky, you may have met someone, perhaps posing as a caretaker but with an altogether different reason for wanting to be near you. If you were unlucky that way, and unwanted things were imposed on you, you may have found that the experience washed over you like a wave and seemed almost to disappear, unable to fix itself as memory in a mind that couldn't fully comprehend it. What I learned when I was floating is that nothing disappears. The experiences our minds can't grasp retreat back into the bodies that bore them, where the knowledge is preserved for us to find another time. Sometimes traces of these events reveal themselves in our personalities; in my case, as a pronounced dislike of being told what to do, and that peculiar fear of floating, an odd corporeal stubbornness, a determination to stay where I put myself and not be moved.

Eventually I did learn to float, but I'll never be good at it. What comes naturally to others will always be an effort for me, a process I have to monitor to keep myself from going under: *if you're sinking, take a breath, relax the neck, and lift the belly.* It's cumbersome, but there's something about it I love. There's a lot to be said for that kind of conscious effort: namely, that it doesn't let you take anything for granted. If you notice when you're sinking, then you'll always know when it's time to rise, and when you finally find yourself aloft, you'll know exactly how you got there. These days, I could float for hours.

Camille Hayes

Camille Hayes is a domestic violence advocate, author, newspaper columnist, and blogger, covering politics and women's issues at her blog, Lady Troubles (ladytroubles.com). In addition to her advocacy work, Camille has experience in teaching and journalism. She holds a bachelor of science in psychology and a master of arts in English. When she's not busy complaining about injustice, Camille likes to cook, make jam, hike, and kayak near her home in Northern California.

Tea and Toast

Jessica Braun

We got married on Independence Day. Our friend, Father Peter, gave a homily that felt like a marriage mission statement: "This is why you were created: to make a new creation; to make something different." I basked in the light of the day, encased in hope and possibility. I was barely twenty-seven, Paul was six years my senior. His magnanimous personality made me feel safe, cared for . . . lucky. This man—smart, charismatic, and kind—had chosen me. Without question, I left my roots in New Jersey to live with him in Pennsylvania. Suddenly, my life path seemed clear. All I had to do was say, "Yes."

By marrying Paul, I joined a large and loyal band of Philadelphia Catholics all living within a ten-mile radius. Before my first family gathering, Paul turned to me and said, "Put on your helmet." The Brauns are competitive partiers. Shouting "Beer Boy!" draws a young nephew to replenish your drink. They talk over each other and eat off other people's plates—a practice called "brauning." Every event—from funerals to First Communions—focuses on good, raucous fun. Either you are in, or you are in their way.

I am one of two girls. My mom is a teacher and my dad an accountant. Wearing fanny packs and plastic ponchos, we spent school vacations touring Civil War battlefields. When Paul *brauned* a dinner roll off my grandmother's plate on Thanksgiving, she practically choked on her turkey. "You were raised in a library," Paul says, "and I was raised in a bar."

By the time I became a Braun, family traditions were firmly established: Oktoberfest, high school football tailgates, and Sunday dinners peppered our calendar. Paralyzed by awkwardness, I kept to the sidelines as my sisters-in-law worked the room like professionals, juggling platters of "ham sammies" and potato salad while sipping cosmopolitans.

The Brauns find any reason to summon the troops for a keg and schnitzel platter, including my daughter's christening. I was content to keep the event low-key, yet suddenly I was hosting the Beer & Bratwurst Baptism of 2010. Washing the dishes in the safety of the kitchen, I listened to the party roll on into the night, punctuated by laughter and the telling of old stories. Surrounded by people, I was oddly alone, an immigrant in a foreign world.

This world was created by Paul's parents: a sassy South Philly girl and sweet North Philly guy who met at a dance at St. Boniface Parish. They grew up in a world of densely packed row homes, where siblings slept head-to-foot in the same bed. Their dream was to plant a family tree with deep roots and arms just long enough to reach Atlantic City.

This is why you were created: to make a new creation; to make something different. Through the years, Father Peter's words would resurface from the dark corners of my mind. As much as I loved my new family, I began to feel consumed by them. I was lost in my own marriage. I wanted to be Paul's partner but had settled for being an appendage, an accessory to his former life. Once a passionate person full of strong opinions, I began to shrink—first emotionally, then physically—when for two years I stopped eating. It was a little-girl response to grown-up problems, a silent but steely rebellion from the trappings of a pre-assembled life. Starvation was my way of communicating what I could not say: "No," and on a deeper level, "Help." But all I did was build a cage with stronger bars than the one I was already in.

Even in the foggy depression that accompanies anorexia, the light of hope and possibility would break through in brief moments of clarity. In one of those rare but grace-filled moments, I checked myself into a treatment center. Years of therapy later, Paul and I finally answered

Father Peter's call to adventure. We needed to give up the comfort of home in order to create our own. Paul began exploring new career paths, and when opportunity knocked in Boston, he answered.

When we told Paul's parents we were moving, his mother was stunned. "Why? Your family is here!" she said through her tears. But his dad, a man of few words but always the right ones, understood: "No. His family is with Jessie and the girls. They have to do what is best for their family."

And we did. We packed up our house in suburban Philadelphia and moved our family of four to a tiny fishing village on the coast of Massachusetts. We were the Pilgrims boarding the Mayflower, ready to stake our claim in an unknown world.

At first, we embraced the new challenges thrown our way: Paul's new job, a new school, a tiny seaside rental cottage with leaky pipes and dark paneled walls. All summer I ran on the rocky cliffs bordering the ocean, drunk on freedom. Who knew this place existed? How can we be anything but invincible?

But endorphins fade quickly, as does the warm magic of the fleeting New England summer. In October, the angry waves of Hurricane Sandy pounded the sea wall, tossing boulders from the ocean like beach balls. By November, the leaky pipes froze and burst. Icicles hung from the toilet bowl during February's blizzard. I felt hazed by Mother Nature.

Paul travels a lot. A Monday-morning departure coincided with the arrival of a plague-like stomach bug that no amount of Lysol could exterminate. With the girls inside clutching their respective puke buckets, I stood shivering in my snowman pajamas as Paul packed his car.

"We talked about this. This type of stuff was bound to happen," he said, cramming his newly dry-cleaned shirts into the trunk.

"I know, I can handle it," I said, fighting back the nausea percolating in my gut.

After he left, I changed the sheets, retrieved the de-puked stuffed bunny from the dryer, and popped in the *Pinocchio* DVD for the fourth time. I called my mother-in-law.

"Oh, Babe," she said, her familiar Philly accent like a salve on a wound, "I wish I was there to help you. I'd make you some tea and toast." The tenderness in her voice felt like a lifeline thrown just beyond my reach. I hung up, pulled on my rubber gloves, and bent down to wipe the floor of the bathroom.

I had thought about what we would gain as a couple by leaving the pack. I had not considered what we would lose: a place to go when your pipes freeze, someone to drop off Pedialyte when both kids are sick or throw in a load of laundry when the only clothing item not soiled with vomit is a pair of old maternity leggings.

This is what we wanted; we asked for this, I thought, as I leaned against the bathroom door and slid down to the floor. My maternity leggings sagged around my nonpregnant waist; the floor was cold against my skin. I removed the gloves, my hands raw and reeking of bleach. I rested my forehead on my knees and cried. Pinocchio chirped in the background: "I've got no strings, to hold me down."

My strings too had been cut. I sat slumped over—limp and helpless without the well-intended impulses of others to control my actions, to give me shape. Pinocchio learned to inhabit his own skin, to become brave and real. I needed to teach myself how to be a grown-up. It started by allowing myself that moment on the floor—to be consumed by fear and loneliness and the overwhelming feeling of "What the hell are we doing here?" My shoulders shook with choking sobs, crying for all that I had left behind and all that I still yearned to know. I held my knees and rocked myself into a calmer place. My tears subsided, and I sat for a moment and breathed, spent but cleansed. Then I got up, washed my face, and went into the kitchen to make my own tea and toast.

Jessica Braun

Jessica Braun is an aspiring writer, former yoga teacher, and mom to two girls. She does most of her writing on yellow Post-it notes while driving or making dinner, many of which end up stuck to the bottom of someone's sock. She lives by the ocean in Scituate, Massachusetts, with her husband, daughters, and semi-comatose chocolate lab.

Single Mother of the Bride

Jane Ganahl

An engagement dinner for my daughter is winding down. Family members embrace each other before heading forth exuberantly into the night air, lifted by the tangible evidence—the sweet opals-and-diamond heirloom ring Erin now sports on her left hand—of true love. An elderly aunt turns to me, the mother of the future bride, hugs me tightly, and whispers in my ear, "I'm sure there's another ring in *your* future, and that your own day will come again."

"God," I blurt out with a chuckle, "I hope not!"

My aunt pulls back, her smile fading, and I catch Erin's eye nearby. She shakes her head and stifles a grin. She knows that there is no greater joy for me than to see her headed to the altar with a wonderful man; she also knows that I have no such desire for myself.

No, I'll never marry again. And I'll have a fabulous life anyway.

I write this with a smile, pleased that after bouts of feeling bereft at being single, I can finally—with midlife in full swing—lay claim to this truth: I am happier this way.

What has changed since my forties? Since my second divorce and the subsequent self-esteem implosion that caused me to incessantly check the schedule for the next bus to the altar? And test-drive man after man after man for marital suitability? Did I become bitter? Do I hate men now?

Not at all.

It's simple, really: I got older. I'm now at an age—Gail Sheehy's "Age of Mastery"—when self-awareness finally trumps societal expectations. When you can own your weaknesses without apologizing for them. When you take the dreams of a giddy youth and hang them on the wall in a pretty frame that honors what they meant to you, even though that meaning is gone.

Take men, for example. Despite my affection for the species, I have let go of all fantasies surrounding them: that they can fix my messy life, or make me brilliantly happy. And in fact, I've concluded that I'm happier without one. At least, the *husband* kind of man.

I know this flies in the face of family values; I know most of the world thinks I should be hitched. But I've been there, done that, and these years, I find more joy in nonwifely things: sharing laughs with close women friends, the sea breeze in my face when I walk the bluffs, organizing literary events, feeding the feral cat colony nearby. And yes, watching Erin take flight—even if that flight takes her down the aisle and into a land from which I'm a refugee.

I think part of my alienation from the marriage myth is because I was not a good wife. Sure, I bent over backwards to make sure both husbands were happy and fed and felt cared-for, but my communication skills hovered around fourth grade level, especially when it came to expressing my own needs. I shopped, I cleaned, I cooked—on top of working full-time and taking care of Erin. But unlike my mother, who seemed to find joy in corralling four kids and a husband, I was acutely unfulfilled, resentful that my needs always took a backseat to his bad day or her school play costume—and was rendered mute by the notion that to complain was to betray the family harmony that I tried so hard to foster. As Tina Fey's character in the movie *Date Night* blurts out: "I just wanted to have *one day* that didn't depend on how everyone else's day was going."

I'm sure hundreds of thousands of women who heard that line groaned audibly. And hearing it myself, I felt a pang of painful recognition. Like so many married women who bought into the myth, I bent over so far backward that I finally snapped like a twig with anger and resentment. I sulked and snapped, withheld my sexual self, had crying jags. Both husbands, champions of non-communication themselves, turned away from my relentless unhappiness, and I withered on the vine. If not for Erin's cheerful affections, I'd have died of loneliness.

To quote Germaine Greer, "Many a housewife staring at the back of her husband's newspaper, or listening to his breathing in bed, is lonelier than any spinster in a rented room."

It must be said: in my nearly fifteen years of spinsterhood, I have never been lonely. Frustrated at times, sure. Tired of not having a honey to share the honey-do list on Saturdays, frequently. Wanting a lover to admire my dimples, most surely. Wondering if I was a loser without a man, definitely. But not lonely.

After my split with husband No. 2, I looked around me and realized that *la vida sola* might actually be *fun*. I could dig out those flowered pillows that he hated, play Mozart all day, buy myself flowers for no reason, leave the popcorn bowl until the morning to clean it. I had no one to answer to but myself.

I soon forgot about the quest for husband No. 3 and instead threw myself into becoming an expert single woman. I networked like mad and forged stronger friendships with women upon whom I could depend for great advice, laughs, and hugs. I bought a book about home repair and learned how to replace a vacuum cleaner belt and hang up a hummingbird feeder. I got involved with a cause—a nonprofit literary festival that I now codirect. I didn't stop until I felt like my network was strong, my tools (both physical and emotional) were sharp, and my life was about something bigger than work and men.

Do I have this single life mastered? I don't think that's possible, any more than it is to truly master married life. Every time I think I might be becoming an *enlightened master*, I get thrown a curveball: most recently, a scary downturn in income that makes me wistful that I have no one to share bills with. And when I'm on a project deadline, it would occasionally be so very nice to turn to someone and say, "Can you get dinner tonight, sweetie-pie?"

But that's unlikely to happen anytime soon, so on I sail, sometimes nearly capsizing in the turbulent seas of solo life.

But oh, what joys it also affords! Deciding to ignore Saturday housework in favor of driving down the coast to a flea market, ignoring the healthy ingredients I bought for a spinach salad dinner and having frozen waffles instead, singing to my cats without fear I'll be overheard and teased, having single friends over for Jane Austen movies, saying goodnight to a lover and sending him home because we both sleep better alone.

It's all about savoring the deliciousness of time to oneself at an age in which we want to dabble, follow long-suppressed dreams, and create brand-new ones.

Like being a mother-of-the-bride. Who knew it would be this much fun? Erin has learned from watching me that she could have a lovely life without the white dress and diamond ring. But she is choosing marriage because she chooses her wonderful Jonathan, not because wedded bliss is the only kind.

For that, I am blissful indeed.

Jane Ganahl

Jane Ganahl has been a journalist, author, teacher, editor, and arts producer in San Francisco for thirty years. She is the cofounder and codirector of Litquake, the West Coast's largest independent literary festival. She is also the author of the memoir *Naked on the Page: The Misadventures of My Unmarried Midlife* and editor of the anthology *Single Woman of a Certain Age*. She has contributed essays to five anthologies and written for *Harper's Bazaar, Spirituality & Health, Ladies' Home Journal, Salon, Vanity Fair, Rolling Stone, The Huffington Post,* and many more. She is chronically overcommitted but thrives on chaos.

The Boardwalk

Judy Johnson Berna

We got there early in the afternoon and walked around inside the Nature Center for a few minutes, learning about tadpoles and stroking samples of real beaver fur. Out the large viewing window we noticed a beautiful boardwalk that led to a pond. Our four children were out the door in a flash, ready to see what kinds of treasures were waiting on the other end of that walkway. I considered going along but knew from the ache in my foot that I had used up all my steps for the day.

It didn't seem to be a big decision when I made it. It was not the first time I'd been left out of a big adventure, and I suspected it wouldn't be the last. My left foot had never allowed me to have the active life I craved. From the time I was a child, I'd learned that when life hands you a deformed foot, your expectations must change. Sometimes you get left behind.

Jack and the kids found the entrance to the boardwalk, and I found the outdoor porch overlooking it. My plan had been to sit in one of the large Adirondack chairs and soak in the beautiful day, such a treat after months of late spring snow.

But then I heard little voices. My children's voices. "Bye, Mommy! Have fun, Mommy! See you soon, Mommy!" I looked over the railing at my family below. Four tow-headed children and their big, strong daddy were headed off on a new adventure, and I was missing out.

At that moment, I realized I was tired of being left behind. As much as I enjoyed some time alone, working on quilting projects or sitting on a pretty deck soaking in the sun, I was missing out on my children's lives. I was missing half the fun.

As my grinning husband and our four little ones ran off to find their adventure, I let my mind wander. For several years I'd been pondering the idea of getting rid of that foot. Just cutting it off and starting over. I kept seeing amputees in the news who could do so much more than I could. But to cut off my own foot—especially a foot that was twisted, but not diseased? Amputations happen after car wrecks and cancer. No one *asks* to have their foot cut off.

I kept telling myself I hadn't tried hard enough to be fit and overcome that tired old foot. For years I'd told myself that if I just lost a little weight, worked out more, or committed myself to stretching out that tight heel cord, I could have a better life. It was my fault that I couldn't keep up with Jack and the kids. There was a lingering doubt that I had not done all I could to make that foot better. And if I had not exhausted all options, I could not have peace about choosing to amputate it.

Then, on that sunny porch behind a beautiful nature center, an amazing thing happened. I believe God had a group of people lined up, just waiting to play their part in changing my mind.

As I simmered in my pity party, I looked below and saw a man walk by with his children. He was a very large man. The kind of large man you might even take a second look at and be amazed that he was hiking at all.

Behind him, right on cue, was a very old woman and her old woman friend. They were strolling along, enjoying nature, and pointing things out to each other along the way.

Next, a very out-of-shape young couple dressed in baggy sweatpants strutted by, hand in hand.

The reality of what I was seeing hit me.

This had so little to do with my fitness level. Had not the old women been able to walk that simple boardwalk? The couple in the sweatpants was enjoying, hand in hand, the beauty all around them. When was the last time I'd walked hand in hand with my patient husband? This had so little to do with the numbers on the scale. The double-sized man had enjoyed the trail with his children. I could lose every pound that kept me from my goal weight and that trail would still be out of my reach.

This had everything to do with the fact that I was born with a birth defect. No surgery was going to make that foot straight and strong. I had exhausted all the other options. I had been optimistic for too long, believing every orthopedist who promised he could make my foot work again.

It might be an overwhelming idea, but if amputation brought me even a hint of a more active life, I was game. If it meant I could have a bionic foot and walk past that heavy man, pass up those old women, and catch up with my children, to see their excited faces discovering the world, then it must be the right move. If it meant I didn't have to miss out on one more minute of their lives—or my own—it was worth doing.

In the glorious sunshine of that spring day, my eyes were opened. I knew what had to be done. I knew the hard choices had lost their sting. It was within my power to get the life I wanted and it was time to stop playing with excuses. My tired old foot had given me enough grief. It was time to get rid of it. It was time to start over.

Twenty-four hours later, I was on the phone, telling my orthopedic doctor I was ready. It was time to schedule my amputation surgery.

Judy Johnson Berna
Judy Johnson Berna is the wife of an archaeologist and mother to four children. She is also an elective amputee. In 2004 she decided to get rid of her deformed foot and start over with prosthetics. Her newly released book, *Just One Foot: How Amputation Cured My Disability*, is an honest glimpse into the life of an active amputee who had to give up her limb to get the life she really wanted. She is a core contributor to GeekMom.com and a writer for the O&P Edge. She currently resides in sunny Colorado with her husband and children.

The Terrifying, Exhilarating Unknown

Kim Bender

Transition. The phase in childbirth when you think you cannot make it. When you want to give up, when you forget what it is that you are doing and want everything to go back to the way it was before you were pregnant. But you can't go back. There is a baby's head between your legs.

Transition. When you get fired from a job and you have no idea what is next, you just know that you can't go back. You don't *want* to go back, but you don't know how to go forward yet—who or what you want to be.

Transition. When you know your relationship isn't right, when you have forced yourself to see things as they *really are*. Maybe you have said things you can't take back. You don't know what is ahead, whether you will be single for the rest of your life, but you know you can't go on with things as they are.

Transition. When your children are supposedly "adults" but still act like adolescents, and you don't see how they can survive on their own in the real world—they don't have any of the life skills that you had at that age—and yet you know you cannot continue to mother the way you always have. Mothering now means (mostly) not mothering.

Transition. When your ovaries are decidedly done with their main job and your hormones are erratic and you are no longer a child-bearer. When your body is shifting beyond your control and your skin is thinning and your hair is graying and the person you see in the mirror is the person you once were and the person you are now and the person you will become all at once, and you don't want to see that because you still feel young inside, you still feel desire, and yet you know everything leads to death.

Transition. The struggle to hang on to life itself when you are at the end of it, and the tunnel of white light is beckoning you. When your organs are quitting but your mind is still alive and commanding your heart to keep beating and your lungs to keep sucking in another breath and your hands to keep grasping at the people and things just beyond your reach, and what you really want is to let it all go but you are so afraid because you have no idea what is on the other side of that white tunnel. Because, probably, you will cease to exist.

I am in transition. Giving up ideas about myself, about my work, about my marriage, about my children. About who I am and what I want. This means forcing myself to open up to who I truly am *now*, and who I want to *become*.

I am fifty-two. I am more than halfway done with this life; that is an undeniable fact. At the same time, I am *only* fifty-two. I am *only* halfway, or maybe two-thirds of the way, into this life, but I still have a whole new set of chapters to write in this long narrative.

Transition mean struggle; it means grasping and clawing and shouting at life for being so cruel and then celebrating the unexpected gifts that lie on the other side of that struggle. Transition means allowing myself the time to grieve the losses, to stay in bed for a day (or the better part of a month), to feel what it means to know someone (or something) is gone forever. To cry out and to mourn, to feel the gaping hole where there was once a piece of me, to feel the edges of that hole, to realize that within that emptiness there is *something else*. That *something* is a place inside where I can go to feel that person who is gone, or that lost childhood, or that job, or that piece of myself that I once shared with someone.

Then, as I become tired of my bed, transition forces me to get up and put on my stretchy pants and go to the gym, to feel the cool air on my face, to push my body, to sweat my tears, to feel my lungs regain their elasticity and my muscles regain their strength. I stretch my tired body, I breathe out all the sadness for the things that are no longer, and

I breathe in the truth of now: the truth of the terrifying, exhilarating unknown.

Kim Bender

Kim Bender is a writer of fiction and screenplays as well as a fundraising and strategic planning consultant specializing in film and media. Kim and her husband of twenty-five years raised their three children in Bolinas, California, a small beach town (population: 1,500), and now live in the mid-Market area of San Francisco. Together they created an artists' live/work community for forty visual, audio, and performance artists and writers, including their three now-grown children.

Mothering Mothers

Lauretta Zuchetti

I should start off by saying that I became a mother long before I gave birth.

I was three and a half years old when my mother left me in the care of a prostitute in the impoverished village of Pavia, Italy. My mother, Pierina, did not travel across the roads of life easily. In turn, neither did I. By the time I was twelve, I had grown accustomed to spending days in isolation with neither heat nor food while my mother's flirtation with alcohol and meth skyrocketed into the most committed relationship she'd ever had. She was frequently inebriated, often delirious, and terminally depressed. I did my best to care for her but I was hopeless. I was lost. I was also determined to find a far less rocky road.

So by the time my daughter Isabella arrived, I had not only secured the benchmarks of success—I'd immigrated to the United States, learned English, French, and Spanish (along with my native Italian), received a master's degree, risen to top sales-executive positions for two of the most acclaimed companies in the world, married a wonderful man, and bought a home—I was tired. No, I was *exhausted*. I was also unwavering in my commitment to raising my daughter under completely different circumstances than I was reared in. She would be comfortable, safe, happy, educated, well fed, and warm. From the first moment I held Isabella in my arms and touched the fragile, pink curve of her ear, I was smitten. I would be unyielding in my decision to give her the best possible life, I promised myself.

Then the inevitable happened. My daughter, my *life*, left for college.

Most parents believe this is a cause for celebration. And yes, I wanted my daughter to go to college, find a fulfilling career, a partner in crime, a home, perhaps children of her own.

I just wanted her to do all of this next door.

Mind you, I'm Italian by birth, and we Italians, I'm convinced, are wired differently. In Italy, kids never leave home—I was the exception. And if they do leave home, they move next door, or, in extreme cases, to the other side of town—which happens to be three kilometers away. Isabella's decision to attend a college not only in a different zip code but what felt like a different time zone was like learning that my next phase in life would be that of a caterpillar. In essence, I would be, well, devolving.

When she left, I didn't allow myself to sink into depression. Instead, I went into Manic Panic Mode. I threatened divorce and left on an extended vacation, where all I did was window-shop for baby clothes and eat grilled-cheese sandwiches. I looked for a new house to buy. I redecorated in bold, offensive colors. I got my advanced scuba certification in Indonesia. I volunteered at the Humane Society, spent weeks researching adopting an infant from Kenya, worked out at the gym until my limbs felt like they would fall off. I. Did. Not. Stop.

Then the frenzy ended, and with it came a torrent of tears. Every time I came home, the silence of the empty space scorned me, and I fixated on cleaning the house and filling the fridge, just in case Isabella made a surprise trip home. I cried every time someone asked me how I was doing. I cried every time I walked into a grocery store and noted that my list was only half as long. I cried when I saw her half-empty box of Honey Bunches of Oats in the pantry. I cried when I walked past the photo I'd taken of her on the beach in Mexico when she was five. I cried when our waiter at the Italian café down the street got my order wrong, when I received a parking ticket, when we were out of milk. When the sun was too hot and the rain was too cold and the wind was too god-damned *windy*.

I cried because the only person I had to mother any longer was myself, and she was behaving badly.

The old adage is true, of course. Eventually, the tears subsided and in teeny, tiny steps, I came around. I stopped having cake for breakfast.

I took up cooking again. Books and newspapers started to make sense once more, rather than being the jumble of black-and-white writing that seemed to demand ransom for Isabella's unharmed return. With time, I was able to walk around the home I'd created with my husband and daughter without breaking down into hysterics, feeling and thinking that everything in this world is so intangible, such an ephemeral, fleeting thing.

I'm now in my second year of having a daughter living a life of her own at a college that isn't a block away—it's a seven-hour drive away, a $300 airline ticket away. And while I miss her intensely, I've reached a point where I can actually enjoy myself. I can sleep in late. I can walk in the woods for hours. I can watch an Italian film, without subtitles, and laugh myself silly. I can fall into a novel without having to worry about picking up Isabella from soccer practice on time. And I do.

What have I gleaned from this? Plenty. I now know, with unshakable certainty, that this rite of passage is huge—for parents as much as for children. Along with this I've learned that self-love is as important as the love we give our children, the siblings we've sibling-ed, the mothers we've mothered. Embracing the empty nest—no matter if it takes weeks, months, years—is in the end an opportunity for growth, for connecting to our inner child in a way that very few talk about. Love *is* all—for others, but just as much for ourselves. It's downright terrifying seeing your kid leave, but it's also exhilarating to find out who *you* might become in their absence.

"What will become of me once they leave?" a friend whose children are on the verge of leaving for college recently asked while she and I and another friend were out hiking.

"I don't know," the second replied, in all seriousness, and our friend's face dropped. "After so many years of neglecting my career and caring for them and for the family and the house, who is going to hire me? Especially at this age?"

"No kidding," the first went on. "What will I put on my résumé? 'Professional laundry folder'?"

They went on like this, fretting, anxiety gripping their voices, as I walked away, the sunlight filtering through the fog and washing over me like grace. I thought back to the last time I'd seen Isabella on my monthly visit, and how she'd given me her cardigan during a movie because she thought I was cold. *I've done well*, I thought as I took the sweater from her outstretched hand and our fingers collided in the bowl of popcorn between us.

What *will* become of us? I can't tell you for sure. But goodness, is it going to be fun finding out.

Lauretta Zucchetti

Lauretta Zucchetti is an author, motivational speaker, and life and career coach who specializes in assisting women through midlife transitions. Her writing has been featured on SoulFriends, A Band of Women, and Thank the Now, and she is currently working on a memoir about her childhood in Italy. Her essay *The Stranded Bird of Pavia* will be published in *Literary Mama's* 2014 Mother's Day issue. She lives in Northern California with her husband and daughter, and plays drums in the band Hot Rocks. To learn more about her, please visit laurettazucchetti.com.

The Unexpected Transition

Megan Calhoun

My mom always said, "There are no accidents—everything happens for a reason." And, as we all know, our mothers are always right (although none of us would have admitted this in our teenage years). I didn't realize until much later how influential her perspective would be as I grew into a woman and a mother, forced to face those times of transition—uncomfortable times filled with uncertainty, doubt, and fear.

The "no accidents" maxim that my mother always referenced in tough times didn't fully sink in until the fall of 1999. That's when I learned to stop hanging on and start letting go.

It was late September, and a great time of year to land in San Francisco. I'd moved west with my boyfriend. This was our second move together since we'd been a couple; we'd dated for years, and I was eager to settle down and move on to the next proper step in life and get married.

But the proposal was always forthcoming. My boyfriend's job kept him incredibly busy, and he spent long stretches on the road. After three and a half years of dating and two moves, I was getting frustrated and fully expected a proposal. Fear crept in. Was I in a relationship with someone who couldn't commit? It will get better, I thought. Boy, did it.

Eager to find a connection in an unfamiliar place, I rang up an old friend from high school who was living in the city at the time. We struck up a conversation, and eventually I came to realize what my mother had been saying all along: there are no accidents in life. Eventually, we fell in love. Instead of hanging on to years invested in a relationship, I simply surrendered to an unknown future with an old friend and new lover. And I got the proposal, just not from the guy everyone expected. I took the next step in life, just not exactly the way I thought it would be. And I wouldn't change a thing.

As a young married couple in a city full of energy and promise, there was never a dull moment in our lives. We gave birth to our first child in San Francisco, our boy Oscar, while living in a third-floor walkup apartment in an "up and coming" (translation: sketchy) part of town. When I got the news that my second child was on the way, my instincts led me to push my husband outside his comfort zone and move us all to the suburbs. Here we were again: making the move from single to married, then married to parents, then city dwellers to suburbanites in just a few short years. There was rarely enough time to get comfortable in any one stage, let alone get comfortable being in a constant state of transition.

We made it to the suburbs just in time for the birth of our daughter, and I quickly realized what was missing. Over the years in San Francisco, I'd developed a strong sense of community, connecting with other moms in our neighborhood there. Together, we bonded over sleep deprivation, the joys and mishaps of nursing, the helpless feeling you get when your child is teething and in pain.

Giving birth to a child in a new town turned out to be a tough experience, despite being less than fifteen miles from the city. Gone were the friends and social connections that supported me through the birth of my firstborn. In the days before smartphones and Yelp really took off, it was a challenge just to figure out what dry cleaner wouldn't ruin our clothes, or how to find a good pediatric dentist. I was in an unfamiliar place with a toddler, a newborn, and an overworked husband (who now faced a healthy commute every day).

That's when another unexpected transition happened. I was telling my husband I was feeling a bit isolated and lost and in need of connecting with other moms. He suggested using social media, specifically Twitter, as a way to connect with other moms. What? Twitter? What's that? Like 99.9% of all human beings in 2007, I had never heard of

Twitter. I mean, I'd just joined Facebook and felt like I was way ahead of the curve.

After my husband explained the service a bit, I told him it sounded like a very nerdy way for hipster dudes to broadcast "where u at" messages as they flocked around different bars in the city. Never in a hundred years would I have thought to use Twitter to connect with moms. Surely, women need more than 140 characters to talk! But I checked out Twitter, and my assumptions were very wrong: I found incredibly engaging, smart women interacting with one another on the service.

Many of these women were former executives, professionals, journalists, authors, entrepreneurs, and more, who were now moms. They relied on Twitter to support each other and stay connected with like-minded souls and other women who shared their interests. I was blown away by how smart these women were—many of them had their own businesses and were creating their own path now that they had left the corporate world. I was inspired by these women and felt there needed to be a place for them to connect further.

While relaxing on our back deck with my husband having a glass of wine, the idea came to me to create an online community for moms where they could support each other and make new connections based on their different passions and interests. That's when SocialMoms was born. Within minutes, I bought an $8 domain name, and my husband cranked out a crude but customized platform that allowed women to discover each other and connect on our site and on Twitter. There was no business plan; if anything, it was a hobby or a service for a bunch of women who needed better ways to find one another. I didn't do research. I didn't talk to investors. I just followed my idea and held zero expectations. I thought after I launched the community, a handful of women would join and that would be it.

I had no idea what kind of transition lay just ahead of me.

I pressed a button to make the site "live" just before driving my firstborn off to his first day of preschool. I cried the whole way home, in awe of how fast the kids were growing up and how our lives were changing moment by moment. I settled down in front of my computer, cleared away the tears, and was shocked by what I saw: *three women had joined SocialMoms.* I had no idea what to do—it was completely unexpected. Why did they join? How did they find it? Who were they? How could I help them? I welcomed each new member as they came aboard, and realized just how special these women were. It became my mission to serve their needs and provide opportunities for these women to make new connections, network with each other, and grow their personal brands.

Within three months, 3,000 moms had joined SocialMoms. We received some great headlines early on—without making a single pitch to a journalist—from *Techcrunch* to *Fast Company.* My phone started ringing. I was getting calls from some of the biggest brands in the world—they wanted to connect with SocialMoms. That's when my unexpected transition from mother to entrepreneur happened. I started SocialMoms by accident and it grew organically, by word of mouth. It was something that I never dreamt I would do—but as my mother always said, *There are no accidents—everything happens for a reason.*

Today, SocialMoms helps thousands of women each year build their personal brands across the social media landscape and earn additional incomes by participating in high-integrity brand sponsorship opportunities. It also provides employment for a dozen people.

One of the biggest lessons I have learned from this experience is that life is full of unexpected transitions, and it's our job to see opportunities in every one of them. Being in a state of transition can be uncomfortable. Often you don't know you're in a period of transition, and they're often thrust upon us by changing circumstances or unexpected life events.

As my mom always said, *There are no accidents—everything happens for a reason.* Yes, it's a cliché. But as with all clichés, there's a kernel of truth in there. Or is it just a justification—a way of comforting ourselves about the way events tend to unfold in our lives? It might just be a matter of perspective, and how we carry ourselves through tough times can drive different outcomes.

Now consider a competing cliché: *Shit happens.* Another common phrase, albeit a slightly more cynical justification we humans use to explain the same sorts of mysteries and experiences that make up the lives we lead.

Both clichés are intended to explain away the same mysterious workings of our universe and provide comfort. Yet they contain very different intentions. To say that *everything happens for a reason* suggests that you simply need to find the gift hidden inside any given life event. To say *shit happens* is to dismiss those very same events—and means that you may never find the gifts hidden in times of struggle, hardship, or transition.

These two clichés give us a seemingly divergent perspective on how we deal with the same hard questions. But in the end, they both encourage us to *let go.* Whether you're a *shit happens* fatalist or someone who always looks for the gifts hidden in life's moments, the underlying insight remains the same: life is best if you don't hang on to it. By whatever means necessary, just allow yourself to let go. You'll be amazed what happens when you do.

Megan Calhoun

Megan Calhoun is the founder and CEO of SocialMoms, a position she has held since the company launched in September 2008. Located in San Francisco, SocialMoms is an active community of 45,000+ influential, web-savvy social media "moms" that reaches more than 200 million fans, followers, and friends in the US. Prior to SocialMoms, Megan spent twelve years in sales and marketing positions, where she worked with Fortune 500 companies including Revlon, Pfizer, Genentech, and Eli Lilly. She is the author of a children's book, mother of two, and lives with her husband in Northern California. Megan is a graduate of Indiana University.

Joe's Donut Shop, by Jan Shively

Artist Statement

In my life, I have lived in some of California's biggest art community hubs: Monterey/Carmel, San Francisco, and Palm Springs, where it seems there's an art gallery on nearly every corner. Rather than create art myself, I was only able to admire the beautiful works of talented others; I thought I was untalented and our family budget wouldn't support my "hobby" while I worked full-time.

It wasn't until my husband and I moved to the Bitterroot Valley in Montana on the eve of retirement in 2008 that I found myself at a place in my life where I could finally indulge myself. It was then that I decided to take a watercolor class for beginners in Missoula, fifty miles from my home. I immediately fell in love with every aspect of the watercolor pigments, teasing shapes into paintings, and realized I wasn't bad. I'm actually extremely talented. (My daughter made me add that.) A passion took hold that has led me to want more for myself.

The shop depicted in my painting, Joe's Donut Shop, was a place I passed each morning on my way to the first watercolor workshop I ever took in Sandy, Oregon. The red-and-white brick building was so colorful abutted upon the thickest green forest I'd ever seen. I smiled every time I passed it. I took many pictures of Joe's to remember my first workshop where I was truly the worst painter, but where I had so much fun becoming inspired and determined to get better. It was in that class that I learned my expertise in watercolor is painting from photographs.

Now, I'm constantly taking pictures. Everywhere I go, I look at my surroundings—people and places—as if they were in a watercolor painting. I consider what my palette would be, what weight of paper I would use. I love becoming anxious to get home to my garage "art studio" to paint my interpretations.

This transition into painting is the first time I have been able to choose the course I want to be on. It gives me something I can do for myself instead of adapting to life's current. This leap of faith wouldn't have been possible without the love and support of my family, who have always seen in me something I am just now seeing: talent for artistic expression. There was my stepson, Jared, who encouraged me when I doubted I could paint "Joe's Donut Shop" and coined my new personal motto, "Why can't you? What's to lose?" My daughter, Kelli, was the first to proudly hang my artwork on her wall and pushed me to overcome my fears by submitting artwork for contests and publication. Because of her encouragement and support I had the courage to enter my watercolors in our local fair for all to see. Not only did they win blue ribbons, but "Joe's Donut Shop" now sits in your hands and represents my first publication. (Thanks to Steve Akry for your technical support to make this happen!)

Jan Shively

Jan Shively, sixty-two, is a health-care assistant working full-time in St. Patrick Hospital's ICU. A California transplant living in Victor, Montana, with her husband and two fuzzy children, Jan has worked in the medical field for nearly thirty years. Always artistic but never confident in her skills, four years ago, with retirement in mind, Jan finally indulged in an art class and discovered a passion and talent for watercolors. To the delight of her four supportive children, she won her first blue ribbons for her watercolors in the Ravalli County Fair in 2013. Her work can be found at janshivelywatercolors.com

The Moment Is a Living Seed, by Silvia Poloto

Artist Statement
The State of Bloom and Shadow
Bud, bloom, poppy sprouting. Wildflower lilac. Roots bursting the earth.

The freshness of the flowers—born perfume of violent beauty corrupting my senses.

The moment is a living seed.

I am on a quest, which may be also yours.
We are all flowers blossoming.
Lifelong search of some memory of the memory of the long-lost memory.

My intent is the brightest flower's opulent blossom, its splendor forever etched on the wall plaster.
Deep inside, the flowers always come back, perhaps to capture their own secret of quiet intensity and visual vastness.

If not as the rose, they come back as the blood of nature, extravagant, mysterious and necessary.

Once sprung, one flower becomes the silence of the other, everything looks at everything, every piece experiences the other, their world utterly reciprocal.

The present contemplating the present.
Everything could be called anything, because anything could be changed into the same resonating muteness.

Since my body is the only way I experience the transparency of all things, every time it feels wilted, another summer opens up.

I live from an obsessed place of invented truth, an inner state of bloom and shadow.

Silvia Poloto

Brazilian-born Silvia Poloto is an accomplished artist working in a range of visual disciplines and with a variety of media. While the Bay Area is her current home, her work has been exhibited throughout the US and several countries abroad, including the United Arab Emirates, France, Spain, Jordan, Italy, Romania, Croatia, Bulgaria, Turkey, Greece, and China, among others. In the Bay Area, her work has been featured in exhibitions at the Yerba Buena Center for the Arts, the Italian American Museum, and the DeYoung Museum, where she was an artist-in-residence. She has also had a solo show at the Triton Museum in Santa Clara in 2012. Silvia's work has been acquired by more than eighty institutional and corporate collections around the US and by more than 900 private collectors around the world.